RARE BREED

RARE BREED
A Chinese Jewish quest

Irene Chu

Copyright © 2016 by Irene C. Chu

Cover designed by John Chu
Chinese calligraphy by Irene Chu
Text designed by Kong Njo

ISBN: 978-0-9951677-2-8 (print)
ISBN: 978-0-9951677-0-4 (electronic)

Publisher and distributor:
Irene C. Chu,
P.O. Box 56515,
8601 Warden Avenue,
Markham, Ontario,
L3R OM6
Canada.
www.irene-chu.com

Printed and bound in Canada by imagingexcellence 2.0.
Electronic edition by Printing Icon.

TO

Father
Djao Singming 赵新民 (1909–1996)

Mother
Florence Rita Shuzhen Yen 严淑贞 (1910–1960)

Brother
Joseph Kun Djao 赵琨 (1946–2003)

FOR

Sisters
Isabelle Ling Wong 赵琳 • Yvonne Fung 赵瑛
Stella Choi 赵瑾 • Angela Wei Djao 赵玮

Sons
John Chu 朱昌年 • Don Chu 朱昌黎

Daughter-in-Law
Ann-Marie Mountford Chu

Grandchildren
Xavier Joseph Mountford Chu 朱敦祥
Bianca Mei Mountford Chu 朱敦华

一個民族忘卻祖先，如一人之沒有卻無統

Contents

Foreword	ix
Preface	xi
Acknowledgements	xv
PART ONE	1
Introduction	3
Kaifeng, China – 1872	5
Chapter 1: Blue-Cap Hui Hui	7
Chapter 2: To Shanghai	27
Toronto, Canada – 2012	49
Chapter 3: Revelation	51
Chapter 4: Searching the Past	65
Nanchang, China – 1872–1927	91
Chapter 5: Nanchang	93
Chapter 6: On Her Own	109
Chapter 7: Inner Conflict	115
Chapter 8: Gande in Ascendancy	121
Chapter 9: SOCONY	131
Chapter 10: A Western Mansion	137
Chapter 11: A Salt Licence	143
Chapter 12: A Knock on the Door	157

Toronto, Canada – 2012   165
Chapter 13: A Project   167

PART TWO   171
Introduction   173

Shanghai, China – 1927–1945   179
Chapter 14: Carefree Days   181
Chapter 15: Destiny Dictates   193
Chapter 16: Marriage & Family   211
Chapter 17: Striking Out on His Own   225
Chapter 18: The World at War   237

Toronto, Canada – 2012   255
Chapter 19: Recollections   257
Chapter 20: Sassoon and Hardoon   287

Kaifeng, Shanghai, and New York City – 2013   301
Chapter 21: Kaifeng   303
Chapter 22: Uncle Charles   327
Chapter 23: Interlude   339

Toronto, Canada – 2013   347
Chapter 24: Welcome-Home Noodles   349

Chronology of Chinese History   361
Chronology of Events Relevant to This Book   363
Notes   370
Chinese Usage and Glossary   388
Bibliography   392

Foreword

WE AS READERS, even as historians, too often assume that the Jewish experience unfolded only in the Middle East and in Europe and North America. In this we are missing an entire page of Jewish history. And that is our loss.

What would be the headlines on that missing page? Jews in India; Jews in Japan; Jews in China. And what we would read on that page – on those many pages – is an almost unbelievable history. For example: Jews lived in India totally free of anti-Semitism for more than two thousand years. In Japan, thousands of Jews lived not only free of hostility but actually welcomed – and this during the perilous years leading up to World War II, when no other country in the world would open its doors to them. And in China? That is the story of this book: the story of just one of the myriad Jewish families who lived for over a thousand years in security in China.

We in the West are blinded by the experiences – often not happy ones – of Jews in the West. The time has come that we look to the East. The time has come to fill in this missing page, to publish the memoirs and diaries and history that tell of the experience of the Jewish people in the eastern world. In this book, Irene Chu has set out to do exactly that by portraying the experiences of her own family, which began in

Kaifeng, China. Kaifeng was the capital of China long before Beijing. And Kaifeng was where the Jews who came east on the Silk Road from Europe and what is now the Middle East first settled.

Ms. Chu has done extensive research on the very early history of the Jewish settlement in Kaifeng and, with authorial licence, has woven into that history the story of her own family. After generations, her ancestors made the long trek from Kaifeng to Shanghai. And after yet more generations, she and members of her family emigrated to Toronto, where they live now.

We applaud her part in spreading an understanding of the hitherto barely known history of the Jewish communities in the East – and to writing a very readable entry on that missing page.

Mary Swartz
Marvin Tokayer
2016

Preface

"THE MOST IMPORTANT THING to the novelist is the preservation of memory," said John Irving, the American writer, during a 2012 interview with Benjamin Percy for *Time* magazine.

"Without memory, we are nothing. No culture, no language, no creativity, all of which is based on what went on before," responded Anthony B. Chan, professor, writer, and filmmaker, commenting on Irvine's statement.

Yet memory is very malleable we are told by contemporary scientists, who warn us of the danger of assuming that memory is a perfect recording of a past event.*

Warnings notwithstanding, I wish to present and preserve memories. Memories of a familial tale that string together two segments of history that have been laid aside by most, namely:

> the Chinese Jews in Kaifeng, Henan Province, China;
> and the Jews in Shanghai during World War II.

It is not that we lack publications on either topic. There are, in fact, numerous books and research papers on both. My attempt here is to thread together the two pieces of history with the story of one particular family, a story that spans four generations and offers a slightly different perspective.

The historic element, with a backdrop harking back to the tenth century CE, moves forward to focus on the hundred years or so between the middle of the nineteenth century and the middle of the twentieth. It was a period of conflicts, of unrest, and of disasters in China, juxtaposed against internal disintegration and external aggression from Western and Eastern foreign powers.

All historic details are researched and are factual. So are cultural customs and traditions. Historic figures are presented as they are generally portrayed in accepted sources.

Two plotlines – one from the past and one from the present – intertwine throughout the book. They are based on an oral history that traces the migration of four generations of my family. The storylines weave together some of my own personal recollections with those of my father, my stepmother, my aunts, my uncle, my cousin, and my siblings. There are, however, dramatizations and speculation about details that have no known record.

Characters are based on my family, but the character traits are mostly fictional; any resemblance to real people is purely coincidental. In particular, the concubine, Ying, and the salt merchant, Liang Jialu, are total fabrications. Their portraits help to reflect and emphasize some of the negative realities in the neo-Confucian society of the day. All conversations are invented. The fictional elements help to enhance the flow of the story, add a degree of richness to the details, and provide a more readable approach to history.

The opening segment introduces one of the last seven clans of the Kaifeng Chinese Jewry at the point of dissolution. In addition to books, research papers, relevant correspondence of missionaries and scholars that stretch from the fifteenth century to the present, a visit to Kaifeng in 2012, interviews with the remaining Chinese Jews, and discussions with contemporary scholars helped me bring the story up to date.

The Jewish experiences in Shanghai from the early to the mid-twentieth century were approached differently from other existing books. Most publications on the Jews in Shanghai during World War II are made up of recollections of the refugees' personal experiences – their harrowing accounts of hardship and helplessness. Not much has been written about the non-refugee Jews in Shanghai during that period. This book offers a Chinese point of view, so to speak. Emphasis is given to the wealthy Sephardic Jews in Shanghai who helped to support the refugees from Europe. It also features some of the Chinese who provided assistance to the wealthy Jews when they had to overcome hurdles during the difficult years from 1942 to 1945.

Bits and pieces of Chinese history, traditions, philosophies, and customs, as well as geographic details, are interspersed in the narrative. (To avoid scholarly apparatus, I have marked with an asterisk those subjects that have a note at the back of the book.) Like a fugue in music, these elements wind in several thematic lines that converge and diverge as they ride the passage of time into a tale of the universal human experience of migration, integration, and assimilation.

Memory enables the past to serve the present and lead to the future. Learning from the past helps to master the present and propels one to embrace the future. In researching the journeys and experiences of their ancestors, the descendants of this particular family strive to establish their cultural and ethnic identity in their present-day pluralistic environment. The knowledge and understanding of the past enable them to appreciate and to treasure the unique strands of yarn that each person brings to this country to weave into the rich and complex social fabric of Canadian diversity.

Irene Chu
Toronto
March 2016

Acknowledgements

FATE BROUGHT ME to Professor Li Qiuyun in 2005. She has been my mentor and the source of my inspiration ever since. My gratitude cannot be expressed in mere words.

Rabbi Marvin Tokayer and Mary Swartz are the two persons to whom I am most indebted. They generously lent me the material from *The Fugu Plan*, the book they co-authored. Both offered invaluable advice and guidance that fine-tuned the accuracy of historic facts and points in my book. I am immensely grateful for the time they spent on reading my manuscript and for meeting with me for discussions, and I am supremely honoured and privileged to include their Foreword in this book.

Through Grant Guo I became acquainted with Professor Guo Changying of Henan University and Professor Liu Bailu, who brought me up to date on the current research on Kaifeng Jews by scholars in Kaifeng. Mary Calder was the first to offer to read my manuscript. I value her comments and suggestions.

Stephen Siu generously passed on to me all of his research material on the Jewish refugees in Shanghai after he completed a photo exhibition of the Jewish refugees in Shanghai some years back.

Andrew Jakubowicz in Australia opened for me an angle on the thousand or so Polish Jews in Shanghai and differentiated them from the refugees from Central Europe.

Laurel Wolfson kindly sent images of the "*Hebrew MSS from China – IV*" from The Klaus Library, Cincinnati, Hebrew Union College of Cincinnati.

Elsie Lo and Sara Irwin connected me to access to the Royal Ontario Museum's collection of artifacts from the Kaifeng Jewish community. Ralph Berrin at the Reuben & Helene Dennis Museum, housed in Beth Tzedec Synagogue Toronto, patiently showed me their collection and explained about the Holy Scrolls. My sincere thanks.

The late Eric Goldstaub of Ergo Industries, Markham, Ontario, kindly loaned me his collection of family photos from Shanghai days.

Harriet Morton shared with me her knowledge on the Russian Jews in Harbin. The books she lent me provided important material in my search for information. As well, Alex Gershtein provided images on Harbin Jews and generously shared with me his personal video on Harbin. Elena Zolotko tirelessly promoted my book in the Russian Jewish community in Toronto.

Sylvia Sweeney's video on her teacher Karl Steiner formed the basis of the story on Karl Steiner and his fellow Shanghai refugees who immigrated to Montreal.

My father, leaving his legacy in the recordings of interviews conducted by my sister Wei Djao and brother-in-law Tony Chan in the 1980s, unfolded much of the family events both in Nanchang and Shanghai. Aunt Randie Chang, Aunt

Winnie Lee, and cousin Zhao Rong narrated anecdotes of their childhood years in Nanchang.

To my stepmother, Alice Djao, I am grateful for all the previously unknown facts regarding her father and her first husband's associations with the Shanghai Sephardic Jews and how they played a part in helping these Jews during the difficult years from 1942 to 1945. My uncle, the late Yan Rendong, provided many details on my mother's family.

My sister Wei and my brother-in-law Tony shared with me their extensive experience and know-how about book publishing. I benefited much.

Dan Wong, my godson, competently designed and managed the website irene-chu.com for me.

My son Don spent a good part of a year researching the various Shanghai Jewish factions during WWII. His contribution was indispensable.

To Patricia Kennedy, my editor, who patiently guided me through the various stages of editing and publishing, I owe a great deal. My heartfelt appreciation.

Kong Njo, my designer, is a master of multi-tasking. Apart from design and layout, he spent time to rescue me from the maze of high technology. A most invaluable associate.

To top it all, I am absolutely thrilled by my son John's design for the book cover.

TO ONE AND ALL, MY INFINITE THANKS.

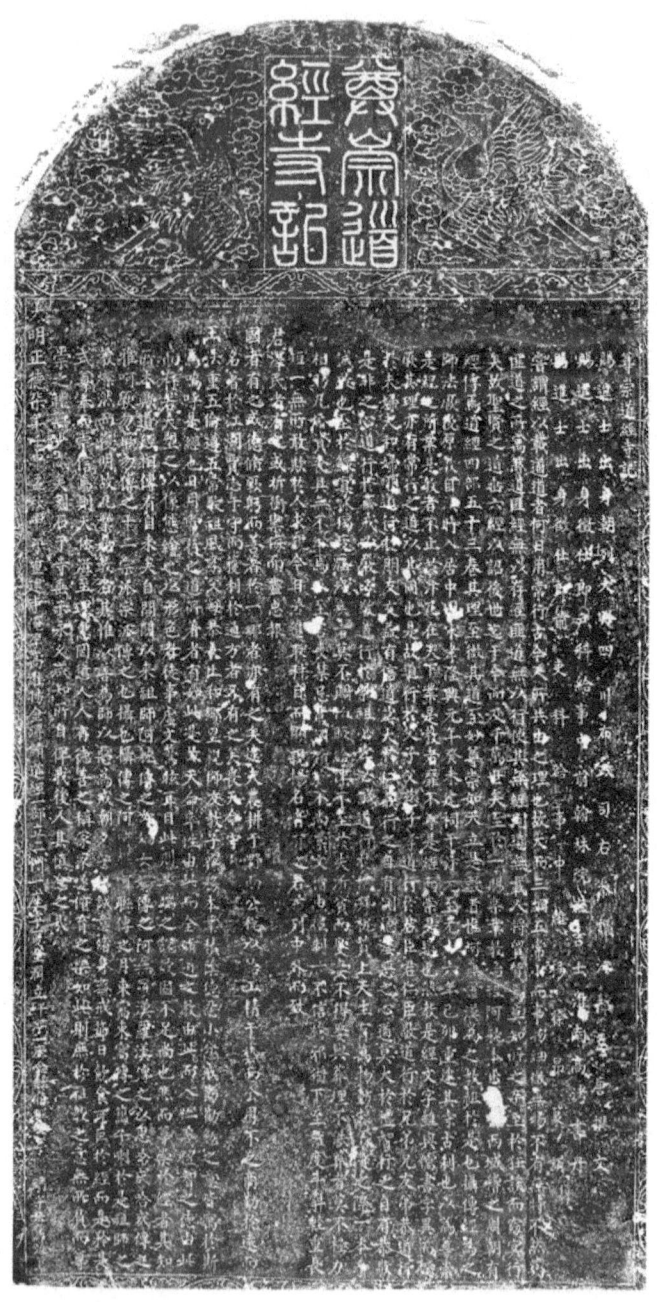

Rubbing of a stele from the Kaifeng synagogue, reproduced with permission of the Royal Ontario Museum © ROM (920.23.1.B-1-ROM 2010).

PART ONE

路盤狹雨綿綿
叢莽夜竹何蹒跚

Introduction

THE CHINESE JEWS are little known to the world at large. Nevertheless, they exist. Their existence has been recorded in Chinese history since the tenth or eleventh century (between 960 CE and 1127 CE). Their descendants have scattered all over the globe, and some have found their way to Canada, a country of many races and countless cultures.

Of all the groups in the Jewish diaspora, the Chinese Jews, classified under "Oriental Jews,"* is probably the least known to most people.

Since time immemorial, traders from the Middle East made the difficult journey eastward to exchange merchandise. Jews were amongst the earliest travellers along what we now know as the Silk Road.

Throughout the millennia, their presence was evident in many Chinese coastal cities, in inland towns, as well as in the interior western provinces. But nowhere did they establish as distinct and as long-lasting a community as they did in the ancient city of Kaifeng in central China. The Kaifeng Jews remained a unique community for close to nine hundred years.

In Kaifeng there are four stone tablets (steles), with inscriptions recording personalities and events in the history of the Kaifeng Jews. Researchers believe the Kaifeng Jews most likely came by sea in the tenth century, when the sea route between the east and the west had opened. A large contingent settled in Kaifeng, then the capital city of the Northern Song Dynasty. They called themselves the Israelites.

In the subsequent nine hundred years or so, the Kaifeng Jews became full-fledged citizens of China, learning the language, studying the classics, participating in the various levels of the imperial examinations, with a number of them attaining high positions at the emperor's court. They had among them scholars, tradesmen, businesspeople, and practitioners of every profession. They suffered no discrimination. The community thrived; they lived well, and in peace, and many prospered. All participated in every aspect of Chinese life.

In 1263, during Kublai Khan's Yuan Dynasty, for the first time the Jews were recorded as Israelites in Chinese official documents. Later, the term *Rudeya* (Judea) appeared. In 1821, during the Qing Dynasty, the term *You-tai* (the present equivalent of "Jews") surfaced.

In the latter part of the nineteenth century, the Kaifeng Jewish community dissipated. What remained were a number of scattered descendants of the last known seven clans. They had no knowledge of their religion or the Hebrew language, but were only cognizant of the fact that they were of a foreign origin, and not of Chinese Han descent.

Our story begins in mid-nineteenth century in Kaifeng. It centres around one Zhao family who is about to send its son, Zhao Yidong, and his bride, Jin Yuchen, on a mission to Shanghai to seek help for the revival of the Kaifeng Jewish community...

Kaifeng, China

1872

一任東西南北各分飛

Chapter 1

Blue-Cap Hui Hui

Jin Yuchen sat on the brick bed, or kang,* lost in thought. Tomorrow would be the big day that would take her life into the unknown.

"What's in store for me?" she asked herself. She had no answer.

It was almost nightfall. In the dusk, the fine drizzle made the distant fields and the huts nearby blend into one grey, indistinguishable blur. How it mirrored Yuchen's heart and mind – in fact, her whole inner self.

"Go away, grey! Go away gloom! Let me be!" she exclaimed under her breath.

"It can't be all bad. I have to make it work. I must! I must! ... I will ..." she vowed.

The newlywed Jin Yuchen was barely past her eighteenth birthday, and her face exuded a youthful radiance, despite her wearisome thoughts. She had a broad forehead, eyes that were larger than usual, not slanted, and a moderately high-bridged, straight nose, balanced by a well-defined mouth with the corners of the lips turned slightly upward. Taken together, these features made up a softly oval-shaped face that was not to be dismissed. In its frame of dark hair, with its fair skin, this face drew attention, admiration, appreciation. By any ethnic standard, it epitomized heaven's blessings.

An orange-pink Chinese blouse and trousers outlined her shapely body as she sat, with a threaded needle in her right hand and a half-finished blue tunic on her lap. She was trying to finish sewing the tunic, but the thought of an unknown future stopped her in the midst of her work. She gazed blankly at the scenery outside the window of her husband's family home – a modest grey-brick house, close by the ruined Qing Zhen Si, or Clear True Temple, in the ancient city of Kaifeng in central China.

What Yuchen worried about was not something that had arisen out of the blue. It had been in the family plan for years, if not decades. She, Jin Yuchen, was a descendant of a people from far away, in the west. Exactly where she could not tell. Ever since she was a toddler, her grandmother had told her repeatedly about her ancestors, the Israelites, God's chosen people. Even as recently as a month ago, the night before her wedding, she was reminded of her roots by her mother.

"Chen-er (little Chen), I know I've said this often enough in the past, but I'll repeat it one last time. You know we've matched you to an outstanding young man, Zhao Yidong. His family is also Blue-Cap Hui Hui,* the same as we are, sons of Israel. So, in future, there will be no conflict between the two of you in bringing up your children according to our religious rites. It is very important, Chen-er."

"But, Niang (mother), our temple is no longer there and we have no rabbi to teach us. We haven't been going to the temple for at least ten years or more. Neither you nor Ba (father) nor anyone else has been able to teach us our religious rituals, our language, or our history. Apart from the dietary observances and the circumcision of baby boys, we know nothing about our religion. How are we to bring up our children in the proper Israelite way? Yidong and I can't practise it ourselves, much less teach our children."

"This is why you and Yidong must leave for Shanghai after the wedding. They say there are many Israelites in Shanghai with abundant silver. The responsibility falls on your shoulders to go and ask them to help us here in Kaifeng. To rebuild the temple and to send us rabbis. Then our people will be able to worship God and practise our religion as before."

"Didn't Granduncle Zhao and some others go there when the temple began to fall apart? I remember Ba talked about them once. What happened to them?" Yuchen asked.

"Yidong's granduncle Zhao Wengui went to Shanghai when Yidong was a year old, three years before you were born. He was in charge of our synagogue then, the keeper of the key. Granduncle Zhao went with his young cousin Zhao Chincheng and stayed at a foreigner's place. They were learning the Hebrew language and the religious rites. Unfortunately, Granduncle Wengui died suddenly and was buried in Shanghai. Chincheng became homesick and returned to Kaifeng shortly after. Nothing was achieved."

Yuchen's mother paused for a moment, then continued. "In the past ten years, a few people have made the trip, but none of them came back with good news. The Jewry in Shanghai is definitely aware of our situation. In fact, there have been letters between our temple and some foreigners in Henan, Beijing, and even England. But no help has reached us. We have seen only those foreigners from other religions who are interested in

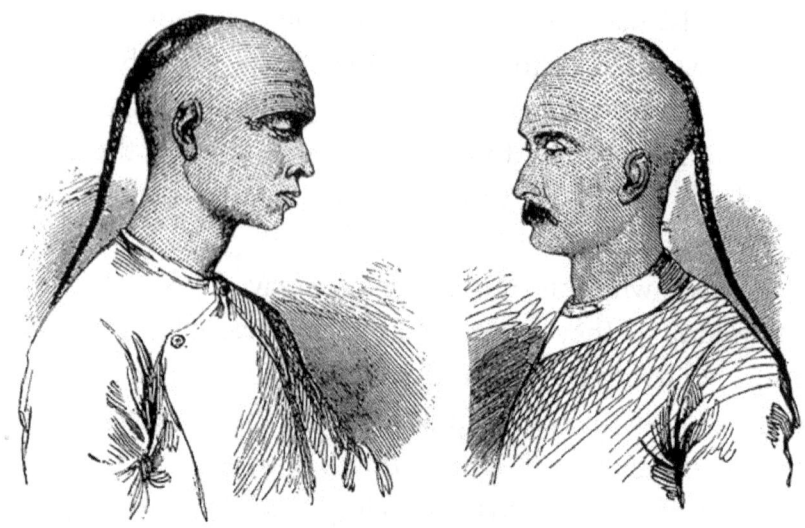

Two Chinese Jews from Kaifeng
(*From the* Illustrated London News, *Dec. 13, 1851, p. 700.*)

getting some of our scrolls and artifacts, as you already know."

Then, as if reluctant to speak, Yuchen's mother went on. "There is another reason, Chen-er, that Ba and Yidong's father are anxious for you two to leave here. We may not have told you before, but as you can see, there is very little future here for young people of our background. Since the opium wars, the foreign powers are so strong that the Qing Dynasty is nearing its end, they say. You remember the Tai Ping Rebellion, which was quashed a few years back? And the riots of the Hui Hui ethnic people in Shaanxi and Gansu against the Qing ruler?"

She sighed and shook her head. "Feelings against foreigners are high, and we are in a very precarious situation. No matter how much we've integrated with the mainstream Han people, we are, nonetheless, of a different origin with a different religion, and will become targets for attacks ... not by local people who know us, but by those rebels from other provinces. They are blinded by their hatred for foreigners. Ba said the second opium war was triggered by the killing of some missionaries in Beijing."

"Then why don't we all leave here and go to Shanghai together? Shanghai is run by foreigners, isn't it? That may provide some protection for us."

"It's not that simple, Chen-er. Yidong's father feels an obligation to rebuild the temple and revive our religion here in Kaifeng. It has been his mission ever since his Uncle Zhao Wengui died in Shanghai and left everything in the air. Yidong's father wants to give it one more try by sending the two of you to seek help, and, we hope, this time there will be some results."

"As far as I can see, Niang, there is not much hope. If the Jewry in Shanghai had wanted to help, they would have done so years ago. Why don't you talk to Ba and see if you two and brother Yuxi can come with us. We'll all start anew in Shanghai. I'll feel much happier that way," Yuchen pleaded.

"It is not that we haven't thought about it. Yuxi is still young. We were thinking, once you and Yidong are settled in Shanghai, and if help is not likely to come our way for the temple, then we may just do that . . . I mean, we may come to join you."

Yuchen remembered only too well this conversation the night before her wedding. The two of them sat at the square mahogany table with the dim flickering of the candle casting light and shadow on their faces as they had their final mother-daughter chat before she was to leave her family to join another.

It pained her to have to part from her parents and her younger brother, even though the Zhao family lived only two *hutongs*, or lanes, away. Just the thought that she could no longer be with them at all times, day and night, gave her a kind of sad longing in her heart. As she realized that, after this night, she would never sleep in this modest house ever again, her eyes lingered on every item with a bittersweet fondness.

Yuchen was excited about her marriage. She and Yidong had known each other since childhood, and they liked each other. When she was only eight years old, her parents had given her Ba Zi* to the Zhao family, and the Zhao's acceptance of it signified that she and Yidong were considered engaged. Her grandmother had told her that several Hui Hui families, including two White Cap Hui Hui (Muslim) families, had asked for her Ba Zi; but her parents would have nothing to do with any of them. They insisted on the Zhao family.

Yuchen distinctly remembered her grandmother telling her that the Kaifeng Jews and the Muslims were similar in many of their beliefs and practices. Both believed in one God; both observed one weekly day of rest. The Muslims prayed five times each day, the Israelites three times. Both refrained from eating pork and had their male children circumcised. Both named the same people – Adam, Noah, Abraham, Issac, Jacob, and Moses – as important personages in their history. Because of this, it was difficult for the Han Chinese to differentiate between the two. During the Tang Dynasty, when traders from the West appeared in China, Hui Hui meant Arab or Persian believers in Islam. By the Yuan Dynasty "Hui Hui" was applied to all people from the "Western Region," including the Jews and the Arabs. The Han Chinese had called the Israelites Blue-Cap Hui Hui, because they wore blue turbans and boots during their religious ceremonies. The Muslims wore white during their religious ceremonies, and were therefore referred to as White-Cap Hui Hui.

Yuchen knew that it was fortunate for both her family and Yidong's, who were determined that their children would marry within their own faith, that Zhao Yidong's Ba Zi and hers turned out to be very compatible. Yidong, being four years her senior, was born in the year of the Dog, and she was born in the year of the Tiger, and hence they were a good match.

As much as Yuchen realized that the Israelites had become quite accustomed to observing many of the Han Chinese traditions and customs, such as Ba Zi matching, veneration of ancestors, and marriage and burial ceremonies, she was told there were certain things that set them apart from the Chinese.

As Blue-Cap Hui Hui, they had their own synagogue – the Clear True Temple, Qing Zhen Si, as they called it – which was first built in 1163 and was now in utter ruin. They worshipped only one God, whereas the Chinese worshipped all kinds of idols, such as the Kitchen God, the Earth God, the God of Mercy, the Fertility Goddess, and many others. The Israelites abstained from eating pork, and they plucked the sinew from the meat they ate. This last practice gave rise to another name "Tiao Jin Jiao" (Pluck Sinew Sect) for their religion.

Yuchen knew her people traditionally had married within their own group for centuries, but at some point during the Ming Dynasty, they had adopted a new practice. As China was a patrilineal society, and the women had no say in the family, they had decided that men would be able to marry someone of a different religion, but the women must marry an Israelite in order to bring up their children as Israelites.

She had been told that, also during the Ming Dynasty, the emperor had decreed that all Hui Hui, Blue or White, had to intermarry with other ethnic groups, including the Han. Thus, many Blue Cap families married outside their community. The Zhao and the Jin clans had pretty much stuck to their own, however, and it was one of the reasons that Yuchen's father was determined to have her marry Yidong.

For ten years, Yuchen had known that one day she was to marry Zhao Yidong. She had quietly watched her future husband and observed him from a distance every time the seven remaining Israelite clans gathered together for some occasions. Yuchen still had some vague memories that, when she was very little, Yidong's grandfather was in charge of the temple. Grandpa Zhao, as she used to call him, had been a student rabbi, who studied the holy books under the tutorship of the then-Chief Rabbi Li, whose clan name was Levi and whose family produced a long line of chief rabbis over the centuries. In 1850 or thereabouts, before she was born, the temple had lost its last rabbi, Rabbi Li.

Grandpa Zhao had reached a level at which he was able to teach some of the Hebrew rites. Yidong's father was to succeed his father in his role, and Yidong, his father. But God did not grant them this wish. Grandpa Zhao died suddenly before he had time to pass on his knowledge and experience to his son. Yidong's father was marginally versed in the holy books, but he did not know enough of the Hebrew language to properly perform the rites on holy days. Besides, he was not a rabbi and did not have sufficient quaifications to teach the congregation.

For years, the temple elders had tried to secure a rabbi from another city. They carried on slow and scattered communications with Israelites in Shanghai, Hangzhou, and Ningpo in search of a properly trained leader, who would be able to carry out all the rabbinical duties at their temple. Their effort was in vain. Hangzhou or Ningpo sent them some holy scripts, but no rabbi. There were some messengers from Shanghai, and two of their own even went to this purportedly prosperous treaty port for a trip. But again nothing came to fruition.

Day by day, year after year, the temple, as if tired of waiting endlessly, began to disintegrate. The roof started to leak; walls crumbled; pillars and balustrades lost their paint and cracked at many places. The terrible flood of the Yellow River in 1854 was the last straw. The entire complex was fast reaching a state at which it could not be fixed, and was turning into rubble. People tried to keep the Holy of Holies and the throne of Moses in good condition – but not for long. With no money and not enough manpower to do the physical work, the temple was in disrepair. Worse still, foreigners from other cities began to pry into their temple and bargain for the few artifacts and scrolls that were still in the temple's possession. By the time Yuchen was eight or nine years of age, the synagogue, the vague image she remembered as a toddler, was all but gone.

The Zhao clan still lived at one side of the temple complex. They – more or less – kept a watchful eye over the last little bits and pieces of their former temple.

Only a couple of months before, Yuchen's younger brother, Yuxi, had come running home in an excited panic.

"Niang . . . where is Ba ? . . . Another . . . foreigner . . . at the city gate," he panted, trying hard to catch his breath. "He wants to see the one in charge of Qing Zhen Si."

"Ba has gone to play chess with Uncle Zhao. Go get both of them. They'll know how to deal with the foreigner. What does this fellow want?"

Yuxi was already out of sight.

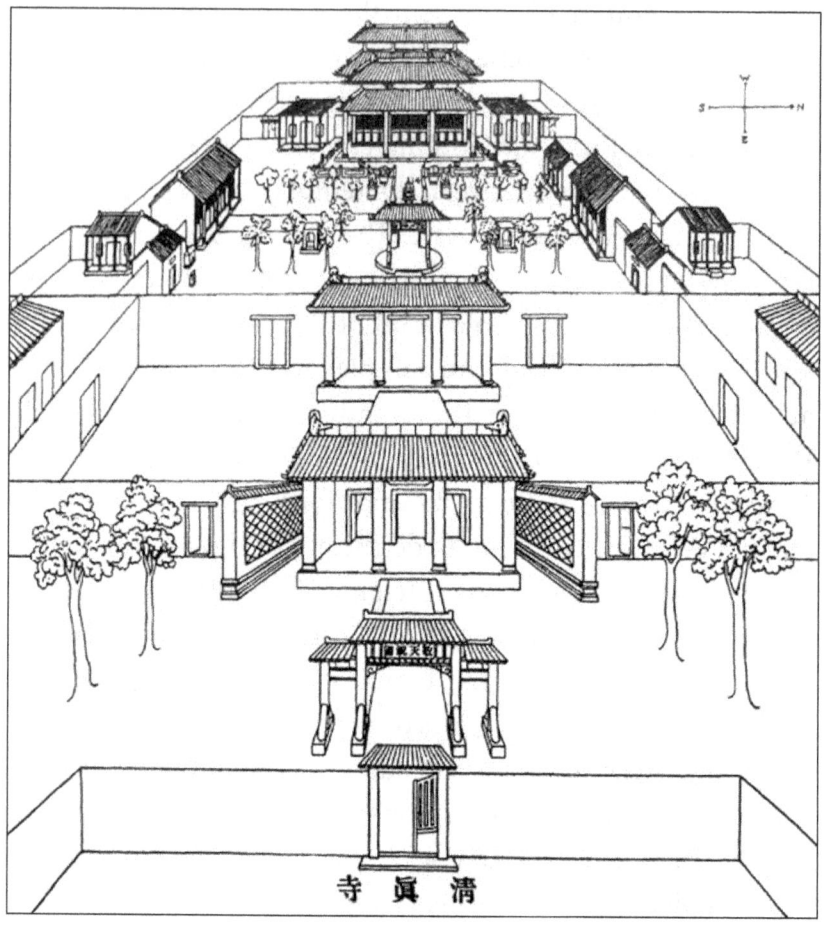

Exterior view of the Kaifeng synagogue, reproduced from Chinese Jews *by William White.*

"To take away from us whatever is left..." Yuchen muttered in a tone of despair.

Her mother sighed in agreement.

It was a daily ritual for Yuchen's father, Lao Jin, or Senior Jin, and Yidong's father Lao Zhao, or Senior Zhao, to walk home together from work and to stop at one or the other's house for a couple of hours before supper.

Lao Zhao owned a little carpentry shop that sold simple furniture, wood utensils, and wood carvings. He was more an artisan than a carpenter. Lao Jin was a merchant for medicinal and herbal goods. Both their stores were on the main thoroughfare of the city.

The two men could not have been more different. Lao Jin was careful and meticulous, always worrying about something – with or without reason. Lao Zhao was happy-go-lucky, and impatient with details. Somehow the opposites complemented each other, and they had been close friends all their lives.

The two did not look very different from the majority of Han Chinese. Their noses might be a bit longer and their eyes slightly larger, but in skin colour and general appearance, they were Han-looking. Since the beginning of the Qing Dynasty in 1644, all males had been required to shave the front of their heads and keep long pigtails at the back. These two men did exactly that. With their full-length tunics of grey cotton, long under-trousers, and homemade cotton shoes, they were almost indistinguishable from Han Chinese.

Lao Jin and Lao Zhao would share a pot of tea, have a few puffs on their waterpipes, and play a game of chess. They found the pastime both relaxing and stimulating. As they made moves in turns on the chessboard they chatted about everything under the sun. Invariably, their conversation would turn to their children and the synagogue.

A few days before the arrival of the foreigners, their discussion had turned to their children's wedding, which was to take place in less than two months.

"I wouldn't take it so lightly, Lao Zhao. You know, Pan Ying's father owns practically all the land outside Kaifeng in the East Village. Pan Ying has a gang of thugs following him everywhere. What if they really carry out their threats to kidnap Yuchen during the wedding procession?"

"He's just bluffing. How can he be so lawless! This is Kaifeng, the city that produced the hero Bao Gong* in the Song Dynasty. We have a tradition of law and order here. Pan Ying can go to jail for what he threatens to do."

"Still, Lao Zhao, I think we have to take some precautionary measures, just in case."

"All right, all right, Lao Jin. For your peace of mind, I'll tell Yidong to have five or six of his kung-fu friends at the procession. They're all experts in Shaolin martial arts. If there's any mishap, they'll take care of it. Now, are you happy?"

Zhao casually picked up some peanuts and popped them in his mouth.

"That sounds good. Shaolin experts are the best in kung fu. However, I'm still worried. You probably didn't know, but this Pan Ying's father also asked for Chen-er's Ba Zi two years back. I wouldn't think of it. Pan is not one of us. Beside, Pan Ying was born in the Year of the Monkey, six years before Chen-er. A six-year clash will not lead to a harmonious union, as most feng-shui masters would tell you," Lao Jin explained seriously.

"O-h-h-h! This is news to me. I was aware that a couple of the White-Cap families were keen to ask for Chen-er's Ba Zi, but not a Han family. Huh!" Lao Zhao frowned as he spoke.

"What happened was that Pan Ying chanced to see Chen-er at the Lantern Festival that year and was quite taken by her. A week later, the request came from his father. I told them right away that Chen-er had been spoken for since the age of eight. Lao Pan (Senior Pan) accepted the refusal graciously, but not his son. Pan Ying still comes around to the market every now and then and tries to strike up a conversation with Chen-er. Chen-er avoids him like the plague."

Lao Zhao sat up straight as he listened intently to Lao Jin's story.

"So, it is more serious than I thought. I'd better warn Yidong about it." His eyebrows remained knotted as he tried to put his thoughts together.

The two men remained quiet for a long while, a rare occurrence. While Lao Zhao was silently reassessing the severity of Pan Ying's criminal intentions, Lao Jin was pondering how best to overcome this pending threat.

At the appropriate hour, as calculated by the feng-shui master, firecrackers were lit and the neighbours came out of their houses to watch the bridal procession. The noisy crackling of the firecrackers heralded the procession's movement from the Jin home towards the Zhao residence. A small band of musicians, playing drums, gongs, and a piccolo, led the way. The bridal sedan chair, adorned with a red embroidered canopy and curtain depicting a dragon and a phoenix, symbolizing a harmonious union, was carried by four muscular men. They followed the musicians closely. The onlookers on the street cheered and clapped and laughed. Joy filled the air. It was a happy day. The community's favourite daughter was being carried to her betrothed.

The procession moved at a good rhythmic pace, every step taking it a little closer to the groom's house. The musicians played as the firecrakers burned – pi, pi, pa, pa, – and the discarded red paper was strewn all over the street, paving it like a carpet. The procession passed the first hutong. It proceeded towards the second. Just as it made the turn to the left, out of nowhere, five large men in kung-fu tunics and tied trousers, their heads bound with turbans, descended upon it.

Pan Ying and his gang lunged at the sedan chair. While his cronies were engaged in fighting with Yidong's helpers, Pan Ying went straight over to lift the sedan-chair curtain, ready to snatch Yuchen and carry her away.

WHAT! He was stunned! Instead of the beautiful Yuchen, resplendent in her exquisite bridal gown, Pan Ying saw two sacs of rice sitting on the chair inside.

No Yuchen! How could that be? Pan Ying was livid. He kicked and smashed and swore and cursed. His men were being defeated too. He had no choice but to call off his fighters and leave, fuming with an unspeakable anger, mortified to the utmost, vowing he would "take care" of Yidong later.

Since the day of the conversation with Lao Zhao, Yuchen's father had been uneasy about Pan Ying, despite Lao Zhao's repeated assurances that everything would be under control. He had insisted that Yuchen be carried in an unadorned sedan chair, without fanfare, at the crack of dawn that morning. Never mind the auspicious hour set by the feng-shui master.

The small dowry the Jins had prepared for Yuchen had been sent to the Zhaos the day before. When the appointed time came, Yidong arranged to have his kung-fu friends play the parts of the musicians and the carriers and walk in the procession with a rice-laden chair. With luck and skill they would take on Pan Ying and his gang before these rascals had a chance to crash in at Yidong's house.

By the time Pan Ying and his gang conceded defeat, Yidong

and Yuchen had already completed the wedding ceremony of Salute to Heaven and Earth (Bai Tian Di), kowtowing first to Heaven, their heads touching the ground, then to their parents, and finally to each other. They were thus legally married.

"It's all arranged, Lao Jin," Lao Zhao assured his friend. "Xiao Gao, has taken the silver for the fare to Shanghai. He's been there before; he knows what to do."

"Can you trust this Xiao Gao, Lao Zhao? Don't forget he is from Gao Ting's family. You know, the traitor Gao Ting, who tried to sell the law manuscript to the foreigner some years back. I heard this rascal often plays dice with Xiao Wang and Xiao Liu, and you know these two are up to no good most of the time."

"Take it easy. Xiao Gao promised he'll accompany them all the way to Shanghai. Too bad Yidong's granduncle Wengui isn't around any more. It was such a shame he suddenly passed away in Shanghai. Otherwise, it would be a lot easier for Yidong and Yuchen."

"Well, if Wengui were still around, there wouldn't be any need for Dong-er and Chen-er to go to Shanghai. Wengui would have made some inroads with the Jewry there about our plight," Jin responded.

After a pause, Lao Zhao muttered, almost as if he were trying to convince himself, "I don't think there will be any problems."

At the first light of daybreak, rosy streaks appeared on the horizon, signifying a fine, bright day ahead. Yuchen had been up since the Mao hour,* between 5 a.m. and 7 a.m. In fact, she had hardly slept at all. Conflicting thoughts and endless questions about the future kept her tossing and turning, even though she tried hard to stay still for fear of disturbing Yidong. She almost hoped that her father and Yidong's father would miraculously change their minds at the last minute and put a stop to this journey, which did not make much sense to her at all.

Yuchen reheated the dumplings left over from their dinner the previous night. It was a Henan custom to serve dumplings for a farewell meal and noodles for a welcome-home celebration. Everyone seemed to be lacking an appetite. As she tried to eat at least two or three dumplings, Yuchen wondered to herself when would she be able to enjoy the welcome-home noodles. Tears welled up in her eyes at the thought.

The two mothers, both with red, swollen eyes, could not stop sobbing. The unknown was too much for them. Would they ever see their children again? Would this parting mean goodbye forever? Up to this date, the planned journey remained a vague event that was to take place sometime in the future. Now that the future had finally arrived, their sudden realization of the cruel reality was too much to bear. Mothers' hearts are never severed from their children's. They are connected for eternity. While they were told by their respective husbands that it was an important and imperative mission that Yidong and Yuchen were to carry out, the thought that they were not likely to see them again for at least a few years, or maybe never again, pierced their hearts with immense pain and a sense of helplessness.

The fathers looked grim and serious. Lao Zhao tried to lighten the atmosphere: "Look at the sky! It's such a fine day! This definitely is a sign, an auspicious omen that your journey will be safe and pleasant."

"Go pay your respects to the ancestors, and then you should be on your way." Lao Jin patted his son-in-law on the back and signalled that he should go inside the house.

They had all gathered in front of Lao Zhao's house. The companion for their journay, Xiao Gao, had hired a four-wheel mule cart and was waiting for them at the city gate.

The group walked slowly, each carrying one or two pieces of baggage. When they saw Xiao Gao and the mule cart, they knew it was time for the young couple to bid farewell. Yuchen had dreaded this moment. She had such contradictory thoughts: she desperately wanted the moment to remain frozen in time, so she did not have to go any further; at the same time, she wished that the parting would be over quickly.

Amidst tears and repeated last-minute reminders, Yuchen's mother quietly slipped a red packet into her pocket and whispered, "For good luck and safe journey!" No one but Yuchen was aware of her mother's action. Yuchen clutched her mother in one last tight embrace.

Xiao Gao helped Yuchen and Yidong climb into the cart. The mule began to trot.

Yuchen and Yidong waved until their parents' silhouettes were mere dots in the distance. Tears continued to stream down Yuchen's cheeks. Yidong took her hands into his and gently stroked them.

"We'll do all right, I promise you," he spoke softly into her ear.

In his mind, he was no less apprehensive about their future, but if he did not put up a brave face, then both of them would end up like flies without heads, confused, with no direction. In that case, who would be there to spur them on.

Yidong looked younger than his twenty-two years. Strong and robust, he still had a touch of boyishness. His slightly square face with its dark, thick eyebrows and long nose was what Chinese fortune-tellers would define as "a manly countenance with a promising future."

Yidong had been in seventh heaven since his wedding day. He had waited for ten years for his marriage to Yuchen to take place. Ever since he was twelve, he had been teased endlessly by his friends about his betrothal to Yuchen, because he was the first among his peers to be "engaged." In the beginning, all the fuss annoyed him terribly, and he found it a nuisance, but by and by he grew fonder and fonder of his future bride and was eager to have her. Often he fantasized holding her in his arms and caressing her. She had grown more beautiful by the day, vivacious and full of spirit.

He had been aware, too, of the fact that many families with sons had their eyes on Yuchen. He was ever so grateful that his parents and Yuchen's had settled on their union. He felt he was the most fortunate young man in all of Kaifeng.

When they were very young, they had played together after gatherings at the synagogue or at some celebratory festivals. With the onset of their consciousness of the opposite sex, they somehow shied away from each other and only dared to steal a glance every now and then. But Yidong knew that, during all these years, Yuchen had him in her heart, just as he held her in his. They simply had to wait till the appropriate time to be joined in marriage. He counted the years, then the months, then the days. The night before the wedding, he was excited yet fearful. He had arranged for his buddies to play their parts to foil any attack on the wedding procession; but then . . . what if? A thousand things could go wrong . . . Then what? The anxiety made him feel that his heart was jumping out of his throat.

And the bliss of their wedding night! Yuchen responded to his unrestrained passion with her own. To his utmost delight, Yuchen revealed that she had been thinking of him often for many years as well. Yidong could relive that moment over and over again for as long as he lived.

Yidong knew that Yuchen too would forever treasure their first night together. In fact, Yuchen was surprised that her first encounter with a man could give her so much pleasure and joy. It was nothing like the old wife's tale that said the wedding night was nothing but pain. To her, it was rapturous. She and Yidong united in body and soul. They had become one and they would remain as one being from then on.

As he sat there in the cart moving along the bumpy dirt road, Yidong wanted so much to hold his wife in his arms to comfort her in her sorrow. But with Xiao Gao sitting across from them, eyeing him and Yuchen from time to time, he felt embarrassed to demonstrate his affection in public, even if that public consisted of only one person.

瀟風悲雨橋平同行到天涯

Chapter 2

To Shanghai

A journey from Kaifeng, Henan, to Shanghai during the late-nineteenth century was an arduous one.

As early as 1864, a British merchant had built a six-hundred-metre-long narrow-gauge railroad in Beijing as an illustration to show the Qing court. It was dismantled almost immediately. Subsequent efforts were similarly unsuccessful. In 1888, the powerful Viceroy Li Hongzhang was able to persuade the Empress Dowager Cixi and overcame the objections from conservative ministers, and railway construction began in earnest. By 1911, there were around nine thousand kilometres of rails in China, built by the various foreign powers in their respective areas of influence. There were also railroads built by Chinese companies with Chinese investments. It would only be after about 1906 that civilians would be able to travel from north to south by rail.

For ordinary people like Yidong and Yuchen, in 1872, land travel was mostly by foot or by carriages or carts. These were drawn by horses or mules, or were pushed by hired labourers. Boats were manually propelled, and were usually not equipped for overnight accommodation. Steamships were in use, but were mostly for foreigners, cargo, and the well-to-do, not the common folk.

Kaifeng had once been a port along the Grand Canal system,* but by the mid-nineteenth century, many sections of the canal were unnavigable due to lack of proper maintenance.

Yuchen and Yidong were told that it would take about a month of travelling the land and water routes to reach their destination. They would travel by land, skirting along the southern shore of the Yellow River for the first part. When they arrived at the Grand Canal, they would take the boat southward down the canal. Passing a major city, Xuzhou, they would reach Yangzhou, a commercial hub at the time. From Yangzhou, they would pass Zhenjiang, Shaoxin, and Suzhou, before reaching Shanghai. Xiao Gao had been hired to look after all their needs and was to bring them to a certain Mr. Medhurst, who had, by mail, promised to connect them to the Jewish community in Shanghai. Xiao Gao had been to Shanghai before; he would not go wrong. They were to simply follow his directions and everything would work out without a hitch.

Their luggage was manageable. One large suitcase between them and several cloth-wrapped bundles (*baofu*), mostly clothing and blankets. Yuchen's mother had sewn a gold ring, a gold bracelet, and two gold pendants into the pocket of her inner garment, and Yuchen was under the strictest orders never to let anyone see them. These were the most valuable items from her dowry; she was to keep them for posterity or, as an absolute last resort, for funds.

In the suitcase, Yidong kept silver nuggets and a few artifacts of foreign origin that his ancestors had brought to China from the West more than eight hundred years before. There was also a letter from his father to whoever was to receive the young couple in Shanghai. The letter set out the misfortune of the Kaifeng Jewry, pleading for help and, at the same time, asking patronage for his son and daughter-in-law. Yidong made sure that he did not leave the suitcase unattended at any time. At night he kept it on his bed for safekeeping.

The journey was a long and tiresome one, but Yidong and Yuchen were happy, despite little discomforts and inconveniences here and there. Being newlyweds, they were content just to be together. Everything else was negligible. The sweetness of love was more encompassing than they realized. The days were idle compared to their usual routine; the nights were filled with passion and tenderness. They were more engrossed with each other than with the scenery they passed or the novelties they encountered. It was an idyllic journey, affording them time to get to know and appreciate each other. Even the pain of leaving their parents seemed to have diminished. They were beginning to look forward to a future of their own.

Yidong was excited to be on the canal. His father had briefly described the journey to him. Yuchen's father had filled him in on the history of the Grand Canal. Lao Jin had said to him in earnest, "Yidong, you should feel very privileged. Neither your father nor I have ever been on the Grand Canal, and you and Yuchen will be going down the canal for a good part of your trip. It's something to remember and to tell your children and your grandchildren about. You know, the oldest canals dated back to before Qin Shi Huang, the first emperor, and they say that the oldest canal, Hong Gou, actually linked the Yellow River near our city Kaifeng to the Si River and the Bian River. Our ancestors travelled the same canal from south China northward to Kaifeng so many hundreds of years ago.

Just think, you're doing the same journey, but the other way round.

"When our ancestors first arrived at Kaifeng, it was the capital, sitting at the juncture of four canals. That was during the Northern Song Dynasty. After the Mongols moved the capital to Beijing during the Yuan Dynasty, that section of the canal linking Kaifeng to Beijing fell into disuse, and now it is no longer navigable. A pity, indeed!

"The Ming and Qing emperors kept the canals in reasonably good condition. But the Yellow River changed course after the flood of 1854. Somehow, fewer people used the canals after that. Now many parts of the canals are also unnavigable.

"Xiao Gao has travelled the route. He'll guide you to take the boat where the canal is still good or to go by land where there is no water route. You don't have to worry."

Yidong reflected on his father-in-law's words and tried to take note as much as he could. The rhythmic sway of the boat over calm water had a hypnotic effect, luring the passengers into drowsiness. Yidong and Yuchen leaned against each other in silent contentment, taking in whatever was going on around them and along the banks.

Occasionally, Xiao Gao would strike up a conversation with them.

"Have you heard of the iron road that the foreigners are trying to build?" he asked Yidong.

"My father mentioned it some time ago," answered Yidong. "He said the Russians, the Japanese, and the British are plunderers in China. It's bad enough that the British forced opium onto the people; now all these foreign countries want to build and own these iron roads and pocket all the profits. He also said there will be 'fire carriages' travelling at top speed on these iron roads."

"No doubt! I heard the fire carriages take only a few days to go from Beijing to Shanghai. That would have made our trip much easier." Xiao Gao continued, "But who knows when all this will happen. I just hope there will be no more fighting. The Taiping Rebellion* was so bad for all of us. I'm glad it is over."

"The Qing government is weak and useless. Both my father and Yuchen's father believe that sooner or later there will be war again. It is horrible just to think about it," sighed Yidong.

Little did they realize that peasant discontent had been rumbling in various provinces and the rebellion called the Boxer Uprising* (Yi He Tuan) was already looming on the horizon. The Boxers would target the foreigners, the treaty-power nations, blaming them for all the woes of the country.

At other times, Yidong would ask Xiao Gao about Shanghai. As they travelled south from Kaifeng, he noticed that people's accents were getting stranger by the day. He could hardly make out what they were saying.

"Do the people in Shanghai speak our dialect?" Yidong asked Xiao Gao.

"No! They speak something totally different. I can't understand them at all. It is not Mandarin. It is their local dialect. But the foreigners can speak some Mandarin. When they speak, it's like they're singing or always posing a question."

"How are we going to communicate with them?" Yidong looked worried.

"Well, can you speak Mandarin?" Xiao Gao asked. "I can make some sense out of them when they speak Mandarin. They also have difficulty understanding my Henan dialect."

"At the Tutelage School (Si-shu), we studied Mandarin. I can understand it, but cannot speak it well," Yidong said.

"You'll be okay, I guess. You can always write it out if you can't say it. As you know, the writing is the same."

"What about food, Gao Shu (Uncle Gao)?" Yidong asked.

"Oh! You'll find that most people in Shanghai eat rice for every meal. Not like us, eating noodles and dumplings most of the time, plus pancakes, buns. They'll eat noodles only sometimes. Dumplings seldom. And their buns are tiny compared to ours. They don't always steam their buns. Some they pan-fry, and they call it 'raw-fried buns' (shen-jian-bao). There are also these 'small basket buns' (xiao-long-bao), a kind of thin-skinned bun with meat fillings and soup inside. Mmmm. They are delicious."

Xiao Gao closed his eyes and sucked in a deep breath as he remembered the savoury taste of this delicacy.

"Meat, eh? They can't be kosher, I suppose," wondered Yidong.

"Not only are they not kosher, I believe they use pork most of the time," answered Xiao Gao. "When I'm away from home, I don't pay much attention to these observances. Besides, everywhere along the coast in China, pork is the most common meat they eat. Can't help it. You know, a lot of Chinese wouldn't eat beef because ox is used to farm the land and they feel it would be sacrilegious to eat beef. And most of them wouldn't touch lamb, because they believe mutton causes body odour. Strange thinking, I must say."

"I wonder what our parents would say about this?" said Yidong. "I know Shanghai is at the mouth of the Yangtze River. They say fish and rice are plentiful in all the land along the river." Yidong turned to Yuchen. "Are we going to change to Shanghai food?"

Yuchen smiled and shrugged as she replied, "If you wish."

Three weeks into their trip, Xiao Gao began to show signs of restlessness. Throughout the journey, by land or waterway, they would disembark at nightfall at a small town or a village and spend the night in a nearby inn. At the crack of dawn the next day they would be on their way again. Xiao Gao always carried some dice in his pocket, and every now and then he would take them out and throw them for fun. Lately, more frequently than before, he had been taking the dice out of his pocket and throwing them in a small wooden bowl to pass the time. Yidong and Yuchen could tell his fingers were itching for action.

One day, as the three of them sat on the deck after dinner, waiting to dock at the next nearest town or village, Xiao Gao took out his dice again. After a while he said to Yidong: "How about playing a hand or two?"

Yuchen immediately tugged quietly at the corner of Yidong's jacket to alert him. She had been warned by her father that Xiao Gao had a weakness for gambling, and she and Yidong were under no circumstances to succumb to Xiao Gao's temptation. If possible, they were to prevent Xiao Gao from playing dice or other gambling games with anyone during their journey.

"We'll play small. A copper each bet," Xiao Gao continued.

Yidong looked at Xiao Gao apologetically and said, "I'm sorry, Gao Shu, I don't know how to play these games."

"I'll teach you. It's very simple . . . " Xiao Gao offered.

"No, Gao Shu, I can't. I don't want to. Really." Yidong's tone was firm and determined. There was no room for negotiation.

Xiao Gao mumbled something about being bored to death, and went to talk to the boatman. Yuchen whispered to Yidong, "We have to be careful now. I think Xiao Gao's addiction is getting to him. I hope he won't get into any trouble."

"I'll try to put in a word or two to tell him the consequences of gambling. I'll talk him out of it," Yidong whispered back in a somewhat optimistic tone. After a minute or two, his cheerfulness disappeared. He said, "Soon we'll be approaching Yangzhou, and I'm afraid he won't be able to control himself once we land there."

"Yes, we have to be extra vigilant," nodded Yuchen.

A day later the barge pulled in at the dock in Yangzhou. Xiao Gao was in high spirits and said to Yidong and Yuchen, "We've been travelling on the canal for so long. It's time to stretch our legs on land. Let's stay in Yangzhou for a few days. I know a comfortable place by the dock. We'll stay there and you can spend some time in this big city. You'll find it fascinating."

"I would rather we continue on right away in the morning," Yidong answered.

"From here it is a short distance to Shanghai down the river. We'll be there in no time. Don't worry. Everything will be fine. Have some fun here. Taste some Yangzhou food; it is delicious. There are quite a few historic sites around too," Xiao Gao insisted.

"No, Gao Shu. Let's just stay the night and leave early in the morning. I'm anxious to get to Shanghai." Yidong would not give in.

"All right, all right. I'll find out about the boats heading south tomorrow and book one to take us," Xiao Gao conceded.

They checked in at a modest inn not far from the dock. Once settled, Xiao Gao said to them, "Treat yourselves to a special meal and get a good night's sleep. I'm going to visit some friends. I'll see you in the morning."

"Why don't you join us for dinner, Gao Shu, and turn in early tonight, so we can get an early start tomorrow," Yidong suggested.

"I can't. I have some urgent business with a friend. I'll see you in the morning," Xiao Gao replied, and with that he hurried out.

"I hope he's not heading to the gambling place," Yuchen remarked.

"I'm pretty sure that's exactly where he's going. What urgent business could he have here in Yangzhou. Just hope he doesn't lose too much. From here, we have only stops at Zhenjiang, Shaoxin, Suzhou, and after that we'll head straight to Shanghai. It's going to be soon, Chen-mei (little sister Chen)," Yidong said, using the affectionate term that some husbands use to address their wives. "Very soon."

Yidong and Yuchen had difficulty waking up the next morning. Their heads felt light and their limbs listless. When they finally managed to open their eyes, they were alarmed that it was already mid-morning. Immediately, Yidong sensed that something had gone awry. He grabbed Yuchen and asked anxiously, "Are you all right?" He eyed her from head to toe and noticed nothing unusual.

"I feel drowsy and weak, Dong-ge. What's wrong with me?" Yuchen looked puzzled.

"Someone must have blown 'sleeping fumes' (mong han yao)* through the paper window into our room during the night. The suitcase..." Yidong checked the bed and found the suitcase gone. Panic-stricken, he dashed for the door. As soon as he opened the door, he almost fell over the suitcase sitting in front of it. He brought it inside and flung it open. The silver nuggets were gone. So were the artifacts from long ago. The letter, books, and personal effects were untouched.

"We've been robbed!" Yidong exclaimed, staring desolately at Yuchen. "It must be Gao Shu. Who else would know we had silver in the suitcase."

Yuchen gently took Yidong's right hand into hers and said, "Let's go find him."

Xiao Gao's room was empty. They hurried to the front to get hold of the innkeeper.

"Did you see Mr. Gao?" Yidong asked.

"He came in last night with two big fellows. They stayed in his room for a couple of hours and left together around midnight. Oh, he left a message for you to go to the dock at noon. By the way, he has paid for the rooms," the innkeeper said.

"Someone came into our room and stole our money and valuables," Yidong stated blankly.

"That can't be! No one has been in here. I locked up and went to bed shortly after Mr. Gao and his companions left. No one else came in. I can vouch for that," the innkeeper responded. Then, as if something had dawned on him, he asked, "I meant to ask you why you left your suitcase outside your door?"

"We didn't. The thief did," Yidong said dryly. "What shall we do? Shall we report the theft to the authorities?" He began to pace impatiently.

"Ah, you mean someone came into your room, took your things, and left the suitcase outside?" the innkeeper asked.

"It looks that way," Yidong answered despondently. "He must have blown some sleeping fumes into our room to send us into a deep sleep. How else would you explain that neither of us was awakened by an intruder in the room. I'm usually a light sleeper."

"Could it have been the two fellows who came with Gao? They looked mean, and I could tell they had been drinking. Not the kind of people you want to associate with, you know what I mean?" the innkeeper speculated.

"Where's the magistrate's office? Can we go there to hit the gong and ask for an investigation?" Yidong asked.

"You don't even have a suspect to be investigated. The officers are not likely to take on such a case. Yangzhou is a big city; robbery happens almost every day. They won't bother to take any action unless it is something sensational," the innkeeper advised. Then he added, "Well, Mr. Gao asked you to go to the dock at noon. Maybe he'll be waiting for you there. You may find out more from him. It is almost noon hour. You'd better hurry. It's too bad that this should happen to you. Frankly, I doubt if you'll ever see your silver again."

"What are we going to do?" Yidong was visibly flustered.

Yuchen took him aside and said calmly to him, "Dong-ge, the innkeeper is right. What we've lost is gone. We'd better go to the dock and continue with our journey. Our things are packed. Let's just leave."

Yidong looked dazed. It was too much of a shock to him. They had not even reached Shanghai, and all their money was gone. How were they going to survive! What to do? He felt like an ant in a hot frying pan.

As is often the case, when there is a crisis, it is the woman who remains more rational and clear-headed. Seeing Yidong standing there looking so helpless, Yuchen took the initiative and more or less led Yidong out of the inn and towards the dock.

The dock looked almost deserted. All the buzzing and haggling of the previous evening had disappeared. There were only a few people around. Most of the boats had left at dawn, and those coming in probably would not arrive till later. From afar, Yidong and Yuchen saw a sampan tied at the post, and a person was sitting there smoking. As they neared the water, they found him to be an older man. As soon as he saw them approaching his boat, he shouted to them, "Young gentleman, are you Mr. Zhao? I've been waiting for you, as Mr. Gao instructed."

The old man spoke in an unfamiliar dialect; a little bit like Mandarin, yet not quite. Yidong thought this must be the Shanghai dialect that Xiao Gao had mentioned. He and Yuchen had difficulty understanding him, but they managed to communicate.

"Where is Mr. Gao?" asked Yidong.

"Ah! Mr. Gao left with the two big fellows. He asked one of them for some money to pay me, and said you'd be here around noon. I'm to take you from here on," the old man answered.

"When did Mr. Gao come?"

"Oh, very late last night. Must have been after midnight. He woke me up and gave me the instructions. Are you ready to leave now?"

"Is Mr. Gao coming?"

"I don't think so. The two men were rushing him. One of them complained when he gave me money and said he should leave you to pay for the fare. Mr. Gao seemed to be afraid of them. Come on now, let me help you with the luggage."

The old man came to the embankment and started to carry some of the bundles onto the deck.

Yidong had hoped to see Xiao Gao at the dock. Now it was apparent that this was not to be. They were on their own from this point on. But didn't Xiao Gao promise his father that he would personally bring them to Mr. Medhurst in Shanghai? Yidong became very weary.

They were glad that there were no other passengers on the boat. They really did not feel like seeing anyone or talking to any strangers. As soon as they were on board and settled, the old man steered the boat away from the dock.

For a while, Yidong and Yuchen sat there in silence, inwardly lamenting the misfortune that had befallen them. By and by they began to discuss what might have taken place. They kept their voices low as they went over all the probable scenarios of the previous night. The only conclusion they arrived at was what they had suspected from the very start.

Xiao Gao must have lost all his money, and probably more, to the two men or their boss. His life must have been threatened. Then, in desperation, he told them about Yidong's suitcase and its contents. That would have been his only source of money. Where else would he have access to cash? Thus he and his creditors devised a way to get to the suitcase. Xiao Gao, with his last little bit of conscience, had probably bargained to pay for the room at the inn and the fare for Yidong and Yuchen to continue on their way. He, in all likelihood, was held against his will and was forced to stay behind to help those thugs to dispose of the artifacts in order to cash out and pay his debt. What a mess he was in.

The young couple sat there assessing their situation and taking stock of what they still possessed. They agreed that all the gold pieces were to stay intact until they were down to absolutely nothing. Yidong counted the loose change in his pocket, which did not amount to much. Luckily Shanghai was within a few days' journey. Mr. Medhurst might help them to find work, they hoped.

Yuchen had quite forgotten about the red packet of lucky money that her mother had sneaked into her pocket on the morning of their departure. She had thought it was just a small token to wish them well. She had not even opened it to check how much was inside. It had stayed in her pocket all this time. Now that money had become critical, every copper was to be hoarded. She opened the packet and was astonished to find a "yin piao,"* a debenture certificate, for ten ounces of silver, payable at any of the money houses.*

Tears streamed down Yuchen's cheeks. This money had to be her mother's private savings* for her old age and, in her generosity, she wanted her daughter to have it. Yuchen quietly thanked her mother in her heart over and over again. If only her mother knew how desperately they needed that money at this very moment. Yidong too was grateful that his mother-in-law had inadvertently given them a lifeline when they were near destitution.

Thinking back, Yidong realized how closely they had brushed shoulders with danger. They could have been kidnapped or assaulted by those gamblers. Or worse still, one of them could have done something to Yuchen . . . he shuddered at the thought.

"Chen-mei, I think we're fortunate in our misfortune. Because neither of us was harmed or injured," Yidong said to Yuchen. "We could have suffered a worse fate. I dare not even think about it."

Yuchen nodded in agreement. With that they put their sadness behind them and were ready to brave the future.

It had been such a harrowing day. From the moment they woke up to the horror of finding most of their valuables stolen until they boarded the sampan, Yidong and Yuchen had been more or less in a state of shock. They had rushed to the dock only to be disappointed that Xiao Gao was nowhere to be found. They took for granted that the old man was taking them to Shanghai. They never even questioned him about the route and the destination.

Although the boat was small, it was fitted with a cabin aft. Obviously, the old man lived on the boat. Because they now had to be extremely frugal, they accepted the old man's offer to spend the nights on the makeshift bed in the shelter. It would only be for about three days at most, they figured, and the weather was fine. There was no reason why they shouldn't save some money this way.

For a couple of days the sky was overcast. It was warm, but there was always a bit of breeze along the river. The old man swayed the pole to propel the boat. At mealtime he prepared simple dishes, mostly salted vegetables, salted fish, and yams, always accompanied by rice. He would also catch fish in the early morning, before they started the journey, and serve it for the noonday meal. Yidong and Yuchen welcomed the novel food and had no complaint. They were also glad that the old man did not serve meat. If he had, they would have had difficulty explaining why they would not eat it. The fact that they did not touch pork and their meat had to be prepared in a special way would have generated too many questions.

On the third day, the sun came out. Yidong and Yuchen felt cheerful, thinking they should be nearing the port of Shanghai soon. But the old man kept on propelling his boat. He made no mention of disembarking. By late afternoon, Yidong noticed that they were sailing towards the sun in a westerly direction. He was bewildered. He knew Shanghai was southeast of Yangzhou. Why then were they heading west. Yuchen prompted him to ask the old man.

Because of differences in dialect, they had not conversed freely with the old man. It was difficult for them to understand each other, and most of the time they just guessed at the meaning of what was said. But this had to be clarified. When the old man took a break to have a cup of tea, Yidong asked, "Are we close to Shanghai now?"

"Shanghai? No, why Shanghai?" said the old man.

"Aren't we going to Shanghai?" Yidong became concerned.

"No, I'm going back home to Nanchang in Jiangxi Province," came the answer.

"But, didn't Mr. Gao hire you to take us to Shanghai?" Yidong's tone was getting more urgent.

"Mr. Gao asked if I was going south, and I said yes, and he said he would pay me to take two passengers, but I had to wait for them till noon."

"Didn't he ask you where you were going?"

"No, he only asked if I was going south, and I was going south, and then southwest to Jiangxi. He didn't have much time to talk to me. The two big fellows were rushing him. He must be in big trouble with those two, I think."

"Are you sure he didn't mention Shanghai?"

"No mention of Shanghai," the old man insisted. "Even

though our dialects are different, I would have known if he had said Shanghai. I thought you were heading south to somewhere near Canton maybe – that you would go as far as I go and continue on another boat."

Yidong and Yuchen looked at each other, stunned.

"But, we're supposed to go to Shanghai!" cried Yidong, almost in tears.

"I had no idea," said the old man, "otherwise I would have let you off in Nanjing, where you could have hired another boat to go to Shanghai. Now we've passed Nanjing. We're in Anhui Province, approaching Anqing. Another three days and we'll be in Jiujiang. From there we'll cross Poyang Lake to reach my home town, Nanchang."

"Can you take us back to Nanjing, please?" pleaded Yuchen.

"Impossible! In nine days, it will be the Mid-Autumn Festival. My wife has arranged for all the relatives and friends to come and celebrate both the festival and, more importantly, the Double-Month party* (Shuang Man Yue) for our first grandson. I must get back before the fifteenth of the eighth month. I can barely make it. Really, I have no time to go back to Nanjing." The old man looked at the young couple and added, "I am so very sorry about this mix-up. We can try to make a stop at Anqing tomorrow, and see if anyone will be heading that way. But I can only refund you a little bit of the fare Gao paid me. Not much."

Yidong and Yuchen made no answer. Their minds went blank. They had no idea what they were supposed to do next. It was a nightmare, and it was all Xiao Gao's fault. They began to blame themselves, too, for letting Xiao Gao leave them in Yangzhou. They should have insisted on keeping him with them for the entire night. But blame all they could, it would not solve their problem.

After a while, the old man said to them, "Look, let me make a suggestion. Why don't you come with me to Nanchang and spend a few weeks there? I'll be making another trip by the middle of the ninth month to bring Jingdezheng* porcelain-ware to Yangzhou. I'll take you with me then, and I won't ask you to pay. Going that way is easier and faster, because it is downstream. What do you say?"

After some discussion between them, Yuchen replied: "We're grateful for your help, Lao Bo (Senior Uncle). Maybe this is a solution out of no solution. You see, Mr. Gao and the two fellows stole our silver, and we don't have enough to hire another boat."

Although Yidong and Yuchen had in their possession the yin-piao for ten ounces of silver, they did not want to show it to anyone. Once they reached Shanghai, they would ask Mr. Medhurst to help them to cash it. Preferably not before that. Once robbed, twice cautious.

"So, you agree we don't stop at Anqing?" asked the old man. His face lit up a little. "That will save us some time. Good."

Navigating upstream was hard work, but the old man seemed to have a knack for it. Apart from taking a couple of extra tea breaks, he manoeuvred the boat smoothly and without incident. At Jiujiang they docked for some supplies, but wasted no time on anything else. Then they embarked onto Poyang Lake,* which would take them straight to Nanchang, as the city sat on its shore.

Poyang Lake, being the largest freshwater lake in China, looked serene and endless. Despite their difficulties, Yidong and Yuchen could not help but admire the awesome beauty around them. The old man told them that they were just skirting along the western bank of the lake system and would not encounter treacherous waters. Traders who traversed the huge expanse of water might well face dangerous storms and big waves, because of the wicked winds from the mountains. Many boats, even large western ships, had been known to disappear without a trace.

"There is one particular stretch which, more often than not, submerges the ships and swallows the men. It's a cursed area. I wouldn't venture near it for any amount of money," the old man concluded.

The lake remained calm as they navigated towards Nanchang. The brilliance of the sunshine added vibrancy to the greenery along the banks. The various shades of green and gold reflected in the water, gradually fading into the blue of the sky. So very picturesque! Beautiful beyond words!

Yidong and Yuchen noticed the birds, a lot of them and so many different kinds. They were intrigued by all the species they had never seen before. In particular, they were taken by the cranes with pure white plumage and a few black spots at the tip of the wings. They had sword-like beaks, brownish yellow, and they stood on long, pink legs. Yidong and Yuchen had seen such creatures in some Chinese paintings, but never in real life.

"Look how tall they are!" exclaimed Yuchen. "I think it's at least five feet or more."

"These are the Black Sleeve Cranes," explained the old man. "They can live as long as seventy years, and they mate for life. We call them the Immortal Cranes. They are a symbol of good fortune. Very precious to us."

"Maybe they will bring us luck too," sighed Yuchen.

"Most definitely they will. I guarantee you," said the old man.

Calm water, balmy weather, beautiful scenery, and the propitious cranes aside, Yuchen began to suffer seasickness. She couldn't hold down any food she ate, and seemed to prefer pickled fruits or pickled vegetables. She felt a bit weak, probably because she couldn't keep food down. Otherwise she looked fine. Yidong, nevertheless, was worried, wondering what to do. He kept bringing her tea and snacks almost on the hour.

"Lao Bo, are we nearing Nanchang soon?" he asked the old man. "I think Yuchen needs to see a doctor."

The old man laughed and told him not to worry.

"Why? She's not eating properly. Maybe she has caught a bad stomach illness. If this goes on, she'll be reduced to skin and bone," Yidong said.

The old man looked at him with much mirth in his eyes and said, "I think the cranes have already brought you good luck. If I'm not mistaken, your wife is going to have a baby. Congratulations."

Yidong's mouth remained wide open, and it took him a while to grasp what the old man was saying. Then he burst out in laughter and jumped into the air, rocking the boat violently. He rushed to hold Yuchen in his arms.

"I'm going to be a father! Is it true, Chen-mei?" he looked excitedly at his wife. "Tell me it's true. I'm going to be a father."

Yuchen felt shy in front of the old man. She blushed and nodded. "I believe Lao Bo is right, although I'm not absolutely certain yet. I'm just worried that this will make things even more difficult for us."

"No, this is the best piece of news since Yangzhou. We will make it work no matter what. As soon as we reach Nanchang, I'll write home and tell everyone about it. Ba and Niang and your parents will be so, so happy. I can't wait! I can't wait!" Yidong was ecstatic beyond words.

Yidong's exuberance gave Yuchen much comfort. She had been aware of her body's changes, but dared not mention it to Yidong, for fear it would load him with yet another burden. Ordinarily, the news of a pregnancy would always be celebrated in the family, but since their future was so uncertain right then, she wasn't sure if an addition to the family would be welcome news. Yidong's positive acceptance reinforced her own joy and happiness. Yes, she vowed, they would make it work.

The three travellers celebrated that evening with a good meal, though Yuchen was able to eat only a small portion. The old man and the young couple had by now become almost like family, and they were more at ease with one another as each became more adapted to the dialect of the other.

The old man's last name was Xiong. "The same character as the bear," he added. "So many strokes to write it."

He and his family lived on a small plot of land just outside Nanchang's city wall. His two sons looked after the farm, and he carried on a small-scale trading business on the side. He would take porcelain pieces from Jingdezheng or rapeseed or kumquats to the big cities of Nanjing, Yangzhou, or even Shanghai. On his return, he would bring back inexpensive fanciful novelty items and sell them locally. He did that twice a year and very much enjoyed the trips.

"And I always bring some salt back. Jiangxi is good for rice, cotton, lumber ... many, many things, but it doesn't have salt.

Those licensed salt merchants are too greedy. It is cheaper near the coast. And we use so much salt to preserve vegetables, meat, fish, and even fruit. The salted kumquats are perfect for the young missus in her condition right now."

Two days later the boat docked at Nanchang.

Neither Yidong nor Yuchen quite expected Nanchang to be the city it was. Whether it was the effect of cruising the ethereal water of Poyang or the charm of the Immortal Cranes, when the young couple stepped on shore, they felt a sense of welcome.

The city was on the west bank of Poyang Lake, and the old man had told them that the city also sat on the bank of the Gan River, which drained into the lake. In the far distance, further to the west, there were the mountains, the old man said. Rice paddies, cotton fields, and orchards crisscrossed the landscape in various shades of golden brown. The season of abundance and of "mellow fruitfulness"* had descended upon them. It was so comforting, so reassuring.

Toronto, Canada

2012

九曲黄河萬里沙

Chapter 3

Revelation

It was a bright, sunny Sunday afternoon at the Toronto waterfront, in early June, 2012. A cruise ship, the *Sea Queen*, was docked alongside the wharf. Along the entire length of the upper railing ran a huge banner, reading "Hui Fook Mental Health Foundation." Four or five volunteers stood guard at the boarding entrances. A merry crowd of about a hundred milled below, scattered in groups of three, five, or more, laughing, greeting one another, chatting noisily. Most were in casual wear – short-sleeved or sleeveless tops, bright and colourful bermuda shorts, or cotton pants with sandals or sneakers. Rhae and a friend, Bill, arrived in similar summer attire.

As soon as they appeared, a few people came forward to greet them. Leen Jin, in a beige cotton suit that hugged her slim body, immediately chaperoned them to an elderly woman sitting atop a low concrete ledge.

"Rhae, come and meet Prof. Li! Professor, this is Rhae Zhao." Leen introduced Rhae to the elderly woman.

Rhae bowed slightly and addressed the professor respectfully: "Prof. Li."

"Ni hao, Ms. Zhao," the professor replied with a broad smile.

A brief glance and Rhae was captivated by Professor Li's appearance. She wore an over-size dark-green cheong-sam,* topped with a light-green sweater. Her attire was obviously Chinese, but her features were not. She had short, curly hair, not artificially permed but naturally curly. Her eyes were greyish-blue, not brown like most Chinese. She wore an interesting stone pendant, not fine jewellery but clearly of some ethnic origin. She spoke perfect Mandarin.

Not quite certain of what small talk would engage this new acquaintance, Rhae retreated to say hello to some other friends. She pondered over the reason for Leen's eagerness to introduce her to Prof. Li. Leen had a knack for finding interesting people, usually those with special knowledge or unusual skills.

By and by people began queuing up to board the *Sea Queen*. As Rhae climbed the ramp to reach the upper deck of the boat, she saw Mena, a Chinese-language television host, and her friend Benoit, a French national, at the front table. Rhae went over to join them.

As the boat slowly pulled away from the dock, buffet dinner was laid out at two stations. People lined up. Mena, Benoit, and Rhae were among the first to fill their plates. They chatted as they enjoyed a selection of scrumptious delicacies.

"I heard you're leaving for France, Benoit. So soon?" Rhae asked.

"Three years in a foreign country is more than enough. I'm quite ready to go home," Benoit replied.

"Any plans?" said Rhae.

"Nothing spectacular, but I signed . . ."

Out of nowhere Leen appeared and, without so much

as a word of excuse, she grabbed Rhae's hand and physically dragged her to the other end of the deck. Leen deposited Rhae on a seat opposite Prof. Li. Then she picked up a folded card with the name "SUPERFARM" printed on it, indicating that the table they sat at was sponsored by Fred Ko's company SUPERFARM. She turned the card over and placed it in front of Rhae.

"Write your Chinese name, Rhae," commanded Leen.

Rhae looked at Leen, puzzled.

"Just write your name."

Rhae knew better than to argue with Leen, so she wrote the two Chinese characters Zhao Yu at the lower left corner of the back of the card. Leen turned it for Prof. Li to see. The latter looked at the two characters and raised her eyes to meet Rhae's.

"Where is your ancestral home, Rhae, may I ask?" Prof. Li inquired.

"Nanchang, in the Province of Jiangxi. But my great-grandparents were from Kaifeng, Henan," came the answer.

Professor Li began to write in the space beside Rhae's name, and in no time four lines of Chinese characters appeared. Fred Ko read aloud:

原籍犹太有天智
挥毕成画可书实
若问仙女居何处
当为瑜女为当任

"Are you aware that you are very likely a descendant of the Kaifeng Jews, Rhae?" Prof. Li said.

Before Rhae had time to answer, all the people sitting at the table exclaimed in unison, "WHAT!"

Fred laughed as he said, "Are you joking, Professor? What do you mean? Rhae not Chinese? She looks two-hundred percent Chinese to me."

Everyone nodded in agreement, but Leen jumped in. "Wait, wait, Fred. Let's hear what Professor Li has to say."

Professor Li was happy to comply. "Have you heard of the ancient city of Kaifeng in Henan Province, which Rhae has just mentioned? It was the capital of at least seven different dynasties, going back many centuries. Well, during the Northern Song Dynasty, it was the capital, and was the most prosperous city in China, if not in the world. It was then that a large group of Israelites arrived at Kaifeng. They settled there and were in Kaifeng for almost nine hundred years, till the latter part of the nineteenth century. Then, somehow, most of the community dispersed to heaven knows where . . . only a handful of clans remained. There . . ."

Fred couldn't help interrupting. "That's fascinating! Where did these Israelites come from? Why Kaifeng?"

Professor Li replied, "I'm talking about ancient history now. If you want, I'll tell you about it."

"Now that you've roused our curiosity, Professor, you'll have to tell us all about it. Especially for Rhae's benefit. She should know about her ancestors," Leen said, and Rhae nodded.

"Please, Professor. Otherwise I won't be able to sleep tonight."

Professor Li smiled. "Very well then. I'll try to be brief. You've all heard about the Silk Road, no doubt. There were several routes of the so-called Silk Road. They were trade routes as well as routes for the exchange of cultures and religions between China and the countries to the west – India, the Middle East, Europe, and so on. There is evidence that these people came from the region of what was then Mesopotamia."

"Where's that?" Fred was impatient again.

"Present-day Iran-Iraq area. The people of Hebrew faith used to travel to China as far back as the West Han Dynasty – that is, about 200 BCE, or even earlier. Over a period of several centuries, some settled along the trade routes, some entered the interior of China. During the Song Dynasty, a large caravan of several hundred . . . "

Everyone was absorbed in listening to Professor Li. More and more people walked over to join the crowd. Professor Li finished her story and pointed to Rhae and remarked, "Look at her ears. She has hardly any earlobes. It is an indication of her non-Han ancestry."

Rhae quickly touched her ears with her two hands and made a face. Leen picked up the card and asked Professor Li to explain the four lines she had written on it.

"It simply says that Rhae is of Jewish ancestry and she excels in arts. I call her a 'xian nv,'* because I think she is a self-reliant . . . "

"Hey, 'xian nv' 'Celestial Maiden'! How do you feel?" Fred joked, obviously finding it most amusing.

"Dumbfounded!" Rhae replied.

Professor Li went on to say: "I must clarify. The term 'xian nv' here is not used in the sense —"

Before she could finish her explanation, Leen turned to Rhae and said, "Rhae, let me properly introduce Professor Li to you. Professor Li is a philologist. She is an authority on Chinese words, each Chinese character's structure, formation, history, development, and meaning. China considers her a national treasure in diaspora. Would you believe, Professor Li is almost a hundred years old, and even a couple of years ago she was still being invited to lecture in Beijing, Shanghai, Hong Kong, and Taiwan."

Rhae bowed with great respect and said, "I'm honoured to meet you, Professor Li. I hope to learn much from you."

Professor Li wrote her name and phone number on the back of the SUPERFARM card and handed it to Rhae.

"Come see me any time, Rhae."

"I'm going to ask Bill to come and see what Professor Li has to say about him." With that Leen hurried away to look for Bill.

It was almost midnight when Leen called. Rhae was reading in bed when the phone rang. Her room was spacious. One wall was lined with bookshelves filled to capacity. On the opposite wall was a large, framed Chinese calligraphy of *"Zhu's Didactics to His Family,"** done in a very neat Dishu* style of calligraphy. Beside the walnut queen-size sleigh bed was an antique night table. On it were some magazines and books.

Leen, in turn, was sitting on her bed, blanket and sheets dishevelled. Her room was untidy, with several stacks of newspaper on the floor leaning against two walls. Clothes were piled up on one chair, and shoes were strewn across the floor. It looked a bit like a teenager's room.

The two were recapping the event earlier.

"How did you meet Professor Li? I never heard you mention her before," Rhae asked.

"She's been here a lot longer than we have. But she wants to stay low-key. I believe she was invited by the United

Nations to come and help with some Chinese books in the Toronto Reference Library, way back in the 1950s. She is of Manchu-Mongolian descent – from one of the Qing royal families—"

"No wonder she looks different, with her curly hair and greyish-blue eyes!" Rhae interrupted.

"Professor Li is very learned. Not only was she tutored by the royal scholars, but she went on to obtain a Ph.D. from Qing Hua University way back when women did not even go to school. She was granted two honourary Ph.D.s from some other universities. She taught at Hong Kong University and also here at the University of Toronto. She's a remarkable person with an incredible amount of knowledge about the Chinese language and Chinese history. She has published four books on the Chinese language. One of them teaches Chinese to the non-Chinese and is rated one of the best on the market. Unfortunately, it was a limited edition and is not available commercially.

"Don't you find her amazing? You can be sure that from now on Fred and the others will tease you to no end about the 'Celestial Maiden' part."

"Stop right there. You hurried off and didn't bother to hear Professor Li's explanation about the 'xian nv' bit. It's not what you think."

"What explanation?"

"What she means by 'xian nv' when she described me."

"What did she say?"

"The character 'xian' that she used in this case is not meant in the ordinary sense you would expect. It is not a fairy or a goddess or some ethereal being that does not belong to this world.

The character 'xian 仙' is made up of the two parts: 'mountain' and 'person,' meaning someone living high on the mountain. In the old days, those who lived on the mountain tended to rely on themselves. They had to solve problems by themselves, do things by themselves, and use whatever resources they could find up there. In short, it only means I am a self-reliant person. No mystery there."

"No matter. Anyway, her analyses of people are usually 99.9999 percent accurate. Reading my husband's writing, she told me Tian is a clean freak. Everything she said about him is right on."

"What does she base her assessment on? It is not really a science to read people's penmanship to determine a person's character or history, as in my case," Rhae asked.

"Professor Li told me that the choice of the characters for one's name is already an indicator of a person's destiny. Because each Chinese character is often made up of two or three or more parts, each part has a meaning and points to the direction of a person's life. She seems to be convinced that the name has a great deal to do with one's eventual choice of career and personality development. She claimed that she learned all these from her teachers, the royal scholars. I can't tell whether it is a special kind of divination or just superstition."

"Fascinating! But I must say I'm not convinced about my Jewish ancestry. She seems so sure of it, and it is intriguing. I'm going to look into it and see what I can find out about the Kaifeng Jews. According to the book of our family tree, we are supposed to be the descendants of Emperor Zhao Kuangyin* of the Song Dynasty. He couldn't have been a Jew."

"Professor Li seems to like you. She is kind of picky about those she associates with. You're in luck if she is willing to teach you a thing or two. You can learn so much from her. I know she will never take me seriously, because my Chinese is so terrible."

"Go on, you, the publisher of a Chinese-language weekly paper, and not good in the language?"

"I just publish. No writing, no editing. I know my limitations."

"It'll be fun to find out how my sisters react to this revelation about our ancestors."

"How so?"

"You know the five of us, all opinionated and headstrong. We are so different in our ways of thinking, it is hard to believe we came from the same family."

"What about writing an article on Kaifeng Jews and your family history for the *Chinese Canadian Weekly*. Readers will find it interesting."

"Sorry, no time."

Rhae did not see her family till late the next week, when she hosted a BBQ in her backyard.

Tables and chairs were arranged on the patio. A built-in brick BBQ sat ten feet off one corner of the swimming pool. Several flowerbeds, separated by huge rocks surrounding the pool, displayed hundreds of peony blossoms blooming furiously in shades of red, pink, white, and lavender. Beyond the pool was a large expanse of grass. The entire backyard was enclosed by tall junipers, interspersed with sumach, maple, oak, and locust trees, forming a solid screen that provided total privacy from the neighbours.

Rhae, her sisters, and their families were scattered about. Winsome, the white German Shepherd, ran excitedly from one person to another, begging and hoping for some scraps of food. The younger generation was dispatched to carry trays of meats and vegetables from the kitchen to the BBQ pit. Wine glasses, soft-drink cans, and bottled water lay on the tables, rocks, benches. Auntie Ellie, short for Eleanor, Rhae's stepmother, sat in the shade enjoying the warm summer air.

Presently someone brought a plate of half-burnt chicken wings over to Ellie. As more food became available, people assembled around the tables to pick their choice items.

"How was the boat cruise last week, Rhae. Sorry I couldn't make it," said Linny, Rhae's eldest sister, as she sat down beside her.

"Oh, that reminds me, I have something quite incredible, literally incredible, to tell you."

"What?"

"I met an extraordinary person on the cruise. A professor, a philologist. A hundred-year-old scholar. Guess what she said?"

"What?"

"She read from my writing that we have Jewish ancestry."

Rhae's four sisters, Linny, Yvette, Sheryl, and Adele all stopped in the midst of what they were doing and exclaimed together, "WHAT!"

Linny was quick to add: "What a ridiculous thing to say!"

Adele: "I don't believe it."

Sheryl: "Mmm, kind of interesting!"

Yvette: "Why did she say that? Based on what?"

"Based on the fact that our great-grandfather came from Kaifeng, Henan. Based on our surname. Based on the strokes, the way I wrote my Chinese name," Rhae replied.

"That's hardly scientific. What else did she say?" Adele asked.

"She told us that during the Song Dynasty, a large contingent of Israelites arrived at Kaifeng, the capital of Northern Song. For close to nine hundred years the Kaifeng Jews thrived. They practised their religion with no opposition. They also adapted to many Han Chinese traditions and became quite 'Chinese,' except for their religion. Most of them changed their original names to Chinese names.

"Towards the end of the nineteenth century, due to widespread sentiments against foreigners and many other factors, the Jews in Kaifeng dissipated. Most left. The last seven clans who remained had among them a Zhao.

"Since our surname is Zhao, and our great-grandfather came from Kaifeng, there is a good probability our family is from that bloodline. What convinced her was the way I wrote my name."

"What's so special about the way you write your name?" asked Adele.

"She pointed out the way I prolong the last stroke of the character Yu. This tells her that our forebears are from a long distance away. Also, she said that I have hardly any earlobes – a non-Han feature. I'm intrigued by her observations," Rhae said.

"That's hardly convincing," insisted Linny.

"Why not?" asked Sheryl. "It's not impossible."

"But improbable, wouldn't you say?" Adele added.

"If this came from anyone else, I wouldn't give it a thought," responded Rhae, "but, Professor Li is so learned. She knows everything about every Chinese written word. She knows so much about Chinese history. It makes you want to find out."

"Wouldn't hurt to look into it." suggested Yvette.

The five sisters had been born within a span of six-and-half years. They were similar in many ways, yet very dissimilar at the same time. They were all on the plump side, and stood about five foot nothing. In their prime they had been at least a third less heavy, possibly an inch or two taller, and, with the aid of three-inch heels, had all looked well-proportioned and attractive. Now, approaching their senior years, they had all become less concerned with their appearance and no longer considered fashion a priority in life. None of them had physical features that would suggest they were anything other than ordinary Han Chinese.

Adele, the youngest, born at the tail end of the Year of the Horse,* looked the fittest. She had a slightly round face, fair skin, light brownish-black hair, and soft features, with a sweet upturned mouth. She had a Ph.D. in sociology from the University of Toronto and had been a professor of sociology for decades. She taught courses on Global Studies and published books and papers. A perfectionist, very down-to-earth and methodical, she tackled issues with an academic, analytical approach.

Twenty-one months older than Adele was Sheryl, born in the Year of the Snake. She had a narrow face, with nicely shaped dark eyebrows over eyes with a twinkle, and a small mouth with thin lips.

Sheryl could be called a non-conformist, which somehow did not sync with her field of study – actuarial science.

Yvette was the middle girl, born in the Year of the Rabbit. Her round face came from their mother, and her skin was a shade darker than Adele's or Sheryl's, but smooth and youthful-looking. When smiling, she showed her impeccably neat teeth, the best in the family.

Yvette was one of the first Chinese executive officers working for the Hong Kong government after she graduated from Hong Kong University. In Canada, she worked as a senior programmer for the Royal Bank.

Born in the Year of the Tiger, under the western astrological sign of Sagittarius, Rhae had a tendency to shoot for the stars in all directions – quite often without focus. She had a longish face with a longish nose and sallow skin. Because of her narrow face, she did not appear to be as overweight as she actually was.

Her degree was in English literature, but her first two jobs after graduation were teaching mathematics in high schools. She dabbled in music and painting.

Linny, short for Carmelina, the eldest, was born in the Year of the Bull. Very true to the Bull's typical characteristics, she was stubborn in the extreme. She insisted on keeping many of the old Chinese traditional practices and customs, even if they were not practical here in Canada. Her bachelor's degree was in psychology.

The five sisters' spontaneous reaction to their possible Jewish ancestry definitively reflected their respective personalities.

千里迢り路漫り

Chapter 4

Searching the Past

Linny's house in uptown Toronto looked stately. Way back in the 1980s, she took great pains in acquiring an old bungalow and demolished it to build her dream home.

The sisters gathered here for a birthday potluck dinner a few weeks after the BBQ at Rhae's. As everyone sat at the dining table, the conversation was almost exclusively about the Kaifeng Jews. Professor Li's suggestion had roused unexpected curiosity and interest. Each sister had taken some initiative to search for and delve into the history, and they were eager to compare notes.

Linny had acquired a copy of *The Chinese Jews* by Bishop William White. This book, first published in 1942, with a second edition in 1966, both published by the University of Toronto Press, had been out of print for many years and was considered rare. She also sourced and purchased another rare book, *The Survival of the Chinese Jews: The Jewish Community of Kaifeng* by Donald Daniel Leslie. She, however, did not read them herself, but gave them to Rhae to read. Both Yvette and Adele had diligently searched online and downloaded a stack of material. Sheryl had purchased two books by Professor Xu Xin of Nanjing University, an authority on the history, culture, religion, and traditions of the Kaifeng Jews. Not an avid reader, she had only glanced at bits and pieces here and there. Rhae bought several books written in Chinese by Chinese scholars and books and DVDs in English.

"I had no idea that Jews were in China as early as the Western Han period. That was about 200 BCE," Adele remarked.

"They were among the traders from the Middle East and Europe along the silk roads." Yvette said. "I read that, in the book of Isaiah, which dates back to the sixth century BCE, there is mention of silk embroidery from Sinia,* which many people think was the ancient Hebrew name for China."

"Actually, that interpretation is outdated, Yvette. It is now widely accepted that the 'Sinim' mentioned in Isaiah does not refer to China," corrected Adele. "As a matter of fact, scholars believe that there is probably no Jewish reference to China before the ninth century."

"While there is no hard evidence of their presence in China so far back, in Bishop White's book it says that the Jews were trading along the silk route as early as the eighth century BCE. I guess we have to differentiate between the Jewish traders who travelled to China and the actual Jewish settlement in China," interjected Rhae.

"The route taken by the traders so far back had to be one of the land silk routes," explained Adele. "It stretched from Antioch, through Damascus, on to to Seleucia on the Tigris River, just south of present-day Baghdad. From Seleucia, the caravan would take either the Samarkand Route to the north or the Balkh Route to the south to reach the Pamir Mountains in central Asia. At Kashgar, which is present-day Kashi, an oasis at the western edge of Xinjiang near the border with Tajikistan and Kyrgyzstan, the traders would again skirt either the northern or the southern edge of the Taklimakan Shamo, a desert in Xinjiang."

Adele paused for a second and continued. "East of the Taklimakan, the two routes converged till they reached Gansu Province. Dunhuang, in Gansu, famed for its numerous ancient cave Buddha sculptures, was one of the major posts as the traders headed east towards central China."

"Professor Li said the Kaifeng Jews originated in Mesopotamia," stated Rhae. "I looked it up and found that it was the area taking in eastern Iran, but also included part of present-day Iraq, plus smaller parts of southeastern Turkey and northeastern Syria. The region was part of the Persian Empire and that of the Parthian Empire started by Emperor Arsaces around the third century BCE."

"There is sufficient evidence suggesting that the Kaifeng Jews came from Persia. However, it was not as if these Jews suddenly decided to leave Persia to go to China. Most scholars seem to agree that the migration process very likely took hundreds of years." Yvette, who had read chiefly about the journeys of the ancient Jews, wanted to tell what she had learned.

She continued, "Silk from China was in mega demand both in the Middle East and in Western Europe. The Chinese traders did not, as a rule, leave the boundaries of their country. It was the Jewish traders who were among the intermediary agents between the Orient and the West. They frequently travelled the silk routes and brought raw silk to Seleucia, on to Antioch near present-day Antakya along the Mediterranean Coast in Turkey, and then dispersed their merchandise to different cities in Western Europe.

"During the Roman Empire, the Roman upper class fancied transparent silk gauze. To make it, the Chinese raw silk was unravelled and rewoven. It was a huge industry. Some raw silks were dyed to suit the Roman taste, others had wool or linen added. They also used silk, as well as cotton and linen, in weaving damask.

"At any rate, there were periods when, for political or economic reasons, the Jews had to migrate or disperse in all directions. Many of them moved eastward—"

Before Yvette could finish, Rhae butted in. "Pardon the interruption, but I have to tell you about this article in the *National Geographic*. I brought the copy with me. Since the beginning of history, the Jews had suffered more than their share of persecution, expulsion, enslavement, discrimination. This article is entitled 'Roman Frontiers,' and has a paragraph on Emperor Hadrian, the adopted son of Emperor Trajan. Hadrian took the throne after Trajan in 117 CE. In 132 CE ... here, Thomas, please read this paragraph aloud. It's on page 122." Rhae pushed a copy of the September 2012 issue of *National Geographic* in front of Adele's husband, Thomas, who began to read.

> In 132 he [Hadrian] suppressed a Jewish revolt in a ruthless, protracted campaign. One Roman historian claimed the fighting left half a million Jews dead and added, "As for the numbers who perished from starvation, disease, or fire, that was impossible to establish." Survivors were enslaved or expelled. The name of the province was changed from Judaea to Syria-Palentina to wipe away all traces of the rebellion.

"That more or less sums up what the Jews had gone through throughout history," Rhae commented. She was about to say more when Thomas stopped her.

"Okay, let's not be distracted by other incidents in Jewish history. Let's get back to what Yvette was telling us."

"No one is yet sure when exactly these Jews left Mesopotamia. Most scholars agree that they very likely took the sea route east. I read that ships began sailing between the Red Sea and India between the first and the sixth centuries. By the ninth century, a maritime route between Canton and Alexandria developed, controlled by the Arab traders. By the tenth century, the sea routes between the east and the west were open. It was estimated that they travelled through the Persian Gulf, the Gulf of Oman, the Indian Ocean, into the South China Sea. Again, it wasn't one continuous journey. They might have settled in a number of cities along the Indian coast or in the southern parts of China. It could have been years or even generations before they moved again."

Yvette took a sip of tea and gave Adele an opening to speak. "There is one research article by a Chinese scholar, Chen Heng, who charted – in most likelihood by speculation, but logical speculation to be sure – a probable route for the Kaifeng Jews. While most researchers are somewhat vague on the exact date of the Kaifeng Jews' arrival, this person pinpoints it to the year 998 CE.

"According to this researcher, there was a large settlement of Jews in the city of Cochin in the southwestern tip of the Indian subcontinent along the Malabar Coast. They had been there for decades, always wanting to get to the source of the Chinese silk. In the year 998, they were able to secure two good-sized ships, each accommodating about two hundred to three hundred passengers.

"From India they sailed through the South China Sea to reach Canton, which was known as Kanfu in the old days. They then went on to Yangzhou at the southern tip of the Grand Canal system, the major waterway linking China's north and south. Yangzhou was a prosperous hub in the tenth century, and a number of the travellers decided to settle down there. But most took the Grand Canal northward to reach Kaifeng, the capital at the time. Kaifeng was known by several names then – Bian Liang and Dong Jing among them.

"The article says that, in the year 998, two major events took place in Kaifeng. There was a change of emperor; Song Zhen Zhong, Zhao Heng, the third emperor of the Song Dynasty, ascended the throne. And, in autumn, around the Chong Yang Festival,* when chrysanthemums bloomed profusely, a large group of westerners appeared in the city. The —"

Rhae broke in. "Actually, another source suggests that the season of their arrival was more likely to be around the Lunar New Year. No way to verify that though. Sorry for the interruption."

Adele continued. "The newcomers were described as having broad foreheads, high cheekbones, and long noses with a bit of a hook. The women wore coloured clothing, while the men wore blue tunics and blue cloth shoes. They raised a lot of curiosity among the locals, but they were well received and treated with civility and courtesy.

"Apparently, the foreigners were so impressed by the prosperity of Kaifeng and felt so comfortable in this city that they sent messengers to other Chinese cities – Dunhuang, Ningxia, Loyang, Hangzhou, Ninpo, Yangzhou, and Canton – where

Jews were known to live, inviting them to come and join them in Kaifeng. Many responded, and the community was said to have had about five hundred families with over seventy different clan names."

Thomas, who had taught in various universities in Canada and the United States and had his doctorate in Chinese history, was listening intently to the exchange of information and could not help commenting.

"You girls are absolutely remarkable in having gathered so much material in a matter of a couple of weeks. Good work! I'm impressed and totally fascinated. Despite my studies, I had no idea about the existence of these Jews. I want to hear more."

"Well, believe it or not, they were actually received by the emperor," stated Adele.

"How did they manage that?" Thomas asked. "As a rule, 'common folks' were not granted an audience with the emperor."

"If you read some of the books, you would think that this group of foreigners arrived in the capital and within days they got to see the emperor. It didn't happen that way. It probably took them years," Rhae said. "One scholar says it was not until 1008 that their leader, Levi, and another person were granted a royal reception.

"Apparently, this is how it happened. After the Jews settled in Kaifeng, they set up all kinds of small businesses. They practised medicine, designed and made jewellery, worked as tailors and farmers, crafted with leather, iron, wood, and fabrics, traded in herbs, spices, medicinal goods, and imported items. They were law-abiding and very disciplined in their daily lives.

"Contemporary documents that I found in *The Kaifeng Jews* by Pan Guang-Dan say that the Jews 'excelled in agriculture, commerce, and magistracies . . . They are highly esteemed . . . for their integrity, fidelity, and strict observance of their religion.'

"It was said that some high officials' wives frequented the shops that carried incense, thyme, fennel, cumin, cinnamon – all kinds of spices, curios, novelties from the West. Through business deals, the Jews gradually befriended some court officials. Over time, from connection to connection to connection, they slowly moved upwards to reach the Court Protocol Office and presented a request to pay homage to the emperor.

"Then again, it was not like the emperor responded quickly with an invitation. The minister had to prepare a comprehensive report on these Jews before he submitted the request to the emperor.

"The emperor was apprised of the lifestyles of these foreigners, probably with details about their beliefs and the practice of their religion. Most importantly, the emperor was assured that these foreigners did not try to propagate their faith; they only practised it themselves. The emperor had to be satisfied that the Israelites did not accept outsiders into their religion. His fear was that, if the Jews recruited converts to their religion, they would be capable of expanding their power base and might one day pose a threat to the state.

"On top of all the details of their lives, what pleased the emperor a great deal were the gifts these Israelites offered him. In the tenth century, cotton was not yet grown in China, but in India and the Middle East it was widely planted and dyed in many attractive colours. These Israelites, originating in the Persian area and having lived in India for many years, knew precisely where to obtain the best-quality, finely spun, beautiful cotton. In consultation with the court officials, Levi and his companion brought along five rolls of dazzlingly bright cotton cloth in rainbow colours.

"The emperor's eyes opened wide when he saw these fabrics. They felt softer than silk, with such a warm touch. He immediately commanded a proclamation to the Israelites:

歸 我 中 夏	Be part of our empire.
尊 守 祖 風	Preserve heritage and traditions.
留 遺 汴 梁	Remain in Bian Liang [Kaifeng].

With the emperor's blessings, the Israelites were granted the privilege of full citizenship in China and given permission to practise their religion and keep their culture."

"Quite incredible indeed!" commented Thomas. "And did they prosper?"

"Extremely so, I would say," replied Adele. "For the first few centuries at least. The Israelites not only adhered to their own traditions and heritage, they also participated in the Han practice of aspiring to become officials. Record shows that many were appointed to high-level ministries.

"And I believe that the Israelites were attracted to scholarly studies, because in China at the time and for many centuries afterwards, people's social ranking was in this order: scholar, at the top, followed by peasant, labourer, merchant, and, finally, soldier at the very bottom. Scholars were highly respected and they were the ones eligible to become officials.*

"At any rate, during the early years of the Ming Dynasty, very likely in the late forteenth century or a bit later, the Israelites reached their peak, with numerous appointments to high posts throughout the country. Their number reached about five thousand, others say close to ten thousand, although this figure has been refuted by some scholars.

"Want to know something interesting about our possible ancestor?" continued Adele.

"Our ancestor? We don't know that for a fact, do we?" retorted Linny. "Anyway, what's so interesting?"

"The origin of the name Zhao, or Chao, for one of the clans," Adele replied. "Care to hear about it?"

"Tell us! Tell us! If Linny doesn't want to hear, she can retreat to the living room." Thomas made no pretense of being polite.

"All right. In 1423, during the rule of Emperor Yong Le of the Ming Dynasty, a Kaifeng Jew by the name of Ai Cheng – some books have An Cheng instead of Ai Cheng – said to be the Chinese version of Hassan, a physician by profession, was given the name Zhao by the emperor. Zhao, as you know, was the surname of the Song emperors.

"It was recorded that Ai Cheng distinguished himself by his compilation of a set of medical journals. But what brought him to the emperor's attention, and his favour, was the fact that he informed the emperor of one of the royal princes' plan to usurp the throne. Out of gratitude to Ai Cheng, the emperor bestowed the name – an immense honour. Ai Cheng was subsequently appointed to the post of lieutenant-governor of the military area of Zejiang Province. Most likely the name Zhao was chosen because the Israelites arrived in Kaifeng during the Song Dynasty, when the Emperor's surname was Zhao."

"Tell me, did most of the Jews use Chinese names at that time?" asked Thomas.

"It was, in fact, during the Ming Dynasty, from 1368 to

1644, that the Jews began to change their names to Chinese forms," Adele answered. "Ordered by the emperor, possibly. But it might well be because by then many of the Jews had been successful in the imperial exams and had been appointed to important posts. To fully embrace the Han traditions and practices, it was natural and logical to adopt Chinese names and the Chinese language."

"Mmmm, Linny Hassan! How do you like that, Linny?" teased Thomas, chuckling.

Linny gave him a dirty look and ignored him.

Yvette went on. "Well, towards the end of the Qing Dynasty in 1912, there were only seven known clans of Kaifeng Jews. Their surnames were:

Ai, Zhang, Zhao, Jin, Kao, Li, Shi.
艾　張　趙　金　高　李　石

"But before that there were more. Some of those include:

Ai 優, Mu 穆, Zhou 周, Huang 黃, Nie 聶, Zuo 左, Bai 白, and possibly a Zhong 鍾, two Jin(s), two Zhang(s). It is kind of difficult, however, to match the Chinese names to the original Hebrew names." Yvette wrote out the Chinese characters as she spoke.

"Are there records of the Hebrew names?" asked Thomas.

"Of course. Records show that the Hebrew names include: Akiba – a rabbi, Aaron, Ezra, Shandiavor, Bethuel, Moses, Mordecai, Phineas – a rabbi, Israel, Joshua – a rabbi, Benjamin, Jacob, Abishai, Eldad – a scribe, Shadai, Simeon Bespristh . . ." recited Yvette from a page in her pile of paper.

"And to which names are those equivalent?" Thomas asked again.

"I only read a few," replied Yvette. "Besides the name Zhao bestowed on Hassan or Ai Cheng, the name Joshua was also translated as Zhao. Ezra became Ai; Levi, Li; Samuel, Shi; Kademiel, Zhang; the rest, I have no idea."

"I just knew you would be interested in records of names, Thomas," Rhae said to him. "I contacted the Hebrew Union College of Cincinnati, where they keep a register of the Jewish congregation in Kaifeng, giving the first names of males, then of women, both in Hebrew and Chinese. It's quoted in Pan Guang Dan's book. Here, have a look at these pages."

Rhae handed Thomas photocopies of a number of pages taken from "Hebrew MSS. from China – IV," which had been sent to her electronically by the university's library. One of the pages read:

11. Prayer book and Name List.
    Manuscript. China. ca.17th century.
    Chinese Hebrew square characters.

    This prayer book for the Sabbath Eve contains a membership list of the Kaifeng Congregation from the time of the Ming Dynasty (1368–1644). The names, written in both Hebrew and Chinese. are an important source of information about the men and women of this community.'

"All these pages are part of Manuscript 926, Prayers for Sabbath Eve from the Chinese-Hebrew memorial book, in the Klau Library, Cincinnati, Hebrew Union College, Jewish Institute of Religion. They were very kind to send me the material.

Cover and pages from Hebrew manuscripts from China.
Courtesy of Klau Library, Cincinnati Hebrew Union College,
Jewish Institute of Religion.

"You'll notice that most of the men's names are among the seven names Yvette mentioned. But the wives or other relatives' names go beyond the seven names," Rhae added.

"Amazing!" Thomas shook his head as he examined the pages. "Adele, Yvette, and Rhae, you form a good research team."

Then taking a shot at Linny again, Thomas said to her:

"Since Huang was also possibly a Chinese Jewish name, isn't it possible that your husband might likely be a descendant of Jews? That would make your children doubly Jewish! Ha, ha . . ."

"Not a chance." Linny snorted adamantly. "My husband's family came from Taishan in Guangdong Province in south China. Had nothing to do with Kaifeng. Besides they have been in Canada for four generations already."

Among the five sisters, Linny strongly resisted the possibility of Jewish blood. She prided herself in being pure Han Chinese, not quite realizing that Han blood is anything but "pure."

Sheryl was at the other extreme. She was proud to be of Jewish descent, claiming that the Jewish element would add intelligence and creativity to her descendants. Obviously she was influenced by some racial stereotyping.

Rhae, Yvette, and Adele fell somewhere between. They were intrigued by the idea and were keen to do some more fact-finding about this little-known piece of history. As they delved deeper into their search, they inadvertently turned their endeavour into a vastly interesting and stimulating academic project, regardless of whether they were personally affected or not.

Both Linny's husband, Jerome, and Rhae's husband, Dean,

had passed away a few years earlier. Both husbands had been medical doctors by profession and history buffs by interest and passion. Had they been alive, they would certainly have entered enthusiastically into the discussion. Yvette's husband, Paul, a chemical engineer, had keen interests in topics such as investments, the housing market, gardening, food . . . but history was not his strong suit. He seldom joined in such conversations. Edmund, Sheryl's husband, was doing a fair amount of textile business in Southeast Asia. He spent more time in that part of the world than in Canada. At the time he was in Bangkok. Then there was their stepmother, Auntie Ellie, who was a bit hard of hearing, but always tried to join in the ongoing chat. On this topic, however, she sat listening quietly to the dialogue. It was hard to gauge how much information she actually took in.

Thomas, married to Adele, was a natural to be part of the discussion group. It was very much his cup of tea. He had an insatiable appetite for knowledge, especially where Chinese history was concerned. As he savoured the taste of his favourite dessert – raspberry cheesecake from Dufflet Pastries – he fired away questions at whoever could answer them.

"Let's see, besides the manuscript, copies of which you obtained from the Hebrew Union College in Cincinnati, are there other records dating from earlier periods?" Thomas asked.

"Yes," replied Rhae. "There are four stone tablets, or steles. Well, now there are only three still in existence. These are inscriptions carved on stones to record people, happenings, and history of the Kaifeng Jews. Respectively, these stone tablets were dated 1489, known as Hongzhi Bei, now in the Kaifeng Museum; 1512, known as Zhengde Bei, also in the Kaifeng Museum; 1663, known as Kangxi Bei, whereabouts unknown, but the rubbing of the tablet is in Shanghai; and 1679, known as the Chao/ Zhao Clan tablet, also currently in Kaifeng. They give quite a bit of history of the Jews' religion and their arrival in China. However, some discrepencies do exist between two of the steles regarding the Jews' earliest arrival in China. The 1663 stone inscription mentions that Judaism reached China during the Zhou Dynasty (1100–771 BCE).

"At any rate, rubbings of the steles were made and the Royal Ontario Museum may have a copy or copies of the rubbings among other Kaifeng Jewish relics in their possession. We should go visit the ROM.

"I also chatted with the curator of the Reuben and Helene Dennis Museum at the Beth Tzedec Congregation on Bathurst Street. I was told they had an exhibition on the Kaifeng Jews some years ago. But now they have only one item, a Hebrew scroll with Chinese symbols, which they are certain is from China. It may or may not have been from Kaifeng. I may go there one day to have a look."

"That sounds good. Now, let's recap. The Jews arrived in Kaifeng in 998 CE, about five hundred families, seventy clans, did you say? Their number grew to five to ten thousand strong by the Ming Dynasty, between the fourteenth and seventeenth centuries. But towards the end of the Qing Dynasty, in the late nineteenth century, there were only seven clans left. Is that right, Yvette? What happened?" Thomas looked at Yvette.

"I concentrated my search on the Jews' travel routes. Didn't read much on the deterioration of the Kaifeng community. Maybe Adele or Rhae can give you some insights," Yvette replied.

"There are bits and pieces on this topic. A lot of speculation of course. I'll tell you what I know, and Rhae can add her thoughts," said Adele. She leaned back a little in her chair as she began.

"Well, from all accounts, the Kaifeng Jews were doing well and living happily and harmoniously along with Han Chinese and other ethnic groups, such as the Mohammedans, as they used to be called. As always, when things go too well, disaster butts in. As far as I can understand, the single incident that dealt an irrecoverable blow to the Kaifeng Jews was the flooding of the Yellow River in 1642.

"Before I go on to tell you about the 1642 flood, I want to clarify something. Even though the community prospered from the tenth to the seventeenth centuries, it does not mean that it did not go through hardships or calamities. Even during the Song Dynasty, the emperor had to relocate his court south to Hangzhou on account of the Jin invasion.

"From 998 to 1644, the Jews had weathered several dynastic changes. They survived the Jin, the Mongol rule of Genghis Khan, and the Ming emperors. With each dynastic change, pillage, carnage, suffering, diseases, and often famine were an inevitable part and parcel of the process. They had their share of hardship, for sure. But they always bounced back, rebuilding their lives and their synagogue. Even after the great fire during Emperor Wan-Li's rule (1572 to 1620), which totally gutted the synagogue and destroyed all the books but one, they were able to rebuild the synagogue and partly repair the books.

"The 1642 flood was exceptional. It was particularly cruel, because it was not a natural disaster but one caused by a heartless army commander.

"The last Ming emperor, Chong Zhen, ascended to the throne in 1627. The following year there was widespread drought in Shaanxi Province. Nothing grew; there was no harvest. People fed on tree roots, field grass, or even mud to survive. Yet, local government administrators would not let up on tax collection. Peasant uprisings sprang up throughout the province.

"That winter, a young soldier by the name of Li Zicheng revolted against his superior and started to recruit all who were willing to follow him. He amalgamated thirteen rebel groups and organized them to rise against the government. Li was immensely popular with the people, and his army became a major threat to the Ming emperor.

"In December 1640, Li led his army to Henan Province, where drought, locusts, famine, and epidemics had driven people to cannibalism and despair. Peasants flocked to join Li's army, and his followers numbered over one million. In February 1641, Li attacked Kaifeng for seven days without success. He tried again in December of the same year, and again, after twenty days of fighting, he was not able to capture the city. Meanwhile, however, Li's army was able to take over several other cities and towns in the province.

"In May 1642, Li made a third attempt to take Kaifeng. Learning from his previous two experiences, Li decided to simply surround the city, anticipating that the siege would eventually force the city to surrender. In June, Li's army won a major battle against the Ming army at Zhu Xian Zheng, a town near Kaifeng.

"Li's victory terrified the Imperial Inspector, Gao Ming-heng, who had been dispatched from the Ming court to supervise civil and military matters in Kaifeng. He dreaded the imminent fall of the city. As it happened, the weather had been miserable; torrential rain had been pouring for over two days and the Yellow River was on the brink of overflowing. Gao thought of a way to counter Li's army.

Seeing that Li's army was camped in the low trough of land surrounding Kaifeng, Gao ordered that the river dike at Zhu Jia Kou, to the northwest of Kaifeng, be broken. Kaifeng sat on the southern bank of the Yellow River. The flood's path was directed towards Li's army camp, and tens of thousands of Li's men perished.

"Li was furious. In retaliation, he ordered his men to go and destroy the dike at Ma Jia Kou, which would send the water gushing directly towards the city of Kaifeng. The flood was so huge that it submerged the entire city. Of the one million residents living in Kaifeng at the time, over three hundred thousand lost their lives. Among them, three thousand Jews.

"The synagogue was badly damaged, and most of the Holy Scrolls were washed away. One brave member, by the name of Gao Xuan, ordered by his father Gao Dongdou, risked his life to retrieve as many of the books as he could. It took them years to reorganize and recompile the various holy books. Although a Zhao Jewish-Mandarin, again possibly an ancestor of ours, undertook to rebuild the synagogue, the community was never the same again."

"The community never fully recovered," echoed Rhae. "Possessions and livestock aside, it was the loss of human lives that was the hardest to bounce back from." Rhae stopped for a minute. Seeing no one was eager to speak, she resumed.

"The two years following the flood were chaotic. War plus natural disasters. By 1644, Li Zicheng had occupied all of Shaanxi Province and established himself as the head of DaShun Empire. He then led one million of his men towards Beijing. By the third month of the year, Ming army desertion was rampant; courtiers abandoned their posts. When Emperor

Chong-Zhen saw a sea of men under Li's command approaching Beijing, he realized it was the end of him and his empire. He hanged himself on Mei Shan in the Imperial Garden behind the Forbidden City. The Ming Dynasty, after 277 years of power, came to an end."

"There must be other factors that contributed to the decline of the Kaifeng Jews," mused Thomas. "The flood, natural disasters, war, change of dynasty – all these had happened repeatedly before. It might have taken them longer to finally recover. But that never happened. There had to be some other reasons why they were not able to bounce back."

"You're quite right, Thomas," said Rhae. "Assimilation!"

"Ah! "exclaimed Thomas. "That makes sense."

"You know, Thomas, I've been lucky. Very recently, I was able to access some of the latest research work on Kaifeng Jews done right in Kaifeng. A friend of mine has a sister teaching at Henan University. She sent me a copy of a recently published book that came out in November 2011. It's called *GuDai Kaifeng Youtairen*, or *Ancient Kaifeng Jews*.* It's one of the most current publications on the subject, and very detailed.

"In the book, they list a number of theories why the Jews assimilated. They give reasons such as the fact that they were an isolated community and had no people of a similar origin to relate to. At the same time, there was no threat of anti-Semitism in China, which led to the Jews' being able to attain success in officialdom. As time passed, the restrictions on mixed marriages with other ethnic groups and the Hans relaxed. And don't forget, it tends to be typical of minority groups that they harbour an understandable desire to receive protection. There were other reasons, but these were some of those mentioned.

"The book then mentioned a contemporary scholar, Mr. L. Gobow, who argues that the primary reason for the Jews' assimilation, above all others, was the close similarities between the Chinese Confucian Code of Ethics and the Hebrew traditional moral code as stated in *GuDai Kaifeng Youtairen*."

"He may have a point there, but I would suggest the answer lies in 'all of the above' rather than in one particular reason," said Thomas.

"Isn't that interesting though, Thomas?" asked Rhae.

"Very."

"Now, even more fascinating, in my humble opinion, is the probable watershed event that accelerated the Jews' assimilation into the Han culture from the early Qing Dynasty onward," Rhae said with a mysterious smile.

"Really! I'm intrigued," said Adele.

"Pray, tell," added Thomas.

"Linny, again it involves someone who might very well be our ancestor." Rhae addressed Linny, who responded with a nonchalant, "No kidding!"

"Before I begin, I want to briefly go over the imperial examination system, so you'll know what I mean when I mention it.

"During both the Ming and the Qing dynasties, the examination system was tightened organizationally, and the management was streamlined. The first level, Tong Shi, was a qualifying exam. It was held locally every year. All aspirants to higher levels had to pass this one. There was no age limit on the candidates.

"The second level, Xiang Shi, was held every three years in the eighth month of the lunar calendar at a provincial capital. Then, in the spring following the second level, the third level,

Hui Shi, took place in the nation's capital. Those who passed went on to the final level, Dian Shi, adjudicated by the emperor himself. If they were selected, the successful candidates were granted a reception with the emperor.

"Those writing the exams were largely students from local schools or from the imperial college in the capital. Those who did not attend school entered as individuals.*

"In 1645, a year after the Qing established their empire, a Kaifeng Jew by the name of Zhao Yingcheng 赵映乘, born in 1619, attended and passed the qualifying level in Kaifeng. On his application form for the higher levels, he filled in his name as Zhao Yingcheng, alias 'Moses,' and indicated his ethnicity as 'Israelite.' He was successful in all the subsequent exams and was received by the emperor in 1650.

"Here I must add that this Zhao Yingcheng was of the sixth or seventh generation descended from the same Zhao Cheng, or Ai Cheng, upon whom the emperor had bestowed the name Zhao.

"Zhao Yingcheng was a lot more than a mere scholar of the Chinese classics. He was well-versed in the Hebrew language as well. He had worked on the recompilation of the Hebrew scrolls after the flood of 1642 and had participated in the rebuilding of the synagogue.

"Upon being told by his minister of Zhao's background, the emperor, very pleased and impressed, became excited. He immediately ordered ink-stone and brush be brought to him and he wrote the calligraphy for a plaque to be installed in the Kaifeng synagogue. He also awarded investiture to Zhao's father, Zhao Guangyu, with some honourary title, and appointed Zhao Yingcheng to the post of 'xing bu lang zhong

刑部郎中,' which, according to Sidney Shapiro, who translated, compiled, and edited the book *Jews in Old China: Studies by Chinese Scholars*, is equivalent to the Secretary of the Board of Punishment.

"When the emperor's representative came to announce the good news in Kaifeng, he rode on a horse decorated with huge red silk bows, heralded by a gong striking and firecrackers popping. He shouted at the top of his voice repeatedly as he rode through the streets of Kaifeng: 'Zhao Yingcheng, a winner! Zhao Yingcheng, a winner!'

"The fanfare drew the entire city out to welcome the imperial messenger and to congratulate the new imperial appointee.

"It was the *culminating* event of the Jews' six hundred odd years of existence in Kaifeng. This single supreme recognition from the emperor brought honour, glory, joy, gratification, pride, and a sense of ultimate achievement to the entire community.

"Zhao Yingcheng was the first Kaifeng Jew who attained the highest level in the exams. He instantly became a hero and a role model for all in this close-knit group of foreigners. Those compatriots who previously objected to the Jews' participation in the exams quickly changed their minds. Children were encouraged to study the Chinese classics from then on, and the parents made it their priority to make sure their sons followed in Zhao's footsteps. Thus, the Kaifeng Jews gradually became lax in their practice of Hebrew traditions and began to abandon their previous study of the Hebrew language and religion. Instead, they redirected their energy and attention to the study of Chinese classics in preparation for the imperial examinations.

"Zhao was later appointed to head the Hunan Hubei Provincial Flood Prevention Bureau, a post he held till his death. Therefore, no doubt, Zhao Yingcheng's success precipitated and accelerated the Jews' total assimilation into the Han culture."

"Wow! It looks like the Zhao clan outshone the others by a long shot," commented Sheryl. "We certainly have illustrious ancestors."

"Not quite," said Rhae. "The Zhao clan had their bad apples too. The book *Gudai Kaifeng Youtairen* records a news item in the inaugural edition of the *He Shen Shi Bao*, or *Henan Voice Newspaper*, which was launched in 1912. A certain Zhao Yunzhong and one member of the Ai clan were accused of secretly selling two of the carved steles, as well as the property of the former synagogue, to an anonymous party for a thousand taels of silver. The two steles were shipped by rail to some unidentified location. This caused an uproar among the Jews, and the other five clans took Zhao Yunzhong and his accomplice to court.

"Then on March 2, 1931, the local-news section of the *Henan Voice* reported that it had been confirmed that the Anglican Church had signed a contract with six of the Jewish clans for the sale of the two steles and the mortgage of the synagogue site for a total of thirteen hundred taels of silver. The Anglican Church planned to build a hospital on the site. The proceeds were to be divided among the six clans, exclusive of the Zhang clan, because none of their members was in Kaifeng at the time. The Zhang clan then took the other six to court, demanding their share.

"By then, the whole incident had become a rallying point for all the residents of Kaifeng, who objected to the sale of the steles, which were considered to be historic relics of importance. Under immense pressure from the public outcry, Bishop White of the Anglican Church agreed to install the two steles in front of the Anglican Church and never to move them outside China. Zhao Yunzhong was arrested for fraud and was jailed. The issue of the steles and the synagogue site came to an end.

"However, rubbings of the steles were done and were sent to the Vatican and Canada. They're right here in Toronto, at the ROM, as I mentioned before.

"The Anglican Church's plan of a hospital on the site never materialized, but years later a hospital was built on the site by the government, and a plaque was installed to commemorate the site of the former synagogue Qing Zheng Si. Only a tiny corner of the previous structure of the synagogue, purportedly the Zhao clan's residence, remains today, and it is occupied by Zhao descendants."

"This Zhao Yunzhong was probably a generation younger than our great-grandfather Zhao Yidong. I wonder if they were related. Great-grandfather left Kaifeng in the late nineteenth century, and by 1912 he had been dead for quite some time already," Adele said thoughtfully.

"It's getting late. Can we call it a day. We covered a lot of ground today. We can talk some more the next time we meet," said Yvette, who lived the farthest away and was eager to go home.

"Wait just a bit," Rhae pleaded. "I have to share this very interesting information with you. It won't take long, and I'm sure you'll enjoy it."

"Be brief, if you can. It is getting late." Sheryl yawned as she said this.

"Do you know, before the temple was built in 1163, the site of the synagogue was a well-known restaurant-hotel by the name of Tie Xiao Luo. It was purportedly run by Israelites, and they brewed a unique wine named 'Yao-Ti,' which was rated one of the three famous wines of Kaifeng. So well-known was this Yao-Ti, because it was brewed differently from the Chinese wines – different ingredients, different method – that even Emperor Song Hui Zong used to frequent the place to enjoy the taste.

"Emperor Song Hui Zong, as you know, was extremely talented in art, calligraphy, and poetry, but a terrible ruler. His ongoing affair with the prostitute Li Sisi was widely known to all his subjects. And it was said that, among other courtesans he bedded, was a Zhao Yuannv, also a well-known prostitute in Kaifeng and possibly an Israelite, according to *GuDai Kaifeng Youtairen*.

"There, end of story. We finish on a gossipy note. Now we can all go home and dream about this ancient Yao-Ti wine."

Nanchang, China

1872–1927

别有天地非人间

Chapter 5

Nanchang

Old man Xiong Xin's two sons, Xiong Yuan and Xiong Ying, and their uncle – Xiong Xin's younger brother – Xiong Xiang, were waiting for him at the embankment. Yidong and Yuchen were warmly received and felt very much at ease in their company. As they loaded their single-wheel cart with all the merchandise Xiong Xin had brought back from the east, they saved one corner for Yuchen and the luggage. Xiong Yuan, the elder son, took it upon himself to push the cart.

Xiong Xin's grandson had been only two weeks old when he left for the coast. His first questions, naturally, were all about the baby: if he was nursing well, if he had gained weight. His sons, on the other hand, were curious about their guests and kept asking questions of Yidong and Yuchen. There was so much chat and exchanging of news that the brisk forty-minute walk took them to their destination without their realizing it.

A simple brick dwelling housed all three generations of Xiong Xin's family. It was very different from the houses in Henan, mused Yidong to himself. Back home, most of the houses in the hutong lanes were in the "si-he-yuan"* configuration, with the rooms surrounding a central courtyard, but here the rooms of each house were in a line, and the roof slanted from one side of the house. It looked strange, he thought. Once inside the house, he noticed they did not have a kang, the heated brick bed covered with clay on top. The winter must be relatively mild, he gathered. There was a large stove along one wall of the cooking area, with bundles of chopped wood laid against the wall. He also noticed the teapot, teacups, and other tableware. They were all of fine porcelain and looked elegant. The furniture was old, but of quality wood.

Xiong Xin's wife, Rong, beamed from ear to ear. She took an instant liking to Yuchen. Taking her hand and scrutinizing her from head to toe, she murmured continuous compliments.

"Ah-y-ia*! What a beautiful young lady! Truly a celestial fairy-maiden among us earthlings! Look at her big, bright eyes that speak . . . such a lovely smile . . . and tall . . . strong hands . . . "

Yuchen was visibly embarrassed. She was immediately aware that both Xiong Xin's wife and her daughter-in-law, Xiong Yuan's wife, Li-er, had tiny bound feet. Yet they were mobile, not a bit hampered by this handicap.

This made Yuchen somewhat self-conscious about her own unbound feet. She knew that all Han women customarily bound their daughters' feet.* The practice had become a symbol of good breeding and fine taste, albeit at the cost of immense pain and suffering to the one whose feet were to be bound. Yuchen's family had shunned this practice. They had adopted most of the Han customs. But foot-binding? A ridiculous and barbarous custom! They would not succumb to subjecting their female members to this tortuous, painful ordeal.

Yuchen had watched one of her playmates, Mingming, who lived in the next hutong, suffering through the entire process of foot-binding. Mingming's agony remained vivid in her memory. Mingming's parents had wanted their daughter to have the properly bound feet, referred to as "three-inch Golden Lotus." Mingming began her foot-binding at age four.

As far as Yuchen understood, on the first night Mingming's feet were washed and her toenails were cut. Then a piece of binding cloth about ten feet in length and two inches in width was applied to force the four small toes to bend into the sole of the foot. Each day the binding cloth had to be changed and the feet washed, and the nails trimmed. Each day the binding would be wound a touch tighter. Every two weeks or so, smaller-sized shoes were forced onto Mingming's feet and she was made to walk in them. This process went on for about two years, until her feet were totally deformed and their growth stunted.

Yuchen remembered that Mingming told her that her mother was extremely careful to make sure there was sufficient blood circulation to the foot to prevent blood poisoning. But Mingming also told her that flesh from her toes would rot and would fall off, and sometimes pus would ooze from the toes. One time, Yuchen was allowed to watch Mingming's nightly ordeal. She was taken aback by the bad odour as soon as the binding cloth was unravelled. She noticed corns on her friend's bent toes and Mingming's mother had to cut them off with a knife. It must have been so painful, thought Yuchen in her recollection.

What Yuchen was not told was that the general belief was that a woman's bound feet stimulated men's erotic desire. As well, it was also claimed that, as a bound-footed woman

*Kaifeng Jewish women with bound feet, 1919.
Reproduced from* Chinese Jews *by William White.*

tottered, it helped to tighten her vaginal muscles and narrow her vagina, thus intensifying sexual pleasure to both the man and the woman.

Neither did Yuchen understand at the time that this hideous practice in all probability started as a measure to restrict a woman's mobility and curtail her freedom. It fitted well with the Confucian philosophy of men's dominance over women throughout the centuries of feudal society.

Yuchen was told that it was not clear as to exactly when or how foot-binding began. Legend had it that it started in the late Tang Dynasty (618–906 CE), with the graceful gait of a prince's concubine. By the Song Dynasty (960–1297 CE), the practice had spread among the upper class. During the Ming Dynasty (1368–1644 CE) and the Qing Dynasty (1644–1911 CE), foot-binding had become a prevalent custom, even amongst the poorest of the populace. A woman with unbound feet was considered an undesirable marriage partner.

However, the Qing rulers were of Manchu-Mongolian bloodlines – the Jurgen clan – a riding tribe from the northeastern part of the continent. The Manchu women did not adopt the foot-binding custom.

What Yuchen would not have known was that, in a few years, in 1895, the first anti-foot-binding society would be formed in Shanghai. Soon, branches would spring up in other cities. Members of this society were allowed to marry women with unbound feet only. In 1912, after the overturn of the Qing government, foot-binding was finally outlawed.

Yuchen was very glad that her family was of a different background. The pressure on them to bind feet was not as fierce. Within the Israelite community, some families, especially those who had intermarried with Han families, opted to follow the trend, while others remained determined not to. Yuchen's grandmother and mother both had large, natural feet, as did Yuchen. I was fortunate to be in a liberal-thinking family, she said to herself. She was rather surprised that Xiong Xin's wife did not comment or show any sign of displeasure at her unbound feet.

Xiong Xin's brother, Xiong Xiang, took Yidong and Yuchen under his wing. His house was a little distance from his brother's, and closer to the city centre. It was a larger and a newer brick house. Xiong Xiang took his guests to the study, which they referred to as the book room, where the young couple was to lodge temporarily.

"My sons will put a makeshift bed in here for you. I hope you will be comfortable. If you require anything, just let my sons know," Xiong Xiang instructed Yidong and Yuchen.

The study was scantily furnished. There was a desk, a chair, and a calligraphy table, all made of mahogany. Scrolls of paintings and calligraphy, mostly Xiong Xiang's work, adorned three walls of the room. The remaining wall had windows that opened to a small garden, with some rockeries and plants. The simplicity of the room exuded a calm, tranquil feeling, much appreciated by the new occupants.

Xiong Xiang also had two sons, Xiong Liang and Xiong Lin, who had both been matched but not yet married. The family operated a tutelage school, or si-shu, and the one classroom abutted their living quarters.

Xiong Xiang was a scholar of sorts. He had attained the imperial exams up to the second level (regional), but had not received any official posting. He was well versed in the classics and in the arts of painting and calligraphy. Both his sons had studied under him and were proficient in the Chinese classics. In the late 1850s, a Methodist mission from the United States had expanded its mission from Fuzhou to Jiujiang and later to Nanchang, where it built and operated two schools. Xiong Liang, the elder son, had been hired as a teacher at their Yu Zhang Academy for Boys.

Liang was two years younger than Yidong, and the two spent much time chatting about the classics and art.

"I'm amazed at your art work, and your father's. They are superb," Yidong said to Xiong Liang as he stood admiring the paintings and calligraphies on the walls.

Yidong had studied the classics and was good at Chinese calligraphy. Although he had worked alongside his father in the carpentry shop, he used to make little wooden carvings as decorative pieces. He had an eye for design, and the art works fascinated him. It gave him pleasure to discuss the colour and composition of the paintings that Liang and his father created.

Time went by quickly. Old man Xiong Xin's original plan to leave by the middle of the ninth month did not materialize, as his order of Jingdezhen porcelain-ware was not ready. His trip would be delayed to the end of the tenth month.

Meantime, Yidong received a letter from his father, who did not insist that they journey on to Shanghai. Having read Yidong's account of their mishap in Yangzhou and the good news of Yuchen's pregnancy, Lao Zhao decided it might be wiser to leave it to the young couple whether they would prefer to go on to Shanghai or simply settle down in Nanchang. Rumour had reached Kaifeng that Xiao Gao had died suddenly in Yangzhou, but no details were given. As well, there seemed to be much opposition from the common people to the foreigners' extraterritoriality in Shanghai. Shanghai was not as ideal as they had thought or hoped it to be.

Yidong did not understand the term *extraterritoriality*, which was mentioned in his father's letter. Liang accompanied him to ask the principal at Yu Zhang Academy. Principal Johnson gave a long history of extraterritoriality.* He explained to them that the practice of extraterritoriality in Shanghai began with the Treaty of Nanking as a result of the first opium war, in 1842. Essentially, it allowed most foreign residents in Shanghai to have their civil and criminal matters handled by their homeland jurisdictions. He quite agreed with Liang and Yidong that the imposition of such practices in China was unfair both to the Chinese government and the Chinese people. But then, there was nothing anyone could do about it.

Lao Zhao's letter mentioned the Anglican Church in Henan and its head, Bishop William White, who had taken a great interest in the synagogue. The church wanted to purchase several items from it, and even expressed interest in the synagogue property. If the synagogue were to lose all these things, Lao Zhao concluded, then there was no hope for the revival of the Israelite religion in Kaifeng.

Yuchen's father had also written with much love and affection. Needless to say, everyone was elated about the forthcoming baby. They just wished they could be there with the young couple.

A few weeks after their meeting with Principal Johnson, Liang was instructed to bring Yidong to the mission again. This time Yidong was introduced to most of the staff and missionary workers at the academy. He and Yuchen were welcome to stay at the missionaries' place if they wished.

To his surprise, Yidong found these foreigners, and the local folks at the mission, to be exceptionally kind and caring. He felt their sincerity and their selflessness. They seemed quite the opposite of the foreign priest he had heard of who had been killed in Tianjin and who had been cruel and oppressive towards the native people. He recalled those foreigners who came to their synagogue in Kaifeng. Most of them were interested only in getting some of the artifacts. The representatives from the Henan Anglican Church, for instance, were there mainly to negotiate a purchase of their scrolls. He did not feel compassion from these foreigners. Yidong was impressed by the Methodist missionary.* He told Yuchen he could trust them with no reservations.

Liang's parents were busy preparing for Liang's wedding in the spring. Liang and his brother, Lin, both urged their new friends to stay on till at least after Liang's marriage celebration.

As it became more uncertain whether they would stay or move on to Shanghai, Yidong decided to accept the offer from the missionaries.

"The principal said that we are welcome to move to the mission for the time being and take time to make up our minds. I think it is only fair that we do that, as Liang and his parents have much to do before Liang's wedding. It is inconvenient to them for us to stay here for too long," Yidong said to Yuchen.

"I was thinking the same thing, Dong-ge," said Yuchen. "But how long can we stay at the mission, and will it cost us money?"

"As far as I understand, the mission often takes in transients or people who have nowhere to go. It is part of their work, they said. They don't ask people to pay. They have several rooms for this purpose."

"That is very kind of them. I think we should take them up on this offer and stay with them till we are certain whether we want to stay or go to Shanghai. What do you think, Dong-ge?"

"That's exactly what I have in mind, Chen-mei. So shall we do that?"

Yidong and Yuchen took a room at the mission. They began to assess their situation and were determined to make the right decision in this all-important matter. It would be something that would affect them the rest of their lives.

Totally engrossed in preparation for the baby, Yuchen had much to occupy herself. She had never been overly enthusiastic about this Shanghai assignment of theirs. Now that she was going to be a mother, all she could think of was how to prepare a comfortable home for the arrival of their first child.

Yidong was undecided.

"I feel I owe it to Ba and the community to go on to Shanghai. Not that I'm that keen on it," he confessed to his wife.

He felt the obligation that was imposed on him, even though there was no longer any pressure from his father or perhaps even any need for him to pursue this venture. At the same time, he was happy to be in this new city, where people had been kind to him. The extended Xiong family and the people at the mission had taken very good care of them. The Xiong female members went out of their way to be helpful to Yuchen in her condition. Even her own mother or sister, if she had had one, could not have done more for her than these new acqaintances. But even as she expressed her gratitude for their constant thought, concern, help, and assistance, Yuchen's longing for her family became even more acute. She so much wanted to share with her mother this all-important period of her life: the carrying of her first child. She so much wanted to ask about her mother's own experience. Such an intimate exchange between mother and a daughter would have meant the world to her. How she missed her mother.

However, everything seemed to favour their staying in this city. In the end, it was Yuchen's gentle persuasion that encouraged Yidong's decision to make Nanchang their home.

Under the guidance of the Xiongs and the people at the mission, Yidong was able to secure a house quite close to Xiong Xiang's house. After he cashed in the debenture certificate that Yuchen's mother had given them, there was sufficient money for Yidong to set up a little lumber shop in the city. Jiangxi had an abundance of forests on the mountains. It would be a shame not to capitalize on it, especially when Yidong's family was in the wood and carpentry business. He felt like a fish in water at his lumber shop, very much in his own element. Things were looking up.

Spring brushed a tender soft green on every blade of grass and on every new shoot covering the ground or on the tree limbs, promising new life and abundant growth. People and animals shook off their winter sluggishness, ready to start the year afresh. The celebration of the Lunar New Year continued on to more cheers and joy. Xiong Xiang's marriage was followed by the birth of Jingde, Yuchen and Yidong's first son.

Happiness upon happiness. Within two years, Qingde, a second son, was born to Yuchen and Yidong.

Yidong's lumber shop was thriving beyond expectation. Hard work, diligence, and a pleasant personality secured him continuing business and repeated customers. His lumber was no longer only for local consumption; orders began to trickle in from out of town, from as far away as Nanjing. Yidong and Yuchen were careful with their money. They lived frugally, and by the time Yuchen was carrying their third child three years later, Yidong was able to purchase twelve mus of land, or about two acres, nearby and hired two men to work the field. Their third child, Gande, was therefore born as a landlord's son no less, albeit a small-scale landlord. A fourth son, Zhende, followed not long after.

Nights followed days, months turned into years. Yidong's family of six was blossoming splendidly. Yidong reached the prime of his life, and maturity brought with it a more manly masculinity. He looked good; he worked well; he loved his family endlessly. As for Yuchen, despite having borne four children in quick succession, she remained as attractive as ever, her soft grace combined with a womanly vibrancy.

On many a quiet evening, when Yidong and Yuchen took time to reflect on their lives, they were ever so grateful at what had turned out to be. Xiao Gao's villainy had long been forgotten. Instead, they often felt that Xiao Gao had done them a favour that led to this twist in their destiny. They were happy. They were content. They had so much to look forward to.

"Men's fortune is as changeable as the weather." This is a proverbial Chinese saying. And those who have read the immortal book *I-Ching** would agree that the only constant in the universe is Change. As the moon reaches its fullness, it wanes, and then it becomes full again. The cycle repeats. Those who manage to sail through life smoothly, with few ups and downs, are considered blessed and fortunate. Ups and downs there will always be. In every person's life. Unavoidable, unpredictable, unforeseeable.

Yidong and Yuchen enrolled their sons in the Yu Zhang Academy for Boys. Books and classics, however, did not excite Jingde, the eldest. He preferred physical enpowerment. He skipped classes to take up martial-arts lessons with some masters, and he became surprisingly skilled in it. By the age of fourteen, he was an acclaimed junior master. From early on, he opted to help his father at the lumber shop rather than attending school. It was the lesser of two evils in his thinking.

Qingde was a born rebel. He was an extremely good-looking lad, with twinkling eyes and well-balanced features. Flawless. But Qingde had no incentive to work. Nothing bothered him, and he recognized no rules or discipline. He could neither sit in classes nor work at the shop. Several times he was suspended from the academy because of misbehaviour. Finally, he was told not to return to school. His parents were not happy, but there was little they could do. He joined his brother at the lumber shop. Even then, he would often disappear when no one was watching him.

All Qingde wanted to do was to be with a group of five other like-minded youths. In the beginning they just played practical jokes on people. It was their idea of having fun. Then they began to dare each other to more daunting feats. Vandalizing private or public properties, petty theft, annoying shopkeepers, or menacing innocent bystanders – all of these gave them a thrill of excitement.

By and by, Qingde was coerced into playing dice for money. Yidong and Yuchen tried everything to keep him from such undesirable company, but met with very little success. No amount of punishment would keep Qingde from his pals or deter him from playing dice. He was in his early teens, and was already a major headache to his parents. What was worse was that Qingde would, at times, encourage his brother Jingde to participate in the dice games.

In those days in China, a whip or a rattan strip was what the parents resorted to when disciplining their children. They believed in the ancient saying: "The whip brings forward a son with filial piety." From generation to generation, this was the accepted method for bringing up a child. As they say, without sculpturing and chiselling, a piece of jade cannot become a piece of art. Reasoning with the child? Gentle persuasion? No one did that, and Yidong and Yuchen were no exception.

Having to deal with the two older boys, Yuchen had, by degrees, become a strict disciplinarian with her children. Because of her second son's misbehaviour, the use of the rattan strip was frequent. To her it was the only way to keep four boys in line. They feared her more than they did their father.

If it were not for the constant trouble their second son brought them, Yidong and Yuchen would have considered themselves perfectly happy in life.

Then the unthinkable happened.

Summer was nearing its end. The fields were mad with growth, every stalk competing to excel in height and in abundance of yield. The hired hands nodded in contentment, anticipating a bumper crop for the harvest. For the moment, they enjoyed a bit of leisure that afforded them time to do repair work on the pigsty and the chicken coop.

At the lumber shop, a huge order had just been shipped out, and Yidong was restocking his inventory in the yard. Two new orders had come in from the coast, and he wanted to have the shipment ready before the mid-autumn festivities.

It was the beginning of September, the lunar eighth month, but the scorching sun had not abated and the summer heat lingered on. Worse still, humidity hung in the air. It was so suffocatingly uncomfortable. Even breathing was an effort. Yidong's team of workers was busy moving the lumber, sorting, marking, stacking each piece.

As always, Yidong worked alongside the labourers. He had felt dizzy in the morning and experienced a kind of tightness in his chest. He blamed it on the weather. He did not feel like eating. Sweat ran from his forehead. How so very unbearably tiresome! He was so anxious to get the work done for the day and go home. He wanted to go home. He wanted to lie down. He wanted to rest. Yet he would not stop to rest; would not take a break. He toiled on, and on, and on ...

He collapsed!

Yidong never regained consciousness. At the age of forty-one, he left the world and his family forever.

蠟炬成灰淚始乾

Chapter 6

On Her Own

No amount of tears, no amount of sadness or grief would bring Yidong back to life. He was gone. Gone forever. Without saying goodbye, without a last word, without a final expression of love or of tenderness.

Yuchen was dazed for weeks. She hardly ate, hardly slept, hardly noticed whatever others did regarding Yidong's funeral, burial, and all the other ceremonies. She went through the motions of being alive, yet the essence of life had been sucked out of her. She felt nothing, thought nothing. She was like the walking dead, a living corpse.

Again, it was the women from the Xiong clan and the Methodist mission who nursed her through this terrible ordeal. They made sure everything was carried out properly and the family was not in need. But as much as they helped to look after the food and the daily chores, they, as friends, were not able to manage Yidong's business or settle his finances. In fact, no one could.

Most of the hired hands were illiterate labourers who simply followed orders. Not a single one of them was privy to

Yidong's dealings with his customers. Neither were the two older sons, Jingde and Qingde. They had no clue about the accounts receivable, the accounts payable, or when, where, and how to collect money or to make payments. The payment part was less of a headache, because inevitably the creditors would come to demand the amounts due. To collect what was owing to Yidong was much more of a challenge – especially from the out-of-town accounts.

The big shipment Yidong had sent out on his last day had reached its destination, but no money was forthcoming. The shipping of Yidong's last two orders was delayed due to the unexpected confusion. Cash flow was tight. Yuchen was faced with the almost insurmountable task of keeping everything going, feeding the family, feeding and paying the hired hands, and making sure that the lumber business stayed afloat. With limited literacy and no experience whatsoever in buying and selling, she felt the weight of her new burden, and she was almost in despair.

Yuchen had hoped that Jingde, the eldest, who was now in his late teens, would take over the helm and direct the business. Big disappointment. Jingde could handle physical work but possessed no business acumen. He needed directions all the time. Qingde, she could not trust with any amount of money. Qingde had the brains, but could she depend on him? Yuchen toyed with the idea of giving more responsibility to Qingde, with the hope that he might be brought to his senses by his father's death, but after much thought, she decided it was not wise to take such a gamble. She had to make sure that she had total control of all the cash, so that it would not end up on the dice table.

Yuchen learned and learned quickly. Xiong Liang was

invaluable in helping her to sort out all the invoices and more or less guided her in taking charge of the lumber shop. Gande, her number-three son, though only in his early teens, surprised her with his understanding and insightfulness in trading and other business activities. Having been a diligent student at the Academy, Gande had acquired an excellent command of both Chinese and English. He was quick with numbers as well. Often Yuchen found herself discussing various business problems with Gande, and she received satisfactory opinions from him. It was a reassuring feeling. By and by she became more and more dependent on this young son of hers in almost every decision.

The Mid-Autumn Festival had come and gone amidst the confusion of mourning and the sorting out of the business mess. By the last month of the lunar year, all the fury seemed to have quieted down and things slowly crawled back to near normal. The three months that had gone by had more or less depleted all the cash. Even the small savings in the bank were down to almost zero. Yuchen was counting on the income from the cash crop off the land. This, she said hopefully to herself, would tide her over the Lunar New Year. Tight though it was, she might just manage without having to go into further debt. The Xiongs would willingly lend her money if she needed a loan, but she wanted to avoid that. If she planned well and used the money wisely, she might just skimp by. After the festivities were over, with business gradually getting back on track, she would try to manage in the new spring. She sighed a cautious sigh of relief.

Yuchen would observe all the rituals in welcoming the New Spring, as all Chinese had throughout the ages. She would, as they always did, spend a large amount of their money in celebration. All debts would be disposed of by New Year's Eve, and all new things would be purchased when the New Year dawned.

By the tenth of the twelfth month, the hired farmhands fetched most of the money from the harvest and handed her the cash. They too were relieved that their mistress would be able to have a reasonably manageable Lunar New Year – and possibly a bonus for them as well.

Yuchen put the cash in a tin biscuit box in the top drawer of the chest of drawers in her room. The coming Sunday would be the big market day for her. New clothes, new shoes for the boys. Pay plus bonus for the staff and the farm hands. Candies, snacks, ingredients for her to make all the special New Year's treats. Firecrackers, for sure, to burn away all the bad luck. Red packets with lucky money inside, too, for her own children as well as those of the Xiong clan. There would be two very busy weeks ahead. The New Year's Eve family dinner had to be as good as when Yidong was around, Yuchen promised herself.

Alas! Yuchen's plans for the Lunar celebration were totally shattered.

It was a busy Friday at the lumber shop. Yuchen did the calculations with her staff and did not get home till almost dark. She had left the soup simmering, and all she had to do was to prepare a vegetable dish and dinner would be ready. They had not been eating much meat or poultry since Yidong passed away. The boys would be anxious to have their food.

As she hurried through the door, she bumped into her eldest boy, Jingde, looking dishevelled and agitated. He shouted, "He took all the money! Qingde stole all the money from the tin box!"

Jingde had seen Qingde leaving their mother's room and rushing out of the house. He had checked his mother's room and found the tin box empty. By the time he ran after Qingde, the thief was nowhere to be seen.

Qingde had taken, all by himself, all the money their mother had managed to gather for the New Year. That money was to buy new clothes for the family, to be spent on special festive food, to give bonuses to the hired hands, to put inside the red packets, and so on. It was a meagre amount that would have to be stretched every which way.

But, before anyone could devise a wise allocation of the money, Qingde lost it all at dice. He took the whole amount and he lost it all. Every single copper of the family's hard-earned savings for the entire year.

Yuchen was livid. She raged out of control. If she could, she would have strangled this rascal of a son with her own hands. To impose maximum punishment, she enlisted her eldest son's help in beating his gambling brother. Jingde, the kung-fu master, probably disgusted with his brother for not leaving him with even one piece of copper to have some fun with, was no doubt a touch too severe in his punches. When the beating was over, Qingde left home, never to return again.

When Qingde had not come home after three days, Yuchen was on pins and needles. She regretted that she had been so careless as to keep the money in the tin box, which was accessible to anyone. She was naïve to think that her boys did not know where she kept her money. She regretted too having ordered Jingde to give his brother a badly deserved beating. She should have taken the matter into her own hands. Even with a rattan strip, her blows would not have been half as harsh as Jingde's. Jingde was, after all, a junior kung-fu expert. She blamed herself to no end, and she kept asking herself why she had done that.

Outwardly, she calmly proclaimed it was good riddance to this unruly, rebellious, good-for-nothing son. Inwardly, her heart was bleeding for the loss. She quietly pleaded with Yidong to help her get Qingde back, but to no avail.

This particular day, Yuchen's lower right eyelid was twitching. It was an ominous sign. She had heard that, if the left upper lid twitches, you could expect an unexpected windfall; but if it was the lower right lid, watch out for bad luck. She was aware too, that people often said that sorrow came not singly, but in a succession of threes. This year had been cursed. First Yidong's death, then Qinde's disappearance. What next? She really could not take any more disasters. Spare me, Heaven, she pleaded silently.

In her state of unsettled nerves, she walked into the kitchen and was alarmed to see her severely myopic son, Zhengde, sitting at the table with his head bent over a pair of scissors. So fearful was she at the possibility that Zhengde might injure himself, that she screamed at him. Zhengde was so startled that his hands jerked in fright at the voice of his mother, and the scissors inadvertently punctured his right eyeball, causing irreversible damage. The irony of ironies.

The cursed year closed on a sombre note.

Chapter 7

Inner Conflict

Ever since they had settled in Nanchang, Yuchen and Yidong had completely forsaken their mission to seek help for the Kaifeng Jews. The few Hebrew religious practices, such as abstinence from pork and shellfish, the removal of tendons from their meat, and the circumcision of the male child were likewise abandoned. They consciously assimilated into the Han Chinese way of life.

On rare occasions, Yidong and Yuchen would broach the subject of their ancestry or their religion. They would make comparisons between their Hebrew practices and those of this newfound Methodist mission. They sensed there had to be some connection between the two, as they both worshipped one God. They speculated it must be the same God. Just like the White-Cap Hui Hui in Kaifeng. Didn't they also worship one God and venerate a number of the Hebrew historic personages, like Abraham, Jacob, Moses . . . The Methodists seemed to venerate many of the same prophets as well. What puzzled them was this Jesus Christ, who was all-important to the Methodists but was never heard of among the Israelites or the other Hui Hui. And, Mary, the Mother of Christ, could she be Esther, who figured prominently in their Hebrew religion? But, more often than not, they simply left all the questions dangling in the air unanswered. Neither did they make any effort to find out if there were any connections or associations among these different beliefs.

When Jingde was born, Yuchen and Yidong discussed briefly if, at some point, their children should be made aware of their ancestry. They came to no conclusion. By the time Zhengde was born, it had become a non-issue. There were so many other necessities that required their attention that the question of ancestry was far from their minds.

At age thirty-eight, Yuchen had now lost a husband and a son. The pain was enormous. The twenty years of her marriage were more precious to her than anything else. Yidong had been a life companion. They had become one being since that first day she was carried at dawn to the Zhao home in an unadorned sedan chair. The twenty years they spent together had bound them closer and tighter. With Yidong's passing, she felt half of her own self had disappeared. She was left with only half the strength and half the willpower to carry on. How she longed for Yidong's presence. In the quiet evenings, when people and animals alike had drifted to the land of dreams, Yuchen sank into dead silence, total stillness, absolute abandonment, complete non-existence. Her whole being would turn numb with the fathomless void in her heart.

Qingde's leaving was like another death in the family. Angry as she was over the loss of money, losing a son was far more devastating. Each morning Yuchen awoke in the hope that Qingde might appear at the doorstep, and each evening she retired to bed disappointed. She would have given anything to have Qingde back.

Jingde's first reaction to Qingde's running away from home was a sense of pride and gratification. He felt like a mighty conqueror who had won an enormous battle. His prowess had given his brother a well-deserved lesson and chased him out of the family.

When Qingde did not return after a week, Jingde began to question his victory. A feeling of guilt gnawed at him. He could tell that his mother had not wanted Qingde kicked out of the family. She was angry at what Qingde had done, but she still loved him as her son. Jingde regretted what he had done to Qingde. In reparation, Jingde spent more time at the shop and worked harder than ever. He no longer boasted about his brawn and his might. He could almost hear people jeering at him behind his back for being so merciless to his brother.

Zhengde, the shy little weakling, became even more shy and more timid after losing one eye. He seldom ventured out to be with people. His short-sightedness prevented him from doing much. Prescribed spectacles might have been introduced to the Qing court at that time, but they certainly were not available to the common folks. As a result, he followed Yuchen or one of the farmhands around and ran harmless errands for whoever asked him.

Out of the chaotic and confusing family situation, Gande, unexpectedly, blossomed forth into a strong and intelligent young man. While his brother Jingde could flex his muscles, Gande was quick with his mind. He had, by then, been at the academy for almost eight years, and he felt he should leave his studies to help his mother run the family business. He was not keen to sit for the imperial exams; neither did he want to leave Nanchang to pursue higher education.

Very sensibly, he first discussed his situation with Principal William Johnson of the academy.

"Principal Johnson, I'm at a crossroads and I have to make a decision. My family has undergone major changes in the last year. I'm contemplating quitting school to help my mother in the lumber shop. I would like your advice, sir."

Principal Johnson looked thoughtful. "I'm very glad that you've come to me. I'm well aware of your family tragedies, Gande, and I am very sorry for what has happened. But I think you are much too young to leave school. Have you considered participating in the county exams in the future? It may secure you a posting from the court? I'm certain you will score high in those exams. I am quite prepared to exempt you from the school fees if you decide to continue your studies," he said kindly, in his heavy Scottish accent.

"Thank you, sir, but I have no interest in becoming an official. Besides, it may take years before I receive a posting. My family's need is immediate. My elder brother works at the shop, but he is incapable of making decisions. I have confidence that I can be of help to my mother in managing the shop. Therefore, as much as I enjoy attending the academy, I'm afraid I'll have to take up my responsibility at home," Gande answered.

"Well, Gande, you have a point there, and I shouldn't insist on your continuing your studies. I wish you well, although I am very, very sorry to lose you as one of our top students. It will not be easy for you either, Gande. Come back any time if you require help or even just to talk things over. I will always have your interests at heart. My door is open at all times."

"There is another matter about which I would like your guidance, sir," said Gande. "Do you think I can become a member of the Methodist church?"

"But, of course, m'boy. What an absolutely brilliant idea! I'm glad you're interested in our church. I'll ask Mr. McEnroy to give you more instruction in the Christian faith and prepare you for baptism down the road. Come to the Sunday service and stay connected." The principal was obviously elated at the thought of a new convert.

For his age, Gande was extremely far-sighted about the socio-economic and political situation of his time. He had observed that the movement of foreign people and business into the Province of Jiangxi had been on the rise. Regardless of whether some people labelled the western influence as an invasion of the Chinese culture, Gande saw that new knowledge and increased foreign trade had benefited the people in certain ways. This trend was going to continue, he speculated, and it would be a good thing to have reliable foreign friends at one's side. Apart from possible material gains, Gande also felt, as did his father, that the Methodist missionaries were exceptionally caring and helpful. He had a genuine admiration and respect for them. He wanted to become like these missionaries – kind, loving, and always willing to provide assistance. He would not want to sever ties with these people.

Gande's decision was met with mixed feelings from his mother. On the one hand, Yuchen was inwardly relieved that Gande would now be at her side more and would take a huge load off her shoulders. She also knew in her heart that Gande was cut out more for business than for officialdom. But she had not anticipated that he would want to step across to join a different religion.

True, the Methodists had been at their side right from day one of their decision to remain in Nanchang. True, she and Yidong had not stuck to their Hebrew religion as their parents had wished. True, too, that they had never mentioned anything about their ancestry or their faith to any of their children. She realized that to Gande it was not a cross-over from one faith to another but an adoption of a religion. She could see Gande's logic in his move. Nevertheless, she felt she had betrayed her parents and her ancestors.

Worse still, because of Gande's initiative, Mr. McEnroy had invited the whole family to join Gande in receiving Christian teachings and being baptized. This led to a major conflict in Yuchen's mind. It was one thing to condone her son becoming a Christian, quite another for her to abandon her own faith and embrace a different one. This would be total betrayal of my roots, she said to herself. What a dilemma!

Yuchen thought of letting all her children join the Methodist church but staying out of it herself. It would ease her conscience somewhat. In the end, she compromised. She sensed that Gande would want her to be there with him and the rest of the family. Besides, she was grateful to the missionaries for all these years that the mission had helped her in one thing or another. The Methodist church was their patron, and she should show her gratitude.

On Christmas Eve, a year after Yidong's passing, Yuchen and her family were received into the Christian fold.

Chapter 8

Gande in Ascendancy

Gande took charge of the shop. Yuchen was amazed as she watched him putting the business back in order so methodically. How on earth did he learn all the skills, she wondered.

Gande reorganized the staff. Each was given specific duties and put in charge of a specific area. There was to be no confusion when a query or an order came in. Each person knew exactly what to do or whom to go to.

He spent time with his suppliers. He studied the people he dealt with and took notes on the quality and the pricing of their merchandise. He charted and graded his suppliers, and the information was updated periodically.

His customers received visits from him, even those out of town. His sincere attitude and his willingness to do his best for them generally impressed the people he met. Because of his knowledge and his accurate calculations, customers found him credible and reliable, despite his youth.

About a year later, all the debts were cleared and orders kept coming in steadily. Yuchen thanked the Almighty for giving her Gande as a son. In an age when appearance superceded other qualities, Gande, unfortunately, was not endowed with attractive facial features or with physical prowess. Jingde had the physique; Qingde, an exceptionally handsome face; Zhengde, a sweet nature and a gentle disposition. Gande had prominently protruding teeth and fiercely intense eyes – not the kind that charmed hearts, but the kind that pierced minds. It could be that the combination of the two created such a solemn and earnest look on Gande's face that people could not but take him seriously. Gande's charm lay in his sincerity and his tireless persuasion. He was never abrasive, never confrontational. He would painstakingly analyze situations and sort out solutions for his customers, most of whom came back for repeat business. The consensus was that Gande was well-liked, well-respected, and trusted.

Years flew by. Jingde had married at the relatively early age of nineteen and quickly produced two offspring. For Gande, business was all that mattered; marriage could wait. By the turn of the century, Yuchen became eager for Gande to start a family. Through the matchmaker, several names of eligible girls from good families were presented to Gande. Without hesitation, he picked Xiong Cheng, the second daughter of Xiong Liang, the loyal friend who had been invaluable to the family since the day Yidong and Yuchen had stepped on shore in Nanchang.

By then, the family business had stabilized somewhat. The marriage celebration was very different from the one Yuchen experienced. There was no threat from the likes of Pan Ying. The grieving for Yidong had lessened. Although at times Yuchen would quietly shed tears for the loss of her second son,

Qingde, the overall atmosphere at the time of this union was one of joy and happiness.

Three days of food and drink left all the guests in high spirits and gastronomically satisfied, albeit mentally a bit woozy. Just about everyone they knew – relatives, colleagues, staff, workers, and the people from the Methodist mission – attended. It was the largest event Yuchen had ever hosted. Though exhausted, she enjoyed every minute of the celebration, despite a tinge of regret that Yidong and Qingde were absent.

Xiong Cheng and Gande were not strangers. Cheng did not go to school, even though her father taught at the Methodist Academy. Nevertheless, she possessed a sharp mind and an incredible memory. In intelligence, she was on par with Gande, who appreciated this quality in her. They could discuss business deals, and Cheng would not be intimidated by her husband's knowledge and skill. Often she would offer a perspective from a woman's point of view that complemented Gande's thinking.

Coming from a more traditional, academic Han family, Cheng had bound feet, literally "three-inch golden lotus." Gande often feared that she might tip over to one side, as she waddled in her gait. Yet Cheng, like her mother and grandmother, was able to handle all kinds of chores and manual work with no difficulty. She also walked long distances, seemingly quite at ease, as she travelled from one place to another.

Cheng was tall for a Chinese woman, about the same height as Gande. She had classic, clean facial features: a straight nose, small mouth, and a tan complexion. She was two years younger than Gande, and the new couple found themselves well-matched and happy with each other.

Likewise, Yuchen was pleased with Gande's choice. She had watched Cheng grow up and was aware that this daughter-in-law was a sensible, hard-working girl, neither vain nor extravagant. These were virtues she valued highly.

Cheng produced four daughters in rapid succession.

However, the times had turned hectic again. The aftermath of the Boxer Rebellion, plus natural disasters in neighbouring provinces, plunged most provinces into hardship. It was a tumultuous period that saw China experiencing stronger antagonism towards foreigners and the Qing court. As a result, political groups of anarchists, socialists, and revolutionaries sprang up, calling for independence from foreign dominance and the Manchu rule.

During the years 1898 and 1899, foreign powers had intensified their imperialistic expansions in China. Germany occupied Qingdao, a port city in Shandong Province, claiming mining and railroad rights in the area. The British had taken over the Weihaiwei harbour on the north side of Shandong Peninsula and demanded a ninety-nine-year lease on the Kowloon peninsula and the arable lands in the New Territories, north of Hong Kong. The French had claimed rights in the provinces of Yunnan, Guangdong, Guangxi, and Hainan Island. The Russians had built fortifications in Lushun to strengthen their hold on Manchuria. Japan had already occupied Taiwan and was hatching plans to penetrate into central China for economic gain. The United States demanded an "open door policy" to allow it equal opportunity with all the foreign powers.

The majority of Han Chinese felt doubly disadvantaged;

they had become involuntary slaves to both the Manchu Qing rulers and the foreign invaders. The treaties with the foreigners signed by the Qing court caused immense bitterness and humiliation to the people. The privilege of extraterritoriality, enjoyed by most foreigners, was considered a shameful insult by most Chinese. The custom regulations were controlled by foreign powers who profited from the tax revenue. In addition, the Treaty Powers were granted rights to station warships in Chinese waters.

There was fear as well as resentment. The Han Chinese watched their country being territorially dissected by foreign powers, the economy controlled and manipulated by the invaders. Rumbles of revolution and uprising stirred among the grassroots.

The Boxers, who called themselves Yi He Tuan, meaning "United in Righteousness" or "Righteous, Harmonius Fist," had come into being in Shandong in 1898 in response to Western provocation. They recruited peasants and workers impoverished by the natural disasters of floods followed by droughts. They targeted the Christian converts and the foreign missionaries, angry at the privileges these people enjoyed. They burned churches, damaged telegraph lines, ruined railroad tracks, and killed Christians – Chinese and non-Chinese alike. They also killed four French and Belgian engineers and two English missionaries.

The Boxers urged the people to support the Qing court and to chase out the foreigners. Empress Dowager Cixi initially welcomed them as a loyal militia, but then flip-flopped between supporting the Boxers and striking an alliance with the foreign powers. When a joint force of twenty thousand troops, made up of soldiers from eight nations – Britain, the United States, Russia, Germany, France, Italy, Austria, and Japan – marched towards Beijing, the Qing court retreated westward to Xi'An. The foreign troops occupied Beijing and forced the Qing court to sign the Boxer Protocol Treaty in September 1901. The Boxer uprising, without proper leadership, modern weaponry, or government backing, was soon crushed.

The Boxer Protocol Treaty resulted in China having to pay an indemnity for the loss of and damages to foreign lives and property of 450 million taels of silver – equivalent to U.S. $333 million at the time. The total payment with interest amounted to close to one billion taels of silver. The Qing court's annual revenue at the time was estimated at about a quarter of that sum.

After the four-year Boxer uprising was crushed by the Qing court, in conjunction with foreign armies, a forceful nineteen-year-old, Zou Rong, came forward, calling for the Han Chinese to take action against the Manchu government. He emphasized the imminent danger to the survival of the Han race. He pushed for an end to foreign dominance. He reminded people that they could take the government, the law, the industries, the land, the military, the resources, all into their own hands and be free of the yoke they had been under.

It was during this period that the U.S. immigration department was harassing and persecuting Chinese residents in the United States and those Chinese immigrants who arrived at the U.S. ports. (In 1882, the U.S. government had passed the infamous *Chinese Exclusion Act*.) In protest against the unfair policy and practices of the United States, a widespread total boycott of American goods by merchants in Canton, Shanghai, Xiamen, Tianjin, and elsewhere, was declared in June 1905.

Products such as cigarettes, cotton, kerosene, and flour were among the goods targeted. The boycott did not last long but did cause much damage to people's livelihood.

Gande's business suffered alongside those of other merchants and traders. The entire country was depleted of funds. Dependence on opium became even more widespread, rendering the ordinary people not only poor but also unproductive. The unpredictability of the political situation kept everyone constantly in suspense, not knowing what was to become of their homes or their villages and cities from one day to the next. Like cattle without a herdsman, masses of migrants moved blindly from one province to another, hoping for greener pastures. Most were disappointed. Life was cruel; days were harsh. Whichever direction they took, they ended up in poverty.

Gande decided the best strategy was to be frugal, by shedding expenses, and to tough it out. But with so many mouths to feed and so little to share, even toughing it out was not easy. It was so difficult that, when their number-three daughter was only four years of age, Gande and Cheng decided to give her as a child bride* to a neighbouring family who was better off and eager to have a girl for their seven-year-old son. It was not a willing decision, but a necessary one. It was not an unusual practice, at the time, for families to sell or give away their daughters to become child-brides to better-off families. In many cases, the child-bride was treated like a bondmaid,* having to do many of the household chores. Gande and Cheng made certain that the family who was to receive their third daughter would treat her fairly, with kindness and affection.

Fortune's pendulum kept on swinging. When it reached one extreme, it began to head the opposite way. A few years after their third daughter was given away, Gande received a huge stroke of luck.

By the turn of the century, many more cities were made accessible to the Western powers. As foreign influence had seeped slowly into China's interior regions, foreign corporations vied to establish their presence in as many regions and cities as they could. In the energy sector, two major oil companies set up distributorships throughout China. Shell, the British-Dutch oil company, dominated Shanghai and the coastal ports. The Standard Oil Company of New York (SOCONY), the predecessor of Mobile Oil, which later became Exxon-Mobile, built their bases in the provinces.

Out of the blue one day, Principal Johnson invited Gande to his house. Tea was served in the parlour.

"Any idea why I asked to see you, Gande?" Johnson asked.

Gande shook his head. "Is there something wrong, Mr. Johnson?" he inquired.

"Not at all. I assume you have seen, or at least heard about, automobiles. Have you not?"

"Oh yes, I have, sir. Mighty powerful machines. There aren't that many around though," Gande answered.

"Well, soon there will be a lot more in all the cities. And this is the reason I want to discuss a business deal with you."

"Selling automobiles?" Gande looked puzzled.

"Not quite, m'boy," chuckled Johnson, "but related. Automobiles are run on gasoline, which also has many other uses. As you know, kerosene stoves are now widely used by most people. Well, gasoline is produced and sold by oil companies, and a U.S. oil company is planning to set up bases in several provinces in China, including Jiangxi. They are looking for someone reliable and intelligent to be the distributor of gasoline in this province. The senior vice-president of the company came to see me the other day and asked me to recommend a candidate. Are you interested, Gande? It will be a lucrative business for sure."

Gande was speechless. His brain was running a mile a minute, but he looked dazed.

"Come, come, my lad. Don't look so bewildered. This is an enormous opportunity to make some good money if you get the distributorship. I am confident that you can do it. But," Johnson took a sip of his tea and looked at Gande intently, "and it is a big but, they do require proof of assets as collateral to ensure your financial capability. I know your family owns some land, but that may not be sufficient. Would you be able to come up with some other assets? Property deeds, bank deposits, and so on."

"How much time do I have to come up with the collateral, and how much collateral do I need?"

"They want to move fast. I would say maybe four weeks. Would that be too soon for you? As to the amount, I'll have to confirm with the company and let you know as soon as they give me the figure."

"I'll try, Principal Johnson. Thank you so much for thinking of me. I'll not disappoint you. May I get back to you within the next two weeks?"

"You certainly may. I'll be anxious to hear from you, my lad. Good luck."

Gande could not wait to tell his wife about this good prospect. While he was elated to be given such an opportunity, he was, at the same time, a bit apprehensive as to how he was to come up with the required collateral.

Without batting an eye, Cheng, his wife, offered to ask her parents, uncles, and cousins for help. Her father, Qiong Liang, uncle Qiong Lin, and their cousins Qiong Yuan and Qiong Ying were all excited at Gande's good fortune. All of them agreed to enter into deals with Gande. They would transfer the deeds to their properties and farmland into Gande's name, and he was to pay them a premium for the transfer. They allowed Gande a period of eighteen months to pay up the premium. It was an act of blind trust on their part.

Principal Johnson was very pleased at Gande's efficiency. Because of his recommendation, SOCONY approved Gande's application for the Jiangxi distributorship immediately. The process went smoothly. Soon Gande met with SOCONY's engineers and things moved along.

Gande was given a mandate to supply oil to eighty-one cities in the Province of Jiangxi. His base would be at Nanchang. With input from the engineers, Gande picked Yan Jiang Road, or Riverside Road, as the location for the first station. This road ran along the bank of the river Gan. On the property, there was a good-sized two-storey building. At the front, on the ground floor, a station was set up. Gasoline would be shipped by tankers along the river to the site and stored in the rear section of the ground floor. The second floor housed the staff and workers.

A new chapter began in Gande's life.

Chapter 9

SOCONY

Not in his wildest dreams had Gande ever imagined that a distributor for a foreign company could be so well compensated. Though it did not happen overnight, the business took off at speed. Cash, cash, cash . . . and more cash. Gande had never seen so much money in his life.

He carefully selected loyal, trustworthy staff to take over the stations in the eighty-one cities within his distributorship region. All the revenues from these branches were accurately and honestly reported to him, and profits were duly forwarded to the main office.

The premiums owed to the Qiong clan were paid up quickly and many of their members joined Gande's employ with well-paid positions. Gande began to amass acres of land in all four regions of the province: north, south, east, and west. Most of the land was good, arable land, and Gande leased it out to farmers to grow rice and gave lenient terms regarding payment from their harvest. A total of twenty-thousand mus* (or Chinese acres) of rice land were registered under his name. Just the documentation of the land titles filled two chests. Surplus rice was shipped to the coast for sale. Inadvertently, Gande became a rice merchant, along with his oil and gas business and his lumber shop.

As his lumber business was also flourishing, Gande's next move was to purchase an entire mountainside for its forest. It made sense to him that he should own the source of his timber supplies. Thus the little lumber shop his father, Yidong, had started grew exponentially and became one of the top suppliers for timber and lumber in the province and beyond.

Besides money in abundance, Gande received yet another much-welcomed blessing. Cheng gave birth to their first son, Xinmeng. In the patriarchal feudal society of China of that era, male offspring were definitely preferred. The joy and happiness of begetting a son after a succession of four daughters was beyond words. Xinmeng became the centre of attention in the family. He was followed subsequently by two younger brothers and two younger sisters.

While money rolled in continuously, and his personal joy was at a peak, the political instability in the country and the provinces deteriorated abysmally.

After the death of Empress Dowager Cixi, the last Qing emperor, Xuan Tong, more commonly known as Puyi, ascended the throne at the tender age of six. His reign lasted three years, from 1909 to 1912.

The consequences of the two Opium Wars, plus all the harsh treaties signed with Russia, Japan, and Germany, led to a total depletion of the Qing treasury. Provinces refused to contribute towards the national coffers. The country's finances were in total shambles. Natural disasters continued to ruin harvests, causing famine and starvation in the countryside. Masses of refugees were on the move everywhere, with no plans and no clue as to where they were heading.

Anti-Qing and anti-foreigner sentiments intensified. Revolution was in the air. In November 1910, the Qing court agreed that it would move towards a fully elected parliament by 1913, but on January 1, 1912, Dr. Sun Yatsen, leader of the revolution, was named the interim provisional president of a totally unstable Republic of China founded by the National People's Party. However, it had not secured the support base of the regional governors, who still pledged their loyalty to the Qing authorities.

Sun Yatsen was advised to enlist the help of General Yuan Shikai,* a regent of the emperor, in overthrowing the Qing government. Yuan's boss, General Rong Lu, controlled the military. If Yuan succeeded, he would be offered the presidency of the Republic.

Yuan agreed to the proposal and moved quickly to force Emperor Puyi to abdicate. After two hundred and sixty-eight years (1644 to 1912), the Manchu dominance of China finally came to an end.

People anticipated rosy days just around the corner. But before they even had time to express their hopes and expectations, the country went tumbling from one disaster to another.

Emperor Puyi abdicated on February 12, 1912. Sun Yatsen relinquished his title of interim president on February 13, and on the following day, February 14, Yuan Shikai became the second interim president of the Republic.

Without delay, Yuan manipulated an election that resulted in his becoming the first President of the Republic, while chaos and confusion throughout the country continued.

Yuan's ambition did not stop with his securing the presidency. He began to negotiate with the Japanese for their support in putting him on the throne, promising the Japanese rights, privileges, control, and the secession of territories in return. He was a traitor with no disguise.

By 1915, Yuan Shikai shamelessly moved to make himself an emperor. With manipulation and bribery he made sure that his supporters would beg him to become emperor. On December 15, 1915, Yuan Shikai accepted the title, inaugurating his new regime on January 1, 1916.

The whole country was in uproar at the re-establishment of a monarchy. Public protests flared up everywhere, and military leaders in the provinces seized the opportunity to proclaim their independence. Foreign powers were disappointed at the political step back, but capitalized on the situation by negotiating with regional powers for their own gains.

Yuan sat on the throne for a brief three months. In March 1916, he had to declare the cancellation of the monarchy due to widespread rebellion. On June 6, 1916, Yuan Shikai died of uremia. He was fifty-six years of age.

Li Yuanhong became the next president of a re-established republic, but he had been in office hardly a year when, in mid-June 1917, General Zhang Xun, a fanatically loyal supporter of the Qing regime, staged a military coup to restore the Qing court and declared Puyi, still a young boy, an emperor again. That attempt too was short-lived. In mid-July, Zhang Xun was defeated by several generals and the boy-emperor was deposed a second time.

While the power of warlords occupying different regions was on the rise, the republic went through a succession of leaders, each of which hung on to power for only a brief period. In 1917 the parliament in Peking (Beijing) was disbanded.

Sun Yatsen tried hard to re-establish his base in the south, with the hope of reunifying the country. His forces did not come together, and in 1918 he was driven out of Canton (Guangzhou) by the feuding warlords.

Sun remained the head of his political party, the Guomindang, which was considered by many as the legitimate ruling party of the country. He escaped to Shanghai in 1918.

The Province of Jiangxi was fought over between leaders Chen Guangyuan and Fang Bencheng.

Adding to regional fragmentation, the nation was further preyed upon by the foreign powers, which seized the opportunity to bribe or manipulate the various factions for their own control of the regions or provinces. With the British in Shanghai, the Japanese in Manchuria, the Russians in the north, and France in the southwest, the United States frantically exerted its influence anywhere it could, trying to grab a colony of its own.

Once again, in addition to the political upheavals and the widespread famines and poverty, opium-smoking became prevalent. China was fast disintegrating and seemed doomed to bondage of all kinds.

The general populace was disenchanted and in despair. In desperation, the young, the intellectuals, the dissatisfied looked to Social Darwinism, Marxism, and Communism in search of change, of hope, and of salvation for their country and the people.*

今朝有酒今朝醉

Chapter 10

A Western Mansion

In 1918, Gande's fortune was assessed at around just under two million U.S. dollars – certainly impressive by any measure. Gande was so wealthy that he even set up his own bank in Nanchang. Many of his relatives worked for him. Juemeng, the eldest son of Jingde the kung-fu master, was the overseer for Gande's businesses. With his prosperity and status comfortably secured, Gande embarked on building a new residence.

Up till then, Yuchen and her family had lived in the house near the river Gong. Two tributaries, the Gan and the Zhang, merge at the foot of the mountain, and then continue as the Gong, which drains into Poyang Lake. Yuchen's house was situated along one bank of the river. As each son married, she would have rooms or sections added on to the old building where she and Yidong had started their life in Nanchang.

"Ma, I'm thinking of building a new house with the latest facilities and conveniences. Our business is so extensive now that we should have a more modern house to entertain our friends and associates. What do you think?" Gande asked Yuchen. He always sought his mother's approval for his projects or undertakings as a matter of courtesy.

"You decide, Gan-er." Yuchen, as usual, left the decision to her son, whom she trusted completely.

"However," she added, "a bigger house means triple the expenses in every way. Do keep in mind it is better not to be showy with money. It invites trouble."

"I quite understand, Ma. I also realize that you're deeply attached to this old house. I'm not going to sell it. Zhengde and his family can stay here. You can always come and visit," Gande replied.

"Have you thought about where to build?" asked Yuchen.

"I'm looking at the land outside the city wall, the area by the Desheng Gate, where the schools and the hospital will have their new buildings."

Yuchen understood right away that her son's mind was made up. She would have preferred to stay where they were, where there were so many memories and where she could still feel the presence of Yidong.

"Do as you wish, Gan-er," Yuchen conceded.

Gande purchased a large plot of land flanked by the three Methodist buildings just outside the city wall. With the added advantage of being close to the police station, they were able to obtain special services and protection from the police for a fee.

It was not clear if Gande actually also funded the Methodist buildings along with his own; but the Methodist missionaries seemed to have a great deal of respect for and gratitude towards Gande, despite his infrequent attendance at church services.

Gande's house and the three Methodist buildings incorporated what were the most modern facilities in the city at the time. Each building was surrounded by walls. In 1918 electricity was already available in Nanchang, but service ran for only a few hours each evening. All four buildings were equipped with their own generators for electricity – a rarity then in interior China.

In the attic on the fourth floor of Gande's new house, a huge water tank was installed, which supplied running tap water to the entire house. All the plumbing fixtures were shipped directly from Montgomery Ward in Chicago.

The living area was about ten thousand square feet. On the ground floor there were three large rooms, plus a Chinese kitchen with a wall-to-wall brick stove and a laundry room with laundry chutes from the second and the third floors.

A huge dining room, which could seat more than a hundred people, and two parlours occupied the greater part of the second floor. Each of these rooms featured a fireplace. On this level there were also a small family room and a kitchen for western-style cooking. This kitchen boasted all the latest conveniences for western cooking that were available at the time.

In the various rooms on this floor, Gande displayed his exquisite collection of curios, antiques, paintings, and calligraphy by well-known artists. Again all the area carpets were shipped from Montgomery Ward of Chicago.

Five bedrooms occupied the third floor. Yuchen had the best room, facing south. Though by now she was in her sixties, Yuchen still maintained her daily ritual of looking after most of the household chores. She refused to be pampered by maids; she kept her modest lifestyle. Gande and Cheng occupied the room at the southeast corner. Gande's sons Xinmeng and his brother Youmeng shared a room next to it. Xinmeng, being the eldest son and Gande's favourite, was assigned a good-sized double bed, while his brother, Youmeng, had to be content with a small, narrow bed. Parental favouritism was a matter of fact and was accepted.

The family moved into the new house in 1919, when Xinmeng was ten years of age. It had already earned recognition as a unique landmark in Nanchang, and was locally known as the "Western Mansion." As there was no western-style hotel in the city, Gande provided hospitality for executives from Standard Oil and their engineers who came to install the oil tanks in the province.

Making one's fortune highly visible is never a wise thing; it invariably invites trouble, as Yuchen feared. Would Gande be immune?

Happy days come and go; carefree days, few and far between. Wealth can buy pleasure and luxury; status can secure access to power and protection; but they do not control the direction of the political winds or provide a shield from the slings and arrows of unpredictable changes.

As early as 1920, Communist activists began to organize in places like Hunan, Hubei, and Beijing, and among Chinese students in Japan and France. In July 1921, the first plenary meeting of the Chinese Communist Party, or CCC, took place in Shanghai.

The Soviet Comintern sent many agents to Shanghai and offered financial and military aid to the CCC. At the time, Sun Yatsen, leader of the Nationalist Party, or Guomindang, welcomed Soviet aid and allowed CCC members to join the Guomindang.

Among the Soviet advisors, Mikhail Borodin was the main instigator who worked hard to bring the communists and the

Guomindang together. He helped to establish the Whampoa Military Academy of which Chiang Kaishek was appointed the first commandant. Subsequently, most of the graduates from the Academy became extremely loyal to Chiang Kaishek.

Sun Yatsen died of liver cancer on March 12, 1925.

It was perhaps the worst of times for the common folks in China. The political turmoil was more than unsettling; the ever-rising foreign debts again drove the government and the people to utter poverty. Yet it might have been the best of times for entrepreneurs, speculators, and those who dared.

A new breed of fortune-seekers emerged: those who had connections to the Treaty Powers; those who spoke one or more foreign languages, even at minimal levels; those who were willing to risk their lives or money on volatile ventures. For all of them, opportunities opened up that allowed them to reap enormous profits and attain a status that had once been impossible to reach.

Gande started out as an insignificant minnow swimming upstream with all his might. But fortune smiled on him, and within decades he was a big catch and had earned a good name in several circles. When they had trouble with money or merchandise, friends, relatives, and associates came to Gande. He helped them solve their problems; he loaned them money to tide them over.

人情翻覆似波瀾

Chapter 11

A Salt Licence

It was late spring. Robins chirped and swallows twittered noisily as they chose places for their nests amidst the shrubs or under the eaves of the pagoda in Liang Jialu's exquisitely manicured garden.

Liang Jialu was the owner of one of the few residences in Nanchang that featured a Suzhou-style house with a designed garden that stretched half a mu and contained intricately crafted rockeries that hugged several large ponds. Two curved wooden bridges spanned the two larger ponds, and footpaths wound in between the smaller ones. Rocks, imported from the Lake Taihu area, were made to represent mountains, which, to most Chinese, possessed some kind of magical power, symbolizing wisdom and immortality. The landscape was immaculately planned, meticulously maintained. As he stood on one of the arched bridges, Liang Jialu, the master of the house, gazed at the koi chasing the colourful little goldfish in the pond and laughed aloud.

Liang Jialu was "lanky" in the truest sense of the word – skin and bone – with the sallow complexion typical of opiate addicts. He wore an off-white silk Chinese tunic that hung loosely over his skeletal body. His right middle finger sported a thick luminescent jade saddle ring* of a rare translucent green, one of the few jewels that was still in his possession. In his left hand, he held a pleated fan, which, when opened up, displayed a landscape painting by the famous artist Qi Baishi.* As he paced slowly along the arched wooden planks, the breeze upturned the bottom corners of his tunic as if trying to carry the wearer into the wind.

He, Liang Jialu, the salt merchant, was cheerful this evening. He was hosting a banquet in his home in Gande's honour – and it was critical that the dinner was a success.

The trading of salt was a much-sought-after business. Salt merchants were licensed, and they were able to reap mountains of money. Traditionally, to be a regional salt minister was an important appointment, made by the emperor. Jiangxi, in particular, having no salt of its own and using a great deal of salt to preserve foods, required a lot of it from the coastal provinces or interior regions. A salt licence was a coveted item, as it guaranteed enviable profits, and there were only a few of these licences available. The licence could be traded as an equity instrument and could garner a good price if it needed to be sold.

Liang's family had held the salt licence for generations, and they were known for their extravagant lifestyle. Alas, easy come, easy go. By the time Liang Jialu inherited the salt business, neither he nor any other male members of the family could conduct business or carry on work related to the business, because they had become accustomed to an effortless life that required no thinking or hard physical exertion. The entire household – the men, their wives, and many concubines – were all hopeless opium users. They had no cares; they suffered no worry. All they wanted from morning to night, from sundown to sunrise, was to lie on opium couches and swallow the smoke that would invariably send them to a perpetual state of delightful oblivion.

Opium was not cheap, especially when Liang and his family were used to the premium-quality opium from India.* They were burning gold away with each puff of smoke.

Lao Yang, the aged house-overseer, who had been in the employ of Liang Jialu's grandfather, tried tirelessly, out of loyalty to his former master, to stop the young masters from sinking deeper into the mire of this horrific habit. Instead of being grateful, Liang Jialu found the aged servant annoying.

"Stop nagging me! Why do you have to repeat the same thing over and over again? I don't want to hear any more. You're a nuisance!" he shouted at the old man.

"Young Master, your grandfather and father entrusted you to me. It is my duty to try and keep you well and on the right track. The way it is going, the family is heading for ruin. How am I going to answer to your grandfather when I meet him in the other world," the servant pleaded.

"You're getting too old. You really shouldn't be working any more," said Liang Jialu.

With that, he dismissed Lao Yang from his service and sent him back to his native village. The replacement for the house-overseer was a yes-man and a thief at the same time. Before long, Liang's cash-flow problem surfaced.

First went the art, artifacts, and rare books from the family collection. Next went the antiques, then the women's jewels ... often Liang would come begging Gande to buy these items from him to help him out. Gande tried to set him straight, but to no avail. More than once, Gande refused to purchase what

Liang had to offer, because he did not want to provide the money that would only further Liang's destruction.

This evening when he was invited as the guest of honour to dine at Liang Jialu's house, Gande was taken aback when Liang put the salt licence on the table.

"What do you mean you want to sell the salt licence, Jialu-ge?" Gande was bewildered. "You're living off the revenue from the salt business. I don't want to be rude, but as far as I understand, you don't have any other income right now. Am I right?"

"This is precisely the reason I want to cash out. I can then start a new business in tobacco," came the answer. "Didn't you always say that you would like to have a salt licence, Gande-di?"

"Sure I did, Jialu-ge, but not at the expense of depriving you of a living."

"No, no, no, Gande-di. You'll be doing me a favour, helping me in my new venture. I've been in touch with a foreign tobacco company. I want to be their comprador, the same way you're a distributor for SOCONY. It has an unlimited future, I tell you. My friend Wu in Shanghai is a comprador for British American Tobacco, and he is doing fabulously well. I don't want to sit by and let the opportunity go to someone else."

"But Jialu-ge, be rational. As the saying goes, a bird in the hand is worth a hundred in the bush. The salt revenue is stable and steady. New businesses face many risks and volatility. It'll be a gamble. You'd better think several times before you plunge into it," continued Gande, trying to dissuade Jialu from selling the salt licence.

"To tell you the truth, Gande-di, I've been thinking a lot lately. I'm waking up. I want to kick my opium habit for good.

I want to spend my energy on a new business. Salt doesn't interest me. But tobacco is a different story. I see a huge market. More widespread than opium, I can assure you."

"You're probably right, Jialu-ge. But . . ." Gande wanted to reason further with his friend, but he was cut short.

"No buts. I'm very determined. You're the first person I'm offering this licence. It will cost you a lot. But if you're not interested, then I'll just have to approach some other people."

It was clear that Gande's words fell on deaf ears. Liang would not hear reason. He was certain he would make a new man of himself with the tobacco business.

So convincing was Liang that Gande half believed him. By the end of the dinner, they struck a deal. In exchange for a handsome sum, Gande secured the licence. It would put a squeeze on his cash flow, but Gande knew he would gain it all back. His only hesitation was whether Liang was on the level with him about turning a new page.

When dinner was done, a pretty young bondmaid, in her late teens, came to serve Gande with wet towels and tea for rinsing his mouth. Gande noticed she was new, and cast several glances at her as she smiled coyly at him. Gande wondered to himself why Liang would acquire a new servant while his finances were in shambles. Well, that was Liang for you. He thought nothing more of it.

About a week after the the transfer of the salt licence was completed, Gande was sitting at home, enjoying some quiet moments with the family, when from the window he saw someone approaching the house carrying a little cloth bundle (bao-fu). Before he had time to speculate who it was, a servant appeared at the living-room door.

"Master, there is a young girl at the door asking to see you."

"A young girl? Who?"

"She didn't say, Master."

"Ask her what she wants."

The servant returned to report: "She said Mr. Liang sent her."

The young girl, Ying, or Nightingale, was the same one who had served him at Liang's. She handed a letter from Mr. Liang to Gande. She was being offered as a concubine to Gande, a gift from Liang with gratitude.

Gande realized that Liang had misread the attention he had paid the bondmaid at the dinner. He tried to return Ying to Liang, who would not have it at all.

Ying stayed and was assigned to be a general help. A few weeks later she was summoned to be Gande's personal maid. By and by the temptation proved too hard to resist. Gande had reached midlife, and his wife, Cheng, after bearing nine children, no longer excited him. Ying was attentive, filled with youthful vitality. Her looks, her movements, her gestures vibrated with a sexual charge that sent every filament of muscle, every blood vessel in Gande's body, pulsating with desire. He found it impossible to ignore her.

Gande was in the habit of taking a short rest every day after lunch, to revitalize himself before he returned to work in the afternoon. One of Ying's duties was to help him disrobe and to get dressed and to prepare a hot towel and a cup of tea for the master when he was about to leave the house.

It was a warm summer afternoon. The humid heat was dizzying. Ying had on a pale-pink silk-gauze top hanging loosely over her body. Her breasts, like two ripe peaches, protruded firmly from underneath the thin, semi-transparent fabric, bouncing ever so slightly as she moved about unbuttoning Gande's tunic and taking it off. Gande felt his body heat rising. His will power faltered. Before he had time to think twice, his hands reached forward and, without quite realizing what was happening, he found himself atop Ying's body, panting away like a ravenous wolf pouncing on its prey.

He, Gande, a man of steel, had succumbed to the weakness of the flesh. He surrendered himself to carnal pleasure. Afterwards, Gande felt every cell in his body coming alive, invigorated and energized. The love-making became a regular ritual, making the siesta period last much longer than it used to.

Ying was only too willing to comply. Ying's parents used to own some land and were relatively well off. When Ying was eight, her father became seriously ill with heart problems and was not able to work. In desperate need of money to feed a family of six, consisting of Ying's grandmother, her parents, her elder sister, herself, and her younger brother, they decided to sell Ying to a well-to-do Li family as a child bride who would eventually marry their sickly son. Her older sister was needed at home to help out with household chores, while her mother devoted more time to taking care of her father.

The Li family treated Ying well. They even allowed her to sit alongside her future husband when the private tutor came to give lessons. Unfortunately, the good days did not last. Three years after her arrival, her intended husband died of tuberculosis before they were old enough for marriage. The bereaved parents went to pieces. The father took to drink and neglected his land. The mother shut herself up in a deep depression. Their own daughter and Ying tried to do as much work as they could and look after the two parents and the elderly grandmother.

But unkind and meddling neighbours and relatives looked at Ying with jaundiced eyes and laid all the blame on her. They called her a "broomstick curse."* She had brought death, grief, and ruin to the family, they insisted, and the family had to be rid of her. As the family wealth dwindled and the non-stop pressure from the relatives and neighbours kept on, the grandmother made the decision to sell Ying as a bondmaid to the Chen family.

Ying was heartbroken. She felt close to the Li family, whose members had treated her like their own. The grandmother's decision to let her go especially pierced her tender heart, as she had grown fond of the old woman. She felt as if she had been dumped in a barrel of icy water.

Ying's new master, Mr. Chen, kept six concubines. All of them began to feel threatened when Ying blossomed into an attractive young woman. Fearing that her husband might eventually take Ying to be his seventh concubine, Mrs. Chen arranged to give Ying to Liang Jialu's wife as a birthday present. Likewise, Liang's wife felt uneasy about keeping Ying. She persuaded her husband to offer Ying as a present to Gande.

Had Ying's intended husband lived to marry her, she might have enjoyed a peaceful life in that family. But because she was purchased as a child bride, she would always carry a stigma in the eyes of the neighbours and relatives. Now she was downgraded to being a bondmaid, a status no different from a slave. For a number of years, she had little hope of rising above the doom of servitude. When Master Liang offered her as a concubine to Gande, she was grateful that finally there was a ray of hope – a way out for her. She made sure that she would cater to Gande's every need and that Gande would find pleasure in her.

Ying knew how to please; she knew how to cast her womanly charm over this middle-aged man who took life so seriously. From serving and observing the two families where concubines competed fiercely for the master's attention, she learned how to attract men's eyes with suggestive looks, gestures, movements, touches. She succeeded. She knew, sooner or later, she was to be, as they say in Chinese, "a crow that morphs into a phoenix."

It was about a fortnight after their first tryst, as Gande lay breathing heavily and recovering from his exhaustion, that Ying whispered softly into his ear, while gently stroking his torso with her fingers: "Master, you will be fair to me, won't you?"

"Don't worry," came the brief answer.

That same evening, Gande announced to the family and the household staff that Ying was to be elevated to "concubine" status. She was no longer a bondmaid.

Ying knelt before Yuchen and Cheng and offered each a cup of tea, representing her plea for their acceptance. When Yuchen and Cheng received the teacups, it symbolized their willingness to allow Ying into the family. Neither Yuchen nor Cheng really had any say in this. Whatever Gande commanded would carry the day.

All servants, from then on, were to address Ying as *Yi Tai Tai*, or "concubine mistress," and all children were to call her *Yi Niang*, or "concubine mother." Gande bought Ying some gold bangles and assigned her a bedroom of her own on the second floor. Thus, Ying leaped from servitude to become the second mistress of the house.

It was not without some degree of inner struggle that Gande had given in to Ying's allure. For one thing, he and Cheng had a close relationship. He did not want to hurt her in any way. Although the prevalent practice of the day was for men to take on several wives or concubines, he was, nevertheless, a baptized Christian, who was to practise monogamy as the church instructed. In a way he was disappointed in himself for giving in so easily.

Gande was doubly remorseful because he remembered that it was Cheng's family and their relatives who had been kind and trusting enough to lend him all their land deeds for him to secure the SOCONY distributorship. Without their help and support, he would have still been working in his lumber yard. He was indebted to Cheng and her family. He felt he had betrayed his wife. But, no man was perfect, he said to himself. He was weak, he admitted. No man was invincible.

Guilt aside, Gande was not exactly sorry for what happened. The excitement he experienced with Ying far exceeded anything he had ever had with his wife. Even though he and Cheng had a good marriage, and they loved and respected each other deeply, their relationship was of a formal nature. So was their lovemaking. Even, stable, a bit tepid. Ying, on the other hand, was like a shot of aged Maotai, the Chinese liquor brewed from sorghum. She intoxicated him and set him on fire, craving for more. He began to understand why men were so prone to take on more than one wife.

To Gande's amazement and relief, Cheng did not make a big deal out of it, showing no visible sign of displeasure or distaste. She offered no complaint. She treated Ying with civility. Gande was immensely appreciative of his wife's understanding of a man's need. He respected her even more.

But Cheng was hurt. Deeply hurt. She quietly shed some tears in private, and put on a smiling face. She said to herself that she should be grateful that all these years Gande had never once joined his friends or business associates in frequenting the brothels. When Gande obtained the SOCONY distributorship and money began rolling in, she half-expected that her husband, like most other men of wealth, would take on a concubine or two. When it did not happen, she counted herself as extremely lucky. She assumed that Gande would remain faithful to her to the end of their lives. Alas, just as she thought that her husband was one in a million where personal discipline was concerned, out of nowhere, Ying was dropped into their midst. Cheng was disillusioned, her inner peace severely disturbed.

What saddened her even more than Gande's new-found interest was the unwelcome realization that she had aged. After ten pregnancies and nine children, every inch of her body showed the tell-tale signs. Stretch marks covered her abdomen, her breasts drooped like two sacks of flour. She had bags under her eyes, and age spots were scattered on her forearms and the loose skin of her face. She thought of the folksong she learned when she was young:

> *The sun sets; it will rise in the morn.*
> *Flowers wither but they will bloom again.*
> *Pretty little bird flies away without a trace;*
> *My youth is gone with the bird ne'er to return!*

Cheng looked at the mirror and sighed a deep, despairing sigh:
"My youth has flown away with the birds – gone with the wind. It will never return!" She conceded to herself that, if

she were a man, she would have looked for a younger body too.

Knowing Gande's temperament, Cheng knew it would be futile to protest or to argue. Besides, it was water under the bridge. "The rice is cooked," as people would say. There was nothing she could do to change the situation. The only sensible option left for her was to accept Ying graciously and hide her own disappointment.

Yuchen, on the other hand, had difficulty condoning Gande's taking a concubine. She had never expected this son of hers, who always adhered to high principals and led a very disciplined life, would even consider bedding a woman who was not his wife. She was hugely displeased with her son's behaviour. She felt angry that Gande was so inconsiderate to his wife of so many years. But would she voice her objections? She knew it would be useless. Cheng, as Gande's wife, had not made any protest over this concubine business, so she, as Gande's mother, would refrain from saying anything negative about it. It would not be in anyone's interest to stir up ill feelings among family members. However, she felt for Cheng, and she tried to comfort her in many small ways. Her efforts were not lost on her daughter-in-law. The two women had always been close to each other. Unlike most mothers-in-law and daughters-in-law who did not get along, Yuchen and Cheng were more like mother and daughter than in-laws. There had never been a word of disagreement between them. They appreciated each other and treated each other with the utmost respect and affection. Yuchen never uttered a negative word about Ying either, yet Cheng knew how Yuchen felt. It did not need to be spoken. Her silence expressed it all. Cheng appreciated her mother-in-law's feeling for her.

Secretly, Yuchen also feared that Ying would bring bad luck to Gande and the family. Lust, she believed, was the forerunner of catastrophic consequences. She sighed. She felt sad. She concealed her feelings, but she kept Ying at a distance.

等是有家歸不得

Chapter 12

A Knock on the Door

In 1927, Gande's number-one son, Xinmeng, had completed his studies at Yu Zhang Boys Academy. Principal Johnson advised Gande to enrol Ximeng in Shanghai University College School in preparation for admission to Shanghai University.

Gande had great plans for Xinmeng. He intended that his son should settle permanently in Shanghai, the one place where the crème de la crème of the rich and powerful congregated, and where it was possible for a young man of wealth and education to distinguish himself among them. He, Gande, would continue to make money in Nanchang. But he would also gradually move some of his assets to Shanghai, where he felt there were limitless opportunities in land development and real estate. He would expand his "empire." Apart from his oil distributorship, which would have to remain in Jiangxi province, his other ongoing timber-lumber, rice, and salt businesses already had existing customers in Yangzhou, Nanjing, and Shanghai. Now he was poised to place a huge bet on this ever-changing city of superlatives.

One morning, Mr. Johnson had summoned him for a chat.

"Here's a letter of recommendation to Mr. Liu Zhanen, the head of Shanghai University. Take the letter to him and he will point you in the right direction," said Johnson, who was by now turning quite grey. Combing his fingers through his silvery locks, he continued, "You asked me the other day what to do to transfer some assets out of Nanchang. I think this is your opportunity to move some silver to Shanghai." Mr. Johnson was always mindful of Gande's welfare. Gande was unarguably his most distinguished and outstanding student, and he was extremely proud of him.

"Thank you, Mr. Johnson. I'll arrange it. I hope it will go smoothly," Gande replied.

Now that plans for Xinmeng's admission to Shanghai University College School were coming to a head, Gande decided to follow Mr. Johnson's advice to transfer a sizeable amount of his liquid assets to Shanghai. Because of the unstable Chinese currency, Gande never kept paper money. He accumulated silver instead, in .999-pure silver bars. It was a hedge against the volatility of the paper money and the uncontrollable inflation.

During these early years of the Republic, there had been a lot of fighting in Jiangxi, and Gande had taken his family to Shanghai on several occasions. Each time he and his family stayed in this fascinating city, he made it his business to get acquainted with the who's who in the Chinese-administered district, the elite among the British and the Americans in the International Settlement, and the top guns in the French Concession. These included a number of wealthy Jewish businesspeople, the police commissioner, the British trade commissioner, the presidents of the banks, as well as a few prominent heads of the underworld. He held lavish banquets and gave expensive gifts, sparing nothing to make sure that people took note of him. He was weaving his network. All these people would one day come in handy, he predicted.

After his conversation with Mr. Johnson, Gande felt that it was urgent that he act promptly.

One bright sunny morning, he went to talk to Mr. Tang, the branch manager of the Bank of China in Nanchang. After the usual customary greetings and the offering of tea, Gande said, "Mr. Tang, I'm starting some business in Shanghai and would like to transfer some silver to my bank account there. Can you arrange to transfer about seven hundred thousand taels of silver for me from here."

"Very well, Mr. Zhao. Let me see. The price of silver today is $1.30 per tael Mexican silver, and . . ." Mr. Tang moved his fingers on his abacus to calculate the exact amount in currency.

"No, no, no, Mr. Tang. I don't want a currency transfer. I want a sterling-silver transfer. The .999 fine silver. Nothing less," interrupted Gande.*

"That is not possible. It's beyond my authority. I'm not able to do it for you," Mr. Tang insisted.

"I have the silver in my safety-deposit boxes in your vault here. They are all .999 pure silver. You know very well that paper money can be worth nothing overnight. Besides, you surely must realize that there is a price disparity between the .999 silver bullions and the Mexican .950. I do not want paper money. I don't even want the Mexican bars. I'll be losing too much." Gande would not give in.

The meeting did not come to a satisfactory conclusion. A couple of days later, Mr. Tang informed Gande that the bank would transfer only the paper currency at $1.30 per tael. "Take it or leave it" was the final word.

Gande was annoyed. The bank was being unfair to him. Giving him worthless paper money for his .999 pure silver was no less than highway robbery. He knew it was the order of the Chinese government officials under Generalissimo Chiang Kaishek to force him to surrender his silver for paper money. The government would stand to make a huge gain from the transaction. They tried to do that to every customer of the bank.

Gande left for Shanghai the next day, carrying another letter from Mr. Johnson. He arranged to see both the head of the Hong Kong & Shanghai Bank and the British trade commissioner. Mr. Johnson's letter requested that the commissioner take care of Gande's problem personally.

The Hong Kong & Shanghai Bank had been established in Hong Kong in March 1865, and a branch had opened in Shanghai a month later. In 1923, the bank built a new, stately landmark building on the Bund, along the waterfront in Shanghai. Thanks to the booming businesses in the city, the general manager of the Shanghai branch wielded exceptional – and unrivalled – power.

The Hong Kong & Shanghai Bank was under British rule. The government dared not interfere, knowing Gande had the backing of the British high officials.

Gande's previous public-relations efforts paid off. Before the week was out, instructions were issued to transport Gande's seven hundred thousand taels of silver from Nanchang to the Hong Kong & Shanghai Bank branch in Shanghai. The bank received a decent commission, the trade commissioner a substantial gift from a grateful Gande.

Such was the sorry state of affairs in China when the foreign treaty powers ruled the day. Even the military or the government officials had to bow to the British or the Americans or the French, shamefully, without self-respect.

Gande got his silver to Shanghai. He bought a house and placed Xinmeng at Shanghai University College School.

After Dr. Sun Yatsen's death in 1925, Chiang Kaishek had succeeded Dr. Sun as the head of the Guomingdang or the Nationalist Party. He was also in charge of the Huangpu Military Academy. Chiang took control of the armies in the southern provinces and planned military campaigns to unify China. His Northern Expedition began in July 1926. The main thrust of the expedition was up the Gan River through Jiangxi Province, across the Poyang Lake basin, and into the Yangtze valley towards Nanjing. The seizure of Nanchang was critical to Chiang's strategy, as the city was at the junction of the north-south axis of roads and rails, as well as on the west bank of Poyang Lake.*

The warlord who controlled Jiangxi and his well-armed troops put up a strong resistance, but by mid-November, at the cost of fifteen thousand casualties, Chiang took firm control of both the city of Jiujiang and Nanchang and planned to establish his base in Nanchang.

In March 1927, he began a relentless and systemic purge of communists or left-leaning nationalists in the areas under his control. Unlike his predecessor, Dr. Sun Yatsen, who allowed members of the CCC to join their political party, the Guomingdang, Chiang was determined to rid his party of all those with communist inclinations.

Jiangxi was the major base for the communists, who had gathered under Mao Zedong and had set up a stronghold in the mountainous area of Jing-Gang-Shan.

When news of Chiang's determination to eradicate all communists spread, Gande debated whether he should once again head towards Shanghai. Ying was pregnant with her first child and was reluctant to leave the comfort of their house. If they were to go, Gande would want to have some of his valuable collectibles packed away for safekeeping. He did not trust Chiang's army.

On a quiet evening, the family had just finished their meal, and the children had left the table to study or play. The adults were sipping tea and thinking. Throughout dinner, conversation had centred on the impending conflict between Chiang's army and Mao's followers.

"Ma, what do you think?" Gande asked his mother. "Shall we all move to Shanghai for the time being? I'm afraid the clash between the communists and the Guomindang will be fierce. We may not be safe here."

Yuchen by now was in her seventies and was old and frail. "You decide, Gan-er. I'll go wherever you think is the best," she replied.

"What do you think, Cheng. Should we go?" Gande turned to ask his wife.

Cheng was concerned about the children and the forthcoming newborn. "Ying's baby is due in two months. It would be better if she could deliver in a safe place. Besides, all the children need to be well-protected. Since Xinmeng is already in Shanghai and he is staying at the college dormitory, we might as well go and stay at the house you bought. It is sitting empty, isn't it?"

"Then I'll have the workers pack up all the antiques, artifacts, and paintings—" Gande was interrupted.

Bang! Bang! Bang! So loud were the raps on the front door that everyone stopped what they were doing and sat up to listen. Before the doorman reached the entrance, there was shouting and swearing outside.

"Open up! General's order!"

Two soldiers with rifles and bayonets barged in and handed a piece of paper to Gande.

"By General Pao's order, you're to leave this house by tomorrow. This will be General Pao's headquarters from now on," commanded the soldier.

"Wait!" Gande stopped him. "We need time to pack. We need at least a week to gather our things and move out."

"Not possible! General Pao is arriving tomorrow at noon. He will come here directly from the train station. You have to be out by then."

"This is ridiculous! It is my house. You cannot just come and take it over," Gande exclaimed.

"General Pao is the chief of the army. He is to prepare this house to receive Generalissimo Chiang, who will be directing his anti-communist campaign from here. If you refuse, you can be shot or jailed. Take your pick," said the soldier. As he turned to leave, he added, "Also, you're not to remove anything from this house except your clothing. If you disobey, there will be consequences."

Ying began to cry. Yuchen frowned. Gande regained his composure and began to direct the servants to pack everyone's clothing. Cheng suggested that they all move to the old house the next day and plan their trip to Shanghai from there.

At Gande's Western Mansion, General Pao and his underlings took control of the oil supply and profited immensely from corrupt dealings. Likewise they carried out other irregular practices, for personal gain, under the auspices of being government representatives.

However, the winds of change blew in various directions. Those who governed would enjoy no more peace or stability than those being governed.

Toronto, Canada

2012

善意嬉怖才

Chapter 13

A Project

The next family dinner was held at Yvette's house in Mississauga, in the west part of the Greater Toronto Area. It was a bit of a drive for the other four, but a gathering at Yvette's was always fun and cheerful, largely due to the warm hospitality of Yvette and her husband. She would prepare so many dishes and set out so many snacks and drinks that it was bound to be a day of indulgence.

Yvette and her husband, Paul, lived in a large house with a sizeable backyard. Paul was an avid gardener, who loved to putter around outside, and both the front lawn and the backyard showcased beautiful perennial beds with gorgeous colours from spring through autumn. It was a real labour of love.

After dinner, everyone gathered in the enclosed sunroom overlooking the garden. It was comfortable and relaxing to be surrounded by pots of greenery and bunches of dried flowers in vases, the preserved products of Paul's labour.

In the middle of the room was a long wooden table that served as a second dining table or a games table. Plates of nuts and chips were placed at the four corners.

As they sat down around the table ready to start a board game, Rhae announced, "I've been thinking. Since we've gathered so much material on the Kaifeng Jews, and most of it is fascinating . . . I wonder if we shouldn't compile it into a book. Any thoughts?"

"I support the idea," said Thomas, raising his hand.

"No harm trying, I guess," Yvette concurred.

"Then we'll have to do more research and make sure details are accurate," Adele said. "But before we jump into it, do you have some kind of a plan how to present the material, Rhae?"

"Yes and no," replied Rhae. "As a matter of fact, I've been toying with this idea of telling the story of the Kaifeng Jews and the story of the Jews in Shanghai during the Second World War. That little bit of history is also not commonly known to most people, yet it is an important piece that fits into the whole history of the Holocaust."

Everyone was quiet for a moment, but no one seemed to take an interest in the board game. They sat there looking at one another.

"How do you propose to connect the two?" asked Adele. "You'd be better off doing two books if you're really keen on the idea."

Adele, who had published several books throughout her working years, had sounded a note of caution. As always, she preferred practical and achievable goals to wild, larger-than-life ideas. Noting the Sagittarius element in Rhae, she wondered what Rhae was shooting for this time.

Pointing to her head, Rhae said, "I do have a structure up here. But I'm not sure if it will meet with your approval." She glanced around the table at each person.

"What do you mean?" asked Linny, her face marked with suspicion.

"Well, I'm thinking, if we simply put the historic facts down, it may be a bit dry to read," Rhae answered. "Besides, we are not historians. But if we weave it into a story threading together the two pieces of history, it may turn out to be quite captivating."

"What story?" insisted Linny.

"What better story than our own family history!" Rhae replied. "Granted, we do not know much beyond grandfather's days in Nanchang. But that part can fall under the 'novel' part, and there a bit of speculation or dramatization would be quite acceptable. Artistic licence, sort of.

"Professor Li's revelation that we might be of Jewish descent triggered our interest in the Kaifeng Chinese Jews. I thought it would be fitting to balance that with the Jews' experiences in Shanghai during the Second World War, when our father befriended and was in close association with many Jews – without the slightest inkling that he might have been of Jewish heritage. Ironic, isn't it?

"Besides, Linny, you and I, and maybe Yvette, should remember quite a bit about the years under the Japanese occupation, and what happened to father's Jewish friends and associates."

"Mmm. There are a few incidents I remember very clearly," mused Linny, eyes brightening. "I still remember Uncle Sassy, Uncle Freddie, and Horace Kadoorie with a hole in his shirt." She giggled at the recollection.

"Thomas and I did some interviews with Dad way back in the late eighties. You're welcome to the tapes we recorded. They may offer some insights," Adele offered.

"That'll be huge! Wonderful! Thanks so much."

To everyone's surprise, Auntie Ellie spoke up.

"I can tell you a few true stories of the Jews during that period. Both my father and my first husband were close friends with the Kadoories, the Sassoons, and the Eliases."

"Wow! That's exciting. It's genuine oral history that should be recorded. But, hold on, Auntie Ellie. I need to have the recording machine set up when you tell us the stories. Are you free on Tuesday? I can come to your place or I'll pick you up to come to my place. What about the rest of you? Can you all come on Tuesday. I'm eager to get this done." Rhae was visibly keyed up.

"Count me in. Hey, Rhae, the second part of your book is taking shape. Awesome!" exclaimed Thomas.

Except for Sheryl, who had a prior commitment, all the others agreed to join the session. Yvette and Paul would pick up Auntie Ellie and they would all assemble at Rhae's at 2 p.m.

"Which year did Dad go to Shanghai to study?" asked Sheryl.

"In 1927. He left Nanchang to attend the Shanghai University College School in preparation for admission to Shanghai University," answered Adele.

"1927!... On to Shanghai!... Here we go!" laughed Sheryl.

PART TWO

崩山裂石

Introduction

SHANGHAI – A MOST UNUSUAL CITY of kaleidoscopic appeal – has, in the twenty-first century, re-emerged on the international horizon, resplendent in all its former glory and much more.

Shanghai is more than a myth or a legend. It is a reality.

Archeological finds in the vicinity of Shanghai date early settlements as far back as the Neolithic period (2500 BCE). The first recorded mention of this mudflat of a place appeared during the Warring States Period (475 to 221 BCE). But it was not until the eleventh century, during the Song Dynasty, that the name Shanghai first came to be known, and the county of Shanghai was officially set up in 1291, during Kublai Khan's Yuan Dynasty.

The city's name came from that of a river that had since submerged. It is believed the former Shanghai River now forms part of the Huangpu River – that portion of the waterfront between Nanjing Road and the Shiliupu Wharf – at the estuary of the Yangtze River as it enters the East China Sea. It was at this point that seafaring people sailed out to the sea, hence the name *Shang Hai*, which means "up onto sea."

From an obscure fishing village, Shanghai grew into a busy trading post. By 1685, the Qing government had set up customs service in Shanghai and the city's population reached two hundred thousand.

The first Opium War of 1840–42 ended with the signing of the Treaty of Nanking, designating Shanghai, along with Ningpo, Fuzhou, Amoy (Xiameng), and Canton (Guangzhou), as treaty ports for international trade.

With the arrival of the Western "Treaty Powers," Shanghai morphed into a metropolis extraordinaire and was launched onto the world stage.

Opium was the one item that played a vital role in making Shanghai such an extraordinary port.

Opium had been in use for medicinal purposes in China as early as the Tang Dynasty, which started in the seventh century. It was first introduced by the Arabs. By the twelfth century, opium use had spread widely and had become recreational. Court officials and well-to-do families would offer a puff to their guests, the same way that liquor is offered today.

In the sixteenth century, when the Portuguese settled in Macao, they imported both opium and tobacco and introduced the pipes that made smoking a mixture of opium with tobacco a lot easier. Opium use and addiction became more widespread.

Emperor Yongzheng was alarmed by the harm brought about by opium addiction. In 1729 he issued the first edict to ban opium importing. At that time, about two hundred chests of opium were imported from India annually.

Later Qing emperors – Jiaqing in 1810, 1813, and 1815, and Daoguang in 1829, 1831, and 1832 – issued repeated edicts banning the use, importation, or trade of opium and set severe penalties for those who disobeyed. But the enforcement of the law was anything but effective. Opium imports were handled by private Hong* merchants – the foreign trade agents – at the ports, mostly in Canton. Through corruption and connections, opium importers and traders were able to carry on their business without much interference.

By the 1830s, the importing of opium reached thirty thousand chests annually. Not only were people's lives destroyed once they became addicts, Emperor Daoguang became aware of the enormous outflow of silver, mainly to Great Britain. That, together with the world shortage of silver at the time, led to economic and currency issues in China and caused a great deal of poverty and hardship.

Emperor Daoguang sent Lin Zexu,* an envoy he trusted, to Canton, where most of the opium landed, to deal with the problem. In March of 1839, Lin publicly destroyed a shipment of opium, and this was cited as the start of the First Opium War.

Shanghai replaced Canton as the main entry point for the import of opium.

Because China lost both Opium Wars, the country and its people became subject to many unfair terms and demands set out in the several treaties and agreements China signed with various foreign powers.

The unfairness of the Opium War has been acknowledged by some in Britain. The journalist Anne Gibson made mention of it in the opening remarks in her presentation of "The Opium War: When Britain Made War on China" on the BBC History channel.* She said:

> In June 1840 a fleet of British warships sailed into China's Pearl River Delta and unleashed a barrage of violence, overwhelming China's weak coastal defences and bringing the country to its knees.

This was the First Opium War in which thousands were killed in the name of free trade.

The thousands she mentioned were, in fact, twenty to twenty-five thousand Chinese versus sixty-nine British.

The future British prime minister William Gladstone attacked the First Opium War in the House of Commons, saying that he had not seen "a war more unjust in its origin, a war more calculated to cover this country with permanent disgrace."

Besides the opening of the five treaty ports, the Treaty of Nanking also demanded that China pay nine million dollars in compensation for the opium destroyed by Lin and forced China to cede Hong Kong to Great Britain.

Shanghai was very much under the control of foreign powers. The French staked out a territory and set up a government of its own. The White Russians, casualties of the Bolshevist revolution in the Soviet Union, came in droves and congregated in the French Concession. The British sat supreme over the Shanghai Stock Exchange, the Jockey Club, and all financial, trading, and commercial activities. The Americans fought to claim an area of their own, but ended up merging with the British to form the International Settlement.

Shanghai became a depository of all cultures, ethnicities, traditions, and values. Each incoming group added a different colour and wove a distinctive thread into the already vibrant and complex fabric of the populace. It was a unique blend of people from all over China, as well as from the West. They brought with them their undaunted spirits, their adventurous boldness, and their inborn entrepreneurial drive. Working hard, playing hard, achieving much, and reaching for the best of the best – this was the winning combination that exemplified the Shanghai style.

The city housed some of the best educational institutions in the country; it nurtured many of the most progressive, forward-thinking leaders of the century. It harboured the revolutionaries who sought and fought for democracy and equality; it groomed countless savvy businessmen to attain immeasurable wealth. Shanghai was a place at the forefront of the newest and the latest, be that intellectual advancements, international trade, fashion, lifestyle, pleasure, or decadence. And along with everything else, Shanghai was the one port in the world at the time that required neither visa nor passport.* In years to come, the city would show its unrivalled humanitarian compassion when its door was opened to the stateless Jews from Europe. And Shanghai would never succumb to Hitler's pressure to espouse anti-Semitism.

Shanghai was a city of contradictions. It was a cradle of lofty ideals and noble acts; it was a cesspool of corruption and depravity.

It was to this place of opposites that Xinmeng came in 1927 to further his education.

富貴必從勤苦得

Shanghai, China

———•———

1927–1945

月檀仙山瓊閣重裏

Chapter 14

Carefree Days

Xinmeng was only eighteen when he arrived in Shanghai.

He was handsome, of medium height, with a trim body. Luckily he did not inherit his father's facial features. Instead, he had a broad forehead, defined eyebrows, medium-sized eyes with no double lids, a narrow, straight nose, thin lips, and even teeth. His hair was parted in the centre, as was the fashion then. His wardrobe held more western-style three-piece suits than anything Chinese. He was a fashionable young man of his time.

Shanghai was not totally unfamiliar to Xinmeng, as Gande had taken the whole family there several times, whenever the warlords, the armies, the monarchists, or the revolutionaries played their tug-of-war in Nanchang and safety became a concern.

Gande very much wanted his eldest son to become a physician. The medical profession was esteemed as the highest achievable goal for any post-secondary student. With wealth and status comfortably secured, it would be undeniably desirable if Xinmeng were to obtain the prefix "Dr." to his name. Icing on the cake, so to speak. Or in the Chinese idiom: jin shang tian hua 錦上添花 – an added feather in his cap.

Even though Gande himself had not finished secondary school, since circumstances at the time compelled him to forsake his studies in order to help his mother run the family business, in his mind, and in the minds of most people of that time, scholars were seen as a cut above the rest, and medical doctors epitomized the top of the top.

Gande discussed his intention with the president of Shanghai University, Mr. Herman Liu Zhanen, who had become his good friend. Under the latter's direction, Xinmeng's selection of courses was concentrated on "pre-med" requirements – subjects such as chemistry, biology, and physics. Xinmeng himself would have preferred something that fit more with his interests. He liked to work with his hands, making things, repairing things, fiddling with machine engines, and such. Alas, he had no say in this decision regarding his future. To become a lowly engineer was out of the question.

It did not matter too much to Xinmeng. Very quickly, he gathered around him a group of young men and women who came from similar family backgrounds and had had similar paths mapped out by their respective parents. They soon became a tight-knit group, which spent as much time together off-campus as in the classroom.

Due to the overwhelming amount of western influence that had been bombarding Shanghai since the First Opium War of 1842, almost all foreigners who had either come under the banners of conquerors or had attained wealth in trading were bent on maximizing their unprecedented advantages in this pleasure capital of the Orient. Their American dollars or

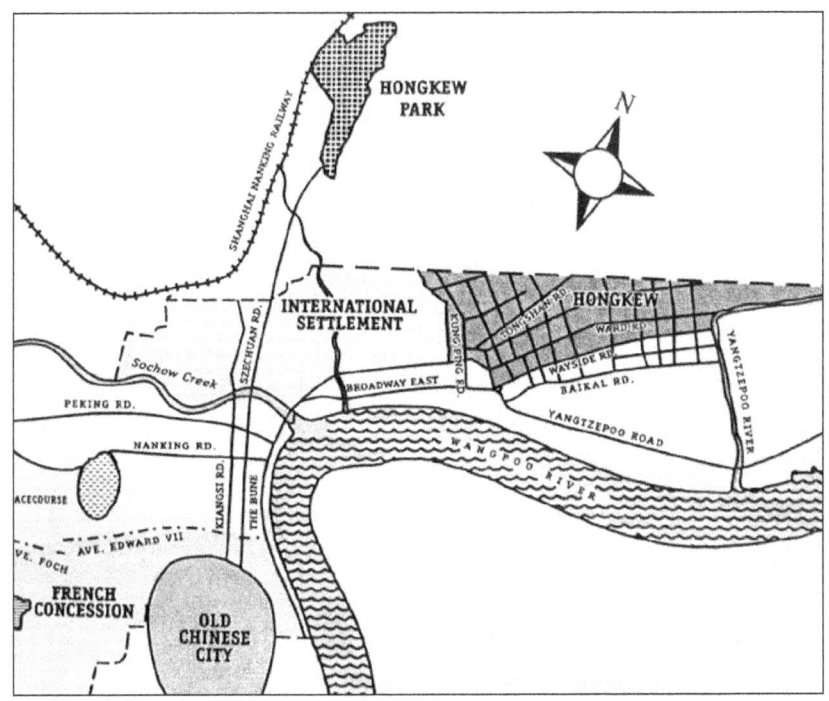

Map of Shanghai, showing different districts. Reproduced from Chinese Jews *by William White.*

British pounds could stretch a long way. Labour was cheap and services were readily available. Consequently, most of them lived in a luxury that they would not have been able to afford in their native countries.

For many wealthy Chinese families, total surrender to consumerism and materialism became the hallmark of fashionable living and modernity. Their unthinking offspring mindlessly embraced this lifestyle as a matter of course. Xinmeng and his friends were among them.

His closest pals included the Nie siblings: Ronnie Nie Guangrong, Teddy Nie Guangyao, and their sister Lisa Nie Guangkun. They were the descendants of the powerful government minister General Zeng Guofan,* who had controlled a ferocious army, with recruits mainly from his native province, Hunan. He was credited with crushing the Taiping Uprising in 1864. However, history portrayed him as a merciless butcher, who massacred over one million people in his campaign against the Taiping rebels. He also allowed his soldiers to rob, rape, and pillage everywhere they went. He himself profited enormously from such atrocities.

In all fairness, history also remembered Zeng as one of the first ministers to initiate the production of weaponry inside China. He energetically promoted the establishment of schools to teach foreign languages. Realizing the importance of human resources, he and his protégé, Li Hongzhang, successfully persuaded the Empress Dowager Cixi to send students overseas for higher education.

Because his army was powerful, Zeng was perceived by certain factions in the Qing court as a threat to the throne. Purportedly, Zeng's daughter, the Nie brothers' maternal grandmother, was kept at the palace as a hostage by Empress Dowager Cixi to ensure Zeng's loyalty to her.

The Nie family was dominant in the textile-manufacturing sector in Shanghai. They also owned thousands of mus of rice land.

The Nie siblings were exceptionally good-looking. Teddy and Ronnie looked very much alike. Dark brows shaded their bright eyes, which were separated by long noses, giving them a very distinguished look. While Teddy was tall, with broad shoulders, Ronnie was of a slighter frame. Teddy, therefore, was tremendously popular among the girls, who all swooned over him. He was the peacock in the group and well aware of his status.

Lisa looked like her two brothers. She was attractive in a sporty sort of manner, not the delicate and dainty type. She had a quick mind and was every bit an equal to her brothers and their companions. With her no-nonsense and straightforward manner, she was always cheerful and helpful.

All three siblings, along with the others in the group, were aspiring to medical careers.

The notoriety of Zeng's protégé, Li Hongzhang, had been based on his dealings with westerners for China's purchases of weapons and other merchandise, which enabled him to profit astronomically. One of his grandsons would occasionally join Xinmeng's group to have some fun.

There was another pair of brothers, Li Peide and Li Peiting, from a different Li family. Their father was a professor at the university at the time, but would later became a minister in Chiang Kaishek's Nationalist government.

Peide and Peiting were fun to be with. The two could not have been more different. Peide, the elder brother, was serious and quiet, always observing but saying little. In appearance, he was average in every way, but the remarks he made were pointed and penetrating.

His brother Peiting was the clown among them. Happy-go-lucky, he raised spirits everywhere he went. He was short and plump, with a round face and ordinary features, but everyone loved him.

And, then there was Yan Tigang, who was nicknamed "the scholar." This was not only because of his academic achievement, but because of his appearance. He was tall and skinny, and wore Chinese full-length tunics most of the time, instead of western suits. Bespectacled, with round horn-rimmed glasses, he looked like a classic Chinese scholar.

Yan Tigang was brought up by his uncle, Yan Shulong, who owned three money houses, or Qian Zhuang, which were the predecessors of banks. He was also a comprador for a French furrier. Tigang excelled in Chinese literature. His calligraphy followed the Shou Jin Shu style 瘦金书 of Emperor Song Huizhong, who had been an outstanding artist and calligrapher. Each stroke of his calligraphy appeared to be dancing. He composed Chinese poetry every now and then, and put all the others to shame.

This group of young people took full advantage of their preparatory and undergraduate years. They were determined to have fun. As there were very few female students at the time, Lisa was the only female among them.

Youth plus wealth plus time equals leisure and pleasure. This was the formula that dictated the lifestyle of Xinmeng and his friends. Their pre-med studies were not overly demanding, and none of them had money issues, so their youthful energy effortlessly glided towards the best in recreational pastimes.

Xinmeng had bought an automobile: a black Ford sedan with a V8 engine, licence plate D5. He also obtained a driver's licence and became one of a handful on campus who not only owned a car but was able to drive it as well. With no regulations on the number of passengers allowed in a car, these young people often squeezed in seven or eight bodies, packed like sardines. Joy-riding was one of their favourite fun things. On campus or off, they were the envy of many people, and they felt like a million dollars as they honked and whistled, speeding past the pedestrians and the rickshaws along the Bund or on Nanjing Road or other busy streets.

Often their destination was a dance hall or a nightclub. Social dancing was very much in vogue at the time. The tea dance was the "in" pastime. Typically, on Saturday afternoons they would head for either the Astor House or YiPingXiang.

"Where shall we go today?" asked Xinmeng the chauffeur. "Astor House?"

"No, Astor House doesn't provide taxi-dancers. We have to bring our own partners, since there are no hostesses to dance with, and we have only Lisa with us," said Peiting. "Six boys and one girl? Even if Lisa is willing to dance every dance, each of us will have to sit out five out of six dances. No fun."

"YiPingXiang it is then," conceded Xinmeng. "Guess I won't get to eat the cakes and pastries at the Astor House today. They are so incredibly delicious."

"I know! But we're not just going for the sweets. I want to dance!" said Peiting.

Social dancing in China had begun with the influx of westerners when the treaty ports were opened in 1842. In the late nineteenth century, it was exclusively a European activity, held in private homes or in western-style hotels such as the Richards Hotel or the International Hotel. Chinese were not welcomed at these places. When Xinmeng settled in Shanghai, YiPingXiang was the first nightclub that had opened its door to Chinese customers. Others then followed suit, and the craze for social dancing surged to feverish heights.

Social dancing was not just a novelty to the Chinese. Along with the abolition of foot-binding, the increasing opposition to arranged marriages, and the success of young women in accessing higher education, social dancing became one of several things that signified the liberation of females from the bondage of many Neo-Confucian traditions and practices.

Rich girls welcomed it as a status symbol, showing that they were at the forefront of fashionable society. Poor girls accepted it as a means of earning additional income by becoming taxi-dancers. Men, well-to-do or not so well-to-do, young or not so young, became addicted to holding in their arms, in public, different and usually attractive-looking young women – some European no less – a thing that had been quite unthinkable only a few years back.

"I hope Suzie is working today. I'm going to book her." Peiting was talking about his favourite taxi-dancer at YiPingXiang. "She's an amazing dancer, as light as a feather!"

"If you're all going to book those dancers, you might as well just take me home right now," protested Lisa. "I don't want to be a wallflower."

"Come on, Lisa. Be a sport," pleaded Peiting. "You know we'll all dance with you. The thing is, at one dollar for three dances, it's a real steal. You can't blame us. We'll all dance with you, I promise."

"Except Ronnie and me, Lisa," said Teddy. "I don't think you'd care to dance with your brothers."

"Why not, Teddy. I do care to dance with my brothers." Lisa was adamant.

"All right, all right. You win, Lisa." Teddy gave in. Then, changing the subject, he continued, "I wonder how much money these girls make each month. Three dances for a dollar is really very little, and they still have to pay the nightclub for the privilege of working there."

"Three dances take less than ten minutes. Each hour they can serve five or six customers if they are popular. In the evening, they charge more and get tips. If they do the tea dance as well as the evening shift, plus all the tips, they can make close to a couple of thousand dollars a month," calculated Yan Tigang.

"That is better than being a clerk. Office jobs only pay a few hundred dollars a month at best," said Teddy. "I know, because I heard my father say that they just hired a clerk for the textile factory for six hundred dollars a month. A university graduate too."

"No wonder so many young girls flock to become taxi-dancers. I suppose some of them are also hoping to catch a big fish among their customers," remarked Ronnie.

"No doubt. So many of my father's friends have taken taxi-dancers as concubines. Some of them have to pay large sums to redeem the girl if she is in debt to the loan sharks. One of them, a confirmed bachelor, is actually marrying a taxi-dancer as his wife," Peiting added.

"My uncle has several concubines, but none of them is a taxi-dancer," said Tigang, "A couple of them are from the brothels. He had to pay extra for virgins."

"Hey, can you guys talk about something else? It irks me to hear about these poor girls being treated like merchandise. So sickening!" Lisa was displeased.

"But that's the reality of life, Lisa," Peide said quietly. "This is the unhealthy side of our society. Men are dominant, and with money they can treat women like dirt. It has to change sometime."

"Not soon enough." Lisa said. "And the women are not helping. I noticed in some of the tabloids and magazines that they actually feature the popular, high-earning taxi-dancers as if they were celebrities, like movie stars or opera singers. The glamour attributed to them works like a magnet, drawing all those young, naïve girls to want to become like them. In actual fact, many of them are no better than glorified prostitutes."

"True, true! But not at the more respectable places we frequent," said Tigang. "We only do the tea dance for fun. Quite harmless, I would say. Besides, my uncle and your parents are all aware of where we go."

"Peiting, don't you get too attached to Suzie or you'll head for damnation with no salvation," Peide teased his brother.

"Tut! Tut! Suzie is just a good dancer. She doesn't get upset when I don't follow the rhythm or step on her toes. And she doesn't seem to mind that I'm so much shorter than she is. Becoming attached to her? Nah! I'm not that stupid," replied Peiting.

"Don't be so sure," Tigang smiled. "Look at all those bankers and taipans* who are supposed to be intelligent, rational heads of corporations. Many of them fall for these girls. You wouldn't say they were stupid, would you? Yet, some become absolutely obsessed with a certain dancer to the point of giving up almost everything for her. Crazy!"

"Can I make a suggestion?" asked Lisa. "Why don't we go for a movie now. I think there is a Greta Garbo film showing at the Grand. Afterwards, we can go back to the residence and get a few girls to join us to go to Astor House. We can dance, we can watch their excellent cabaret, and Xinmeng can have his fill of their pastries."

Before anyone could respond, Lisa added quietly, "I dislike being in the company of taxi-dancers. People may think I'm one of them."

"Lisa has a point," Teddy defended his sister. "Let's not do the tea dance today."

With that, Xinmeng the driver navigated towards the Grand Theatre.

Movies, dancing, and cabaret were three of the top weekend pastimes for these young people. Because of the large influx of White Russians, who had left their homeland after the communist revolution and had settled in Shanghai via Harbin in northeastern China, many of the Russian girls became dancers, because cabaret had become a popular entertainment – especially in the French Concession, where most of the White Russian refugees lived. They were truly professional in their high-calibre performances. Most respectable nightclubs set a cover charge; some offered free desserts with it.

As for movies, the group would go to Hollywood films most of the time, even though Shanghai was, at the time, the movie capital of China and had produced some outstanding films during this period. Xinmeng and his friends often opted to go to the matinee. Occasionally, they would go to the 9:00 p.m. show. It was customary that on weekends those who attended the late evening show would dress up elegantly and extravagantly. It was as much fun trying to identify who was who and to watch the ladies in their stunning fashions as seeing the movie itself. Xinmeng used to say, "It's like watching two shows for the price of one."

Such were the casual and carefree days that slid by in a wink.

秋風愁水魂欲斷

Chapter 15

Destiny Dictates

Gande could not have been more pleased with Xinmeng's studies. After two years at the College School, Xinmeng was successfully admitted to Shanghai University. He excelled in physics and mathematics, always placing first in the class. Other subjects he passed with flying colours as well. He had just started his junior year, and from all indications he would, in two years or so, have a degree in medicine.

Gande felt so proud of his number-one son. He had discerned that Xinmeng was of a mild and gentle temperament and easy-going – often showing signs of indecisiveness. He was not cut out to be a businessman. It was just as well that he had chosen medecine as a profession for Xinmeng. That could not go wrong. Xinmeng had compassion for the poor and the suffering; he also possessed good interpersonal skills. In Gande's mind, these were the two essential qualities for a good doctor.

Lately Gande had been giving some thought to who would eventually succeed him to take care of the business. Well, there was still plenty of time to make the decision. Ying had given him a new son who had just turned three. It was too early to tell.

"Who knows," Gande mused to himself, "maybe Xinmeng will produce a son who will be my successor. Wouldn't that be ideal! ... That reminds me. I should start looking for a suitable match for him. He should marry as soon as he graduates."

Gande was not unlike other traditional Chinese of the time; the first son enjoyed an unrivalled position in the family. The first son of a first son was even more privileged; he would be the little prince, second in line to the throne. Often, in the distribution of inheritance, the first son might secure a double portion, whereas daughters might be left out altogether. In some cases, the entire inheritance would be left to the first son, who would manage it and take care of the family. And again, the first son of the first son might be bequeathed a substantial portion of the assets, when all other grandchildren might not even be mentioned in the will. Such was the enviable status of the first son, and likewise the first son of the first son. It was a feudal tradition practised by most of the well-to-do.

Because Gande was still living in Nanchang, far from the glamour and modernity of Shanghai, he was hardly aware that young folks in fashionable Shanghai were determinedly against arranged marriages. When he broached the subject to his wife, Cheng, she only suggested that Xinmeng might prefer some young ladies in Shanghai to anyone in Nanchang. That set Gande thinking, mentally making a list of all the important people he had befriended in Shanghai and trying to recall who would have daughters of marriageable age.

While Gande was pondering his plan for his son's eventual

marriage and Xinmeng was happily and mindlessly enjoying a life of ease, disaster struck once again.

It was 1932. Generalissimo Chiang Kaishek, on the advice of German general Hans von Seeckt, had successfully surrounded Jiangxi province with five hundred thousand soldiers, who had built trenches and cement blockhouses and were advancing slowly. There was no fighting, but they were closing in on the Communists. The strategy was to strangle the Communist's Red Army and their sympathizers. General Seeckt's plan was working well. The Communists were losing ground and would soon begin their now famous "25,000 Li (Chinese Miles) Long March"* from the JingGang Mountains in Jiangxi to Shaanxi province.

Chiang's troops were now being deployed all over the province, and Nanchang became less important in the overall plan. Gande and family, who had returned to the old house, were counting the days until they could move back to the Western Mansion.

It was a Sunday afternoon. Gande was discussing some renovation details with Yuchen and Cheng, while Ying kept interrupting their conversation with her demands for her two young children.

"They will need separate rooms . . . they will need separate maids . . . they will need . . . they will need . . ."

The fact that she had given birth to a male offspring three years before had encouraged her to presumptuously – but quite erroneously, because she was only a concubine – assume her entitlement to all the best things, not in the least aware of the annoyance she was causing.

All of a sudden, the cook burst into the room, huffing and puffing and firing off words that made no sense.

"Lao Ye! Bad, bad ... fire ... fire ... go ... go ... go see ... the fire ..."

Everyone followed the cook and arrived to see a large crowd gathered near the grand Western Mansion, watching it being engulfed in orange-red flames.

Soldiers were posted around the perimeter to prevent anyone from trying to put out the fire. Gande tried reasoning with the captain, who simply sneered and said, "Go talk to General Pao and get a permit from him to enter the building!" He laughed.

Everyone stood there, stunned, totally helpless and speechless as the stately structure with all its contents crumbled to ashes.

Chiang's officials and soldiers were to depart from Nanchang the next day. General Pao did not want to leave behind any traces of their corrupt activities. The commander mercilessly set fire to Gande's house and burnt it down. Gande's collection of antiques and paintings went up in smoke, along with all the furnishings from Montgomery Ward.

Thus ended the brief life of the Western Mansion. Yuchen's warning to Gande regarding building an ostentatious mansion had come true.

Although by then Ying had been Gande's concubine for six years, and had borne him two children, Yuchen secretly blamed Ying for what had befallen the house. Yuchen had no doubt that this young "fox spirit"* had brought bad luck to Gande and the family.

The loss of the Western Mansion struck a major blow to everyone in the family, and was particularly hard on Gande and Yuchen. It was bad enough to have had strangers occupying their home against their will; now these uninvited marauders had the nerve to totally demolish it – building and contents – and there was no recourse for such injustice. Loss of the valuables aside, it was the amount of thought, energy, planning, and execution that were involved in erecting such a monumental structure, and which represented many years of their hard work, that brought tears and heartbreak. In those days, there was no such thing as property insurance. It was a total non-recoverable loss.

For the first time since he took the helm of the family lumber business, Gande felt dejected and without direction. Should he or should he not make plans to rebuild something out of the rubble? Should he create a "phoenix" rising from the ashes? Or should he just let things be, since his larger plan was to spend more time in Shanghai. If he were to build something special, he would rather do it in Shanghai. He was over fifty now, no longer a young man with boundless energy. Besides, who was to know if the same thing would not happen again, with the Nationalist government and the Communists at each other's throats and the Japanese invaders poised to sweep all over China.

After years of enjoying western conveniences, living in the old house without modern comforts had been hard for both the old and the young. All along they had thought that this was just a temporary shelter for a few months or, at the most, a year or so. Once Chiang's officials left, they would return to their home and enjoy all the luxuries once again. Now it dawned upon them that they were to remain in the old house permanently. The Western Mansion was no more! It was a bitter pill to swallow.

Gande decided to add toilets to the old house and do away with the use of outhouses. Neither Yuchen nor Cheng breathed a word of discontent; they went about their daily chores as if they never had it any other way. Ying, on the other hand, often sighed in displeasure over their downgraded lifestyle, but no one paid much attention to her.

A few months after the Western Mansion was burned down, Yuchen took ill and passed away. On her deathbed, she asked to see Gande's eldest daughter, Shuyi, and his eldest son, Xinmeng. She held their hands and muttered something about the west and Youtairen (Jews).* Neither of her grandchildren could make sense out of what she mumbled to them. With her passing went the final link that connected the family to their Jewish origins.

Yuchen's funeral was followed by that of her eldest son, Jingde the kung-fu master, who also died unexpectedly. As misfortunes followed on one another's heels, relatives began to feel nervous; some became alarmed. Would there be a third death in the family? "Tragedies come in threes," they whispered. In order to deflect such a curse, they hired monks and exorcists to cleanse the house and chase away the evil spirits.

1932 was a lamentable year.

Word buzzed around on the campus that Xinmeng's father was seriously searching for a bride for his son. Excitement abounded within Xinmeng's little group. Xinmeng himself was not sure whether he should laugh it off or take offence at all the teasing he received.

It was not unusual for parents to arrange matches for their children before they graduated. Some students were even married during their undergraduate years. But because of the new sense of freedom, many chose to stand up to their parents and refused to accept their arrangements. In this period of transition from a traditional neo-Confucian mentality to a more liberal western outlook, many arranged marriages ended in tragedy that brought nothing but utter misery to all concerned.

Xinmeng did not have a girlfriend. He liked Lisa a lot, but more in a brotherly way. He did not object to his father's attempt to set him up with someone, but he felt he was not quite ready to take that step. He would have preferred to finish his degree before considering taking a wife.

But Gande felt a sense of urgency. He was not so much anxious to see his number-one son settling into a family life as he was eager to whip up a reason for some kind of celebration. A wedding would no doubt generate excitement, joy, happiness, a ray of hope, and a feeling of exuberance, all of which were so very badly lacking after the sad events that had taken a toll on the family and cast a shadow of gloom that just would not dissipate.

One weekend, Xinmeng and his usual group gathered for a dinner at a new restaurant. Yan Tigang "the scholar" and Peiting, sitting side by side at the round table, whispered secretively together. Peiting kept staring at Xinmeng with a mischievous and mysterious smile. Lisa noticed their unusual behaviour and demanded to know what was going on. Peiting giggled and pointed to Tigang.

"Ask him! He has a fantastic idea! Hei, hei, hei . . ."

Everyone turned to Tigang and waited. Tigang wriggled in his chair, took a sip of tea from the cup, and looked sheepishly from Xinmeng to Teddy to Ronnie to Lisa, without uttering a sound.

"Come on! Out with it, Tigang. Don't keep us in suspense," Teddy ordered.

"I think it'll work, Tigang. Tell them," encouraged Peiting.

"What will work? Why are you being such a sissy all of a sudden, Tigang?" Teddy pressed on.

"All right, all right. But don't get mad at me if you think it is a stupid idea," Tigang conceded.

"Well, we'll have to know what it is first." Teddy was getting impatient.

"Let me see, how should I put it . . . it is about Xinmeng . . . you know . . . match-making . . ." Tigang was still hesitant.

"What about it? Do you have someone for him?" asked Ronnie.

"As a matter of fact, I do," admitted Tigang.

"Then, tell us. Who is it? Do we know her?" said Lisa.

"Well, it's my cousin Flora. You know, ever since my father passed away when I was very young, my uncle has taken care of me. He is my guardian, and Flora is like a sister to me. She is a couple of years younger than we are. I think she'll be a good match for Xinmeng."

"Why? Did she ask you to be the go-between?" asked Ronnie.

"No! She doesn't know anything about it. As a matter of fact, I haven't even consulted my uncle about this. The idea came to me when I realized that Xinmeng's father is serious in looking for a suitable daughter-in-law."

Tigang continued. "I'll tell you why I think it is a good match. My uncle is from Ningpo. He owns three money houses here in Shanghai and is a comprador for a French fur company. Financially, her family is not beneath Xinmeng's. Xinmeng is quite westernized; so is Flora. Xinmeng, you mentioned once that you took piano lessons in Nanchang, right? Well, Flora took violin lessons, though I have no idea how well she plays. She attends McTyiere Girl's School, the most prestigious girls' school here. She's in Senior Middle One, two and half years from graduation. Her English is as good as any of us. And I'm not boasting, her Chinese tops you all. She writes Song-style poetry, and her calligraphy is excellent. Above all, she is very refined and proper. No nonsense."

"Wow! Sounds extraordinarily fitting! Jolly good choice, Tigang. When can we meet her?" said Lisa excitedly.

"Wait, wait, Lisa. It is a match for Xinmeng, not for you," Teddy reminded his sister.

"We can still meet her, can't we? We'll all help Xinmeng to assess her," offered Lisa.

"Flora is quite shy. If all of us meet her, it may scare her off," explained Tigang. "I am thinking maybe I can arrange for Xinmeng to have tea with her, and they can go to a movie together or something like that. What do you say, Xinmeng."

"I'm flattered, Tigang, that you think I'm worthy of your cousin. She sounds interesting. Sure, I'd be happy to meet Flora. If I like her, I'll tell my father about her, but not before."

What Tigang did not tell the group was that, ever since he had set foot at Shanghai University, his uncle had entrusted him with a mission to find a good husband for his cousin. But Flora was still attending high school; Tigang felt it was premature to even think about it – until Gande's intention became public knowledge.

Tigang liked Xinmeng. He picked Xinmeng over Teddy, whom he considered a bit on the arrogant side, and over Ronnie, who was clueless in many things. Peide was too serious, and Peiting, though fun to be with, was more suitable as a friend than a life-mate. Tigang did not want Flora to miss this opportunity, and so, without prior consultation with his uncle, he took it upon himself to approach Xinmeng directly.

Xinmeng and Flora met for high tea at the Palace Hotel on the Bund on a weekday afternoon. On weekends, the Palace Hotel's tea dance was popular, and there would have been no guarantee that they would not bump into someone they knew. Tigang made sure none of their usual crowd was privy to the time and place of this blind date. He did, however, arrange for his uncle to sit in an obscure corner in the mezzanine, so he could have a peep at this prospective candidate who might well be his future son-in-law.

Mr. Yan had three children, none of them by his wife, who had died young with no issue. He subsequently elevated the first of his eight concubines to be his wife, but she too bore no offspring. Concubine number two gave him a daughter, who had been married the previous year. Her husband was a man whom he not only disliked intensely, he actually suspected this son-in-law of being connected to the underworld. It was only at his daughter's insistence, reinforced with threats of suicide, that he had reluctantly given his blessing and a huge dowry.

Flora and her brother, Charles, were from concubine number three. Mr. Yan was very fond of both – Charles as his only male offspring and Flora because she was docile and sweet-natured. He wanted to make sure that Flora did not follow in the footsteps of her half-sister. He wanted a good, well-educated gentleman for her.

Xinmeng took all the advice and suggestions that Tigang provided. He made sure not to take Flora to a sad movie, because she would cry buckets when watching a tragedy. Knowing that Charlie Chaplin was among Flora's favourite stars, he took her to see *City Lights*, in which Charlie Chaplin not only played the lead role, but for which he also wrote the story and the score and directed. They would have much to chat about afterwards.

Xinmeng found Flora exactly as Tigang described her. She was not a ravishing beauty, but had a pleasant appearance and a sweet, winsome smile. She had a round face with a low-ridged nose and smooth skin, a tint on the dark side. She was well-dressed, well-groomed, and well-mannered.

She wore an embroidered Chinese-style jacket and a skirt with a touch of western influence in the tailoring, which was very becoming, and sported the latest Hollywood hairstyle – short, at mid-ear length, with one side sweeping down to cover part of her eye. She was petite and slim and used practically no make-up – just a slight dab of lipstick and possibly a light brush of rouge.

Flora listened more than she talked, but her conversation was interesting and sincere. They spoke in the Shanghai dialect, but Xinmeng could tell that Flora's English was good. Because *City Lights* was a silent film, there was no need for the use of earphones for simultaneous translation during the film for an audience who did not understand English, but it still required some proficiency in language to fully appreciate the film. Also Flora had read Charles Dickens, George Eliot, Jane Austen, and many other English classics. Xinmeng was convinced that her command of the English language was probably superior to his own. He felt a degree of admiration for this young lady.

Mr. Yan, perched in the mezzanine, scrutinized Xinmeng as much as he was able to without betraying his presence. His first impression of this young man was positive. He was handsome and gentlemanly. His manner was refined and pleasant. He could tell Xinmeng's three-piece suit was from the most distinguished – and also the most expensive – tailor, Baromon, whose clientele included many well-to-do businessmen and bankers. He could not hear what they talked about, but he sensed that they were comfortable in each other's presence, very much at ease and without pretense. With the added knowledge provided by his nephew that Xinmeng was a top student in their class, Mr. Yan was well-pleased.

A native of the old seaport city of Ningbo, Flora's father, Yan Shulong, had been born into a poor fisherman's family. He was born decades after Ningbo had been opened as an international treaty port in 1842 as part of the Treaty of Nanjing.

Uneducated, but extremely quick, intuitive, and money-wise, Yan watched all the foreign ships sailing into port with intense curiosity. He decided to become a seaman. He instantly sensed the importance of being able to converse in a foreign language. With unwavering determination, he taught himself to speak English and tried to strike up friendships with the foreign traders on the ships. Diligent and obliging, Yan made friends easily and was well-liked.

On the ship, Yan met his future father-in-law, Mr. Ruan, who was a wealthy landlord and an astute businessman. Mr. Ruan recognized the potential in Yan, and offered his only daughter, Wen, to be his wife. Wen brought with her a substantial dowry of land deeds and certificates of deposit. On top of everything, Mr. Ruan gave Yan two thousand taels of silver and told him to try his luck in Shanghai.

In Shanghai, Yan went into partnership with a Frenchman, M. Beauchamp, and opened the Oriental Fur Company, trading in lambskin, broadtails, and karakul (caracul), a Central Asian breed of sheep that produces lambs with soft, curly black fur. Broadtails are the pelts from premature or fetal lambs. They are supple as velvet, and the leather is thin and delicate. They are worn more for appearance than for practical purposes.

As Shanghai was at the forefront of fashion and luxury, the fur business boomed. Mr. Ruan had not been wrong about this young man.

At about the same time, there had been a large influx of Ningbo merchants migrating to Shanghai. They had an extensive network in Shanghai and a large number of them went into the banking business. Just about every Chinese bank in Shanghai was headed by someone from Ningbo.

Yan was in that network. But instead of taking a job at the bank, he took ownership of three money houses, which were the old-style Chinese banks of the early twentieth century. Unlike the regular banks, these institutions were not protected by limited liabilities, and were therefore exposed to high risks and volatility.

At its height, Yan's assets totalled in excess of two million taels of silver.

Xinmeng enjoyed his outing with Flora. It was not exactly love at first sight, but he felt the warmth and gentleness of this girl, who was obviously intelligent and possessed a congenial personality. He found her delightful and was quite ready to ask her out again. He even considered writing to Gande about Flora. But, at the back of his mind, he wondered if he should allow himself to meet a few more prospective brides.

The next day, Xinmeng was in the chemistry lab all afternoon. Feeling exhausted and wanting to share his dating experience with his pals at dinner, he headed for the dormitory to wash his face and change to some casual wear before going to the dining room. No sooner had he entered his room, and before he had time to take off his clothes, there was a rap on the door. A messenger boy delivered a telegram.

"Father ill stop charter plane home immediately stop."

Something must be seriously wrong, Xinmeng figured. Such urgency. Travelling by train from Shanghai to Nanchang would take more than a day, and the scheduled runs each week were not always on time. Planes, on the other hand, could be chartered for a fee. Xinmeng left immediately on an army plane and arrived at Nanchang early in the morning.

Gande had suffered a stroke and was at the Methodist Hospital. The mobility on his left side was hampered and his speech was slurred. However, his mind was clear and his vision unaffected.

The doctors' initial prognosis was pessimistic, because they anticipated a second stroke to follow. But Gande somehow recovered a bit. He was anxious to speak to his son. He instructed Xinmeng to stay in Shanghai after his graduation and establish himself there. The business in Jiangxi would be looked after by his able staff.

He drew Xinmeng close to speak with special emphasis. "Xinmeng, you're the eldest son in the family. Under you there are six brothers and sisters that you must take good care of. Will you do that?"

Xinmeng nodded. "I will, Father."

"I want you to promise that you will make it your business to see to it that all of them attend prestigious universities and obtain a degree each. You hear me? Will you do that?"

"Yes, Father. I will."

"The silver I shipped to Shanghai will stay in Shanghai. You manage it. But, first and foremost, education for all of your brothers and sisters. Will you promise that?"

"I promise, Father."

"All of them must go to university and get degrees. All of them . . . Remember that . . ."

"I will remember, Father."

Everyone expected Gande to die soon. Xinmeng stayed on, thinking his father's death was imminent. Four weeks passed, and Gande was still alive. There was no marked improvement, but no serious deterioration either. Fearing he was missing too many classes, especially chemistry lab work, Xinmeng decided to return to Shanghai, hoping Gande would gradually recover from the stroke.

Before he left, he made it known to his father that he had met a very nice girl and described Flora and her family to Gande, who was happy with the news.

"If you think she is a suitable girl for a wife, make a decision and marry her soon. Maybe a happy event will chase away the bad luck," said Gande.

Xinmeng understood that his father would like him to get married as soon as he could, hoping the marriage would bring good luck for his recovery. It was a common superstitious belief in those days.

"I will do as you say, Father. Do get rested. I'll come back to see you as soon as I catch up a bit on my classes."

"Yes, that is important. Go. I have enough people to look after me here."

Xinmeng returned to Shanghai with a heavy heart. He was worried about his father's health, but he was also worried about all the lectures and lab work he had missed. On top of everything, he now felt an added urgency to propose to Flora – if that was at all possible after only one meeting between them.

Much as he tried, he could hardly keep up with all the ongoing classes, not to mention catching up on those he had missed. He was easily distracted and found himself unable to concentrate on his studies.

He asked Tigang to arrange another date for him. He debated with himself whether or not to propose marriage to Flora, although he knew it was premature and inappropriate. It was so stressful.

But before Tigang was able to fix a second date for him with Flora, another sudden telegram arrived, summoning him back immediately. Once again a chartered army plane carried him to Nanchang.

Gande was on his deathbed. He had suffered a second stroke and heart failure and kidney failure on top of it. He drifted in and out of a coma. When Xinmeng arrived, Gande opened his mouth, trying to say something, but no words came out. He closed his eyes again.

Three days later, Gande died in his sleep, at peace now that his number-one son was there to send him off.

People sighed that no one could fight destiny. Three deaths in a row. "Destiny dictates!" they exclaimed with humble resignation and bowed their heads in submission.

Being the number-one son, Xinmeng had an extensive role in the funeral and burial services. Notwithstanding the fact that Gande and family were baptized Christians, relatives insisted on having Buddhist monks chanting prayers for seven weeks. They burned paper money, paper houses, paper food, and paper servants, to make sure that Gande would continue to enjoy a life of ease in the other world.

Even though Gande's staff managed the businesses in Jiangxi with competence, they wanted the number-one son to be apprised of the goings-on in the different sectors – the SOCONY distributorship, the lumber yard, the salt business, the export of rice . . . It was close to two months after Gande's passing that Xinmeng was finally able to leave for Shanghai.

On the train, alone by himself, Xinmeng came face-to-face with reality. What was to become of him! He had missed so many classes and lab work, he could see his medical degree disappearing. To repeat a year and continue, or . . . ?

Upon Xinmeng's return, Principal Herman Liu asked to see him.

"Please accept my deepest condolences, Xinmeng. It must be terribly difficult for you. Your father was a good friend, and I'll miss him. Have you given any thought as to what you'll do?" asked Principal Liu.

"My mind's still in a muddle, Dr. Liu," replied Xinmeng. "I'm sure I won't pass the exams this year. Which means I may have to repeat a year and complete my medical degree in three more years instead of two. I'm not sure if this is a wise choice under the circumstances. But, if not, then what? It'll be such a waste to give up everything just like that."

"May I make a suggestion, Xinmeng?" said Principal Liu. "I would not encourage you to repeat a year and pursue a medical degree. It takes a long time, and you now have added – and shall I say, unexpected – family responsibilities that may interfere with your studies. I looked at your records. You're only a couple of credits short of a Bachelor's degree. That is, if you give up chemistry and biology – because it will be impossible to make up the missed laboratory work – and take two courses in economics and commerce, I think you can earn a degree at the end of this year. This way, all your previous credits will not be wasted. You'll have a degree and you can go on doing business, trading, or whatever. What do you think?"

"Do you think that is possible, Dr. Liu?" asked Xinmeng. "I hesitate to approach the professors in the Commerce Department. What if they say no?"

"Leave it with me. I'll give directions to Professor Hardy and Professor Endicott, and I'm sure it will work out. This is the least I can do for you and your late father. I think he would approve of this arrangement."

"Thank you very much, Dr. Liu. I think this is the best I could ask for. I'm very grateful. I'll prepare myself to meet with Professor Hardy and Professor Endicott."

In 1933 Xinmeng graduated with a Bachelor of Commerce degree. Neither Gande's wish to see his son become a doctor nor Xinmeng's ambition to be an engineer materialized. Heaven has a way of twisting a person's destiny.

Chapter 16

Marriage & Family

Gande had not lived to see his number-one son graduate from university. Nor did he live to attend Xinmeng's wedding.

When Gande died, Xinmeng no longer felt the same pressure to rush into marriage. His priority was to make sure he had sufficient credits for a Bachelor's degree. Courting Flora was put on the back burner.

After a few months passed, Xinmeng was able to complete all the required courses. Graduation was now just around the corner.

Mr. Yan became increasingly restless, anticipating that, once graduated, Xinmeng, a very eligible bachelor, would definitely receive many marriage proposals. He knew Flora was fond of Xinmeng and was waiting nervously for something to happen. He himself would certainly welcome their union. Determined to make it happen, he pressed Tigang to expedite the process if possible.

Tigang hinted several times that Xinmeng should see Flora again, but Xinmeng made no response. Finally, Tigang came right out and suggested to Xinmeng that it was time for him to resume his courtship of Flora – and perhaps come to a decision about whether Flora was the right girl for him. Somehow this triggered Xinmeng to spring into action. He and Flora went out for tea, a movie, and dinner several times.

One day, Tigang forwarded a message to Xinmeng from Mr. Yan, asking whether Xinmeng was serious about Flora. If there was no intention on his part to take the relationship to another level, then, very sorry, Flora would not go out with him any more. It was an ultimatum of sorts.

Meanwhile, Mr. Yan asked Tigang to get Xinmeng's Ba Zi, the eight characters representing his birth date and birth hour, and secretly consulted a feng-shui master. The feng-shui master told Mr. Yan that Flora's Ba Zi was not compatible with Xinmeng's. Their union would cause conflict with Xinmeng's mother, Cheng. Mr. Yan was taken aback by this unwelcome prediction. It was a death sentence for his daughter's happiness. Mr. Yan demanded remedy.

"I'll create a new Ba Zi for your daughter. This Ba Zi will be a perfect match with the other party's. But you, your daughter, and anyone who knows your daughter's real birthday must be sworn to absolute secrecy. The boy's side must never find out her real Ba Zi. Is that possible?" asked the feng-shui master.

"Yes, it is possible," answered Mr. Yan resolutely.

"All right, then. From now on, Miss Flora's birthday is the second day of the fourth month in the Year of the Pig, 1911. You must destroy all evidence that indicates that she was born on the twentieth day of the eighth month in the Year of the Dog, 1910. Miss Flora must be persuaded never to reveal her real birthday to her future husband or anyone else. It is very important," the feng-shui master warned.

That same evening after dinner, Mr Yan summoned Flora, Tigang, Flora's personal maid, Jin, and the cook, Ah Fang, to his study.

"From now on, Miss Flora's birthday will be the second day of the fourth month. And she was born in the Year of the Pig," Mr. Yan commanded.

"No, Lao Ye, Miss Flora was born in the Year of the Dog," protested Jin, who had been with the family since Flora's birth.

"That was before. From now on, she has a new birthday. Understand? And from now on, no one must remember her old birthday or ever mention her old birthday to anyone. Jin, you and Ah Fang are both loyal servants and you want Miss Flora to have a good and happy life, do you not?"

"Of course we do, Lao Ye," Jin and Ah Fang answered together.

"Then make sure you remember this. Make sure you never mention Miss Flora's old birthday ever again. Do you understand? I'm counting on you."

"Yes, Lao Ye."

Although Jin and Ah Fang did not understand the reason behind this sudden change of birthday, they would not question the master's decision. They would simply obey the master blindly, as most loyal servants did in those days.

It was Mr. Yan's plan that, when Flora married, Jin and Ah Fang would be part of her dowry. They would accompany Flora to her husband's home and continue to serve her there. Mr. Yan was aware that Xinmeng had many siblings. Now that the father had passed on, since Xinmeng was the number-one son, there was a real probability that the whole family would live with

Xinmeng and Flora. Conflicts, large or small, within the family were inevitable. He, as Flora's father, had to take measures to protect her by placing one or two persons who were totally loyal and devoted close to her. They would be her confidants when disagreements arose and, in an extreme case, if the whole Zhao family was to turn against her. In-law politics.

Jin was like a second mother to Flora; she would have died for her. Flora had not seen her biological mother, Mr. Yan's number-three concubine, since the age of six or seven. Her mother had had an affair with Mr. Yan's chauffeur and was banished to live in Ningpo by herself after the affair was exposed. Both children by this concubine were cared for by the number-one concubine, who had been upgraded as Mr. Yan's wife by then. However, Flora was much closer to Jin, who showered her with unconditional love and devotion.

Ah Fang used to be a chef in one of the top restaurants in Hangzhou, where Mr. Yan had a villa on the banks of West Lake. Because he liked Ah Fang's cooking so much, he paid a large sum to release Ah Fang from his contract with the restaurant. Ah Fang had been with the family from before Flora's birth. He was revered as Master Chef at the Yan residence. All other servants were at his beck and call. Flora always addressed Ah Fang as "Uncle Fang" and never treated him like a servant.

These two people had to be entrusted with the secret of the changed birthday. As it was customary for the cook to remember every family member's birthday and make sure that he served "longevity noodles" for the birthday person, Ah Fang had to have the correct dates embedded in his head.

Both Tigang and Flora were told the reason for this altered birthday. Tigang shrugged and gave his word that he would never reveal the secret. Flora was not too happy about it. She felt it was not honest. But would she want to tamper with her future happiness? She dared not.

Two weeks after Mr. Yan's ultimatum, Xinmeng asked Tigang for Flora's Ba Zi. He had discussed the matter with his mother, Cheng, and had shown her Flora's photo. Cheng offered no objection. She smiled cheerfully and encouraged Xinmeng to go ahead with wedding plans.

The wedding date was set for Friday, March 13, 1934, by the feng-shui master, who was totally unaware of the western superstition regarding Friday the thirteenth. The wedding banquet was held at XinYa Hotel, a brand-new hotel equipped with the latest luxuries.

As Gande was no longer alive, and Jingde, Gande's eldest brother, had also died, Zhengde, Gande's younger brother, blind in one eye, substituted as the parent of the groom. Cheng, his mother, or women as a whole, did not count.

Peide was the best man, and the two Nie brothers, Teddy and Ronnie, were the groomsmen. Mr. Yan was beside himself with joy. As far as he was concerned, Flora's future happiness, without a doubt, had been sealed.

Xinmeng and Flora rented a three-storey townhouse in a gated complex of fifteen residences on Yu Yuan Road. The compound was named "Yong Quan Fang," which means "the bubbling brook place." When spoken, it sounds close to "ever-flowing money place" – reflecting the typical Chinese wish for, and obsession with, never-ending prosperity.

The double iron gates at the entrance were closely guarded by the security person, Lao San, during the day, and by his son, Junior San, at night. Lao San was a robust fellow from

Shandong Province, where people were said to be honest and loyal – indispensable qualities for a security guard. On each side of the double gates were two small iron gates, one of which remained open throughout the day for the convenience of pedestrians. Inside the gates, to one side of the ramp, was a brick shelter with a small glass window. Inside it was fitted with a narrow bench bed, a stool, and a tiny table.

Lao San normally sat outside the shelter in his wicker chair, chatting and exchanging gossip with the passersby or chasing off mischievous youths playing around. In the afternoon he might indulge in a nap or have a snack inside the shelter. Most of the time, however, he was ready to respond to the horns of the cars waiting to gain entry to the compound or to spot an unfamiliar face that had appeared through the small gate. Beggars from the street were strictly denied entrance.

After coming through the gates, the ramp continued as the central driveway, from which lanes stretched sideways to reach all the dwellings. These were grouped in rows of two or three, numbering from three to eighteen – odd numbers to the left and even numbers to the right.

At the very end of the compound sat number twenty-four, a single, majestic mansion on a large property with a huge landscaped Chinese garden and an enormous expanse of lawn, all behind a stretch of stone wall with a closed iron gate. This was the residence of Mr. Chen Chuxiang and his family. Mr. Chen owned the entire compound, and thus was the landlord of all the families living there. He also owned the Beauty Brand cigarette factory.

It is interesting to note that, with the preoccupation of people from Hong Kong since the 1950s with the unluckiness of numbers containing the digit four, the residents in Yong Quan

Fang certainly had no qualms about living in houses numbered four, fourteen, or twenty-four.

As a matter of fact, to the people in Shanghai or northern China, the number four is an auspicious number. In the old days, people believed that the sky was round and the earth was a square. The number four represents wholeness, because it encompasses all four directions of north, south, east, and west. It stands for completeness, as a cycle of four seasons completes a year. Also, as most chairs, tables, and motor vehicles are built on the basis of four supporting elements, four, therefore, implies stableness and security. Again, in feng shui (geomantic theory), a square is the preferred shape, primarily because all sides are of the same length and all angles are of same degree – thus representing discipline and exactness. Hence squares also denote honesty and righteousness. In ages past, Chinese coins were cast in a circular shape with a square hollow in the middle, expressing a fundamental Chinese principle – round outside and square inside 外圓內方 – that dictates a person's behaviour. Simply put, a person should be diplomatic in appearance and carriage when dealing with other people; at the same time, he should maintain a high standard of discipline and integrity within his inner self. Conclusion: Number 4 is harmless. In fact, it is a good number.

In Yong Quan Fang, curiously, number thirteen, was conspicuously omitted, thus reflecting the Western superstition. It was an obvious indication of the imposition of foreign influences on the cosmopolitan metropolis of Shanghai in the 1930s and 1940s.

Such gated compounds of townhouses could be compared to subdivisions in North America. Each compound was called a NongTang 弄堂, meaning "lane" – a very specific name that is used only in Shanghai. A Hutong in Northen China is a close equivalent to a NongTang. Lanes were of varying sizes, and they were widespread throughout the metropolis of Shanghai. Yu Yuan Road ran in the area west of the city core.

Yong Quan Fang was a microcommunity of its own. Most of the residents were fairly affluent, by and large business people with a few professionals. Because there were only fifteen residences, as compared to over a hundred in similar compounds, it was considered an exclusive, upscale enclave. Many of the families were either close relatives of Mr. Chen, the landlord, or distantly connected. Flora's brother, Charles, was married to the sister of Mr. Chen's son-in-law.

Interestingly, all the houses in the compound had their front entrances facing Mr. Chen's house at the end of the compound. Thus, on coming in from the street, one would be confronted by the back entrances. As a result, the front entrances were almost never used. It was confusing to the children that the door at the front was called the back door and the door at the back was supposed to be the front door.

This design plan might have had something to do with feng shui, as all the houses had their official front side facing south. Chinese geomantic theory gives preference to buildings on a north-south axis, preferably sitting with the front facing south. Or perhaps Mr. Chen did not fancy looking out of his window onto the backs of the houses. Even more significant was the configuration of the rows of houses in relation to Mr. Chen's mansion. It suggested an emperor looking down at his subjects paying homage, or, on a lesser scale, a teacher standing in front of a class of students. At any rate, Mr. Chen's residence possessed a definite air of superiority.

At the official front of each house was a little courtyard

surrounded by stucco walls capped with a row of Spanish-style red-brick roofing tiles. A metal gate opened at the centre of the wall and led through the courtyard to the living room. Some courtyards sported a lone, sickly tree; others were used to store piles of rubbish. Xinmeng's courtyard had one evergreen tree and the rest of the space held large piles of coal. None of the courtyards showed a cultivated garden or a grass patch. There was hardly any green, a reflection of the residents' lack of interest in nature or landscape.

As Mr. Yan had predicted, Xinmeng's family moved to Shanghai and lived with Xinmeng and Flora. With the exception of Youmeng, Gande's second son, who chose to stay in Nanchang to take care of the family business, all the other siblings, along with Cheng, took up rooms at number fifteen Yong Quan Fang and attended high schools or universities as Gande instructed. All eventually would graduate from prestigious universities. As for Ying, she remained in Nanchang, while her two children were taken care of by Cheng in Shanghai.

Three years into the marriage, came their first child, a girl. Flora then gave birth to four more daughters within a span of six-and-a-half years. The neighbours referred to her as the perpetually pregnant woman at number fifteen. At Yong Quan Fang, all residents were referred to by their house numbers.

"Number seventeen is hosting a big banquet tonight," Ah Fang would tell Jin when he came back from the market, where he had chatted with the cook at number seventeen.

"The mistress at number four has a message for Tai Tai (the mistress of the house)," Ah Gui, the housekeeper, said after answering the phone.

Flora's daughters would become the five girls of number fifteen.

Flora tried desperately to produce a son for the Zhao family. When the first girl, Linny, arrived, there was excitement and good cheer. Everyone pampered her. When Rhae was born, there was a collective sigh from all. Mr. Yan was disappointed. With Yvette's birth, the servants whispered that the mistress was unable to produce a male offspring. Mr. Yan was very displeased.

To Mr. Yan, it was shameful that Flora failed to have a son. According to the general belief at the time, the woman was held accountable for the sex of the newborn. If the woman could not bear sons, she was a disgrace; she brought dishonour to her family. Mr. Yan was no different. He blamed Flora for producing daughters only.

"Your womb is a disgrace. Why can't it bring forth a son," Mr. Yan demanded. When Flora delivered Sheryl, the fourth girl, Mr. Yan was so upset he refused to visit Flora and the baby in the hospital.

The pressure on Flora was tremendous. Since Xinmeng was the number-one son, it was paramount that he should have at least one son, if not half a dozen. Although Xinmeng never once complained about having only girls, Flora knew better. The whole family was anxiously waiting for her to deliver a male. However, it just did not happen. Every time the obstetrician proclaimed "It's a girl," Flora's heart sank and she cried, thinking she had once again failed her father.

Mr. Yan passed away before Adele's birth, but even without his presence, Flora was laden with guilt and sadness. To have a son was imperative. At all costs. She would do anything to have a son. So ingrained was the idea that she must have a son that when, three years later, she did give birth to a very sick and severely mentally-challenged boy, she would go out of her way to make sure he lived. The story would reflect many of the attitudes that still held sway, even in cosmopolitan Shanghai after the war.

In 1946, Flora was thirty-six. She delivered her sixth child and only boy on June 26 (the sixth month in the western calendar), which fell on the sixth day of the sixth month in the lunar calendar. Six being an auspicious number denoting smooth sailing, Flora was in seventh heaven. Her womb had finally complied to give her a son.

The infant ran a high temperature right at birth. Dr. Wang the obstetrician noticed some physical deformity in the child and observed he was exceptionally weak. His breathing was uneven, and he hardly made any sound when he cried. She did not expect him to live through the night.

Difficult though it was, Dr. Wang had to break the news to Flora, who was heartbroken. After so many years, she finally had a son and he was not to live more than one day. How totally cruel! Flora, who was prone to tears, cried buckets. She could not stop. She was devastated.

"Don't be sad, Mrs. Zhao. Wipe your tears. This child has problems; even if he lived, it would be a very hard life for him and for the family," Dr. Wang consoled Flora. "You're still young. You'll have plenty more children and you'll have sons for sure."

Flora was unconsolable.

All the servants shared her grief. They were only too aware how their mistress longed to have a son. They felt her sense of despair and they wanted to help. The news that the young master was to die within hours sent them scurrying for anything miraculous that might alter the boy's fate.

Ah Fang burned more incense before the Earth God statue in the kitchen to secure protection for the young master. Gui, the housekeeper, led all the nannies to the Guan Yin Temple to supplicate for mercy. Niu-Niu, the chauffeur, ran around seeking unconventional healers who might possess some supernatural powers.

At nightfall, when darkness enshrouded the city, accompanied by the deafening thunder and lightning of a summer storm, Jin and Gui, stealthily smuggled a shrivelled old woman into the hospital. Purportedly, this old medicine woman pricked the infant's tongue with mercury and pressed hard on a number of acupoints along the meridians of the boy's body. The next morning, Dr. Wang was incredulous when she was told the baby had survived the night, although he was still running a fever and was terribly weak.

It was right after the Second World War and penicillin had just come on the market, but it was not readily available to ordinary people. Xinmeng used all his connections with the U.S. and British military officers in Shanghai and obtained a few vials. The antibiotic brought the fever down, and the child lived.

The entire household was filled with exuberance when Flora brought her son, Kun, home. She was proud to have a male offspring at last, regardless of how limited this boy's mental capacity would eventually be. Xinmeng was extremely fond of Kun, despite his deformed right thumb and his low intelligence. Everyone pampered Kun to no end, treating him like a little pet.

Kun's mental capacity would never develop past that of an eighteen-month-old child. He was able to walk and could use a spoon to shovel food into his mouth, but he could not speak, only making unintelligible, incoherent sounds. He could not dress himself or use the bathroom by himself. He drooled constantly. In short, he required twenty-four-hour care and supervision.

Flora was always aware that her son might not live to maturity. She did not care. The fact she had a son was sufficient, no matter how long or how short a time he was to last. The servants suggested to her that, when Kun reached puberty, they would help her to buy a peasant girl of robust stock and have her mate with Kun to produce heirs for the family. Such was the primitive feudal thinking of the time. Women did not count, and their main function was to produce children. Flora neither condoned nor opposed such an idea.

At this point, the war was over. The family was well-off and there was plenty of money to hire people to serve and care for Kun for as long as he lived. Little did she anticipate the tumultuous changes that were to take place on the nation's political scene, which would gravely and adversely affect the family wealth and the future of every individual member.

白雲無盡時

Chapter 17

Striking Out on His Own

While Flora was giving birth to one daughter after another, Xinmeng was busy trying out one business after another. All along, he had expected to follow his father's wishes and enter the medical profession. The unexpected change to a degree in Commerce was confusing and unfocused for him.

Unlike his father, Gande, who had gone through years of hardship with little to fall back on, Xinmeng had been born into a worry-free life. He did not have to struggle or to resort to extreme measures in order to provide for the family. He was a typical fashionable young man of that era, not quite in touch with the real world.

Xinmeng did not inherit Gande's sharp business acumen. Gande knew when to be lenient and when to be ruthless; Xinmeng was kind and forgiving towards everyone – his clients, his suppliers, and his partners. Gande had probably been right that Xinmeng was more suited to be a compassionate physician than a skilful businessman.

Right after graduation, with plenty of silver in the bank, Xinmeng and two friends pooled a total of a hundred thousand dollars to open Zhong Jie Trust Company on Maybeck Road. With a referral from a branch manager of the Shanghai Commercial Bank, the company lent small amounts of money, at interest higher than the bank rate, to government employees, post-office workers, or other civil servants who did not qualify to secure bank loans.

Theoretically, it was a win-win situation. The borrowers did not have to go to loan sharks, who charged exorbitant rates, and the trust company deducted interest right at the outset. Unfortunately, inflation was way beyond what they had estimated. With a staff of ten, the Zhong Jie Trust Company made no profit. The two partners pulled out, leaving Xinmeng to deal with the shortfall.

Next came tobacco and cigarette ventures. As Gande's friend Liang Jialu, the salt merchant, had predicted, cigarettes had become the new opium in China. Just about everyone – young or old, rich or poor, man or woman – was puffing away. Xinmeng was certain he could not go wrong this time. Without executing proper due diligence, Xinmeng purchased the Eugene Cigarette Factory, which carried the Paradise Brand, only to find out that the factory owed the tobacco supplier some thirty thousand dollars that he had to repay. He was in a hole before he even started.

In an attempt to cut his losses, Xinmeng went ahead and purchased the Kun Lun Brothers Cigarette Factory in the International Territory. He was told the business was worth a hundred thousand dollars and the asking price was less than thirty thousand dollars. What a fabulous steal he said to himself, not quite questioning why something purportedly worth a hundred thousand was on the market for less than thirty thousand. He amalgamated the two factories, hoping that he would profit from this manoeuvre.

But Xinmeng had not done his market research thoroughly enough. There were far too many cigarette producers in Shanghai, and the competition was fierce. In addition, the British American Tobacco agents were bringing in all the British and American brands. On top of the competition, Xinmeng gave the retailers thirty days net to pay, whereas his competitors allowed no credit. By the time he collected his debts, money was worth less than half its original value. Once again, the return was negative.

While Xinmeng did not inherit his father's business sense, he did inherit Gande's business friends. All the connections Gande made were now within Xinmeng's reach – British, Jewish, American, or Chinese.

He took the advice of Gande's Jewish business associates and, with the general manager of SOCONY and Mr. Liu, the taipan at Quan Gong Bank, as guarantors, Xinmeng purchased a seat on the Shanghai Stock Exchange (SSE).

SSE was a British-controlled stock exchange that was registered in Hong Kong. It did not have a Chinese name and the board limited the number of seats to one hundred. The owners of the majority of the seats were either British or Jewish. It was enormously difficult for a Chinese to obtain a seat, and there were perhaps a total of five or six seats under Chinese names. Xinmeng secured one for about twenty thousand dollars.

Xinmeng opened Lambert Danbur Company Ltd., a stockbrokerage firm with an office on the Bund. He co-brokered both the Shanghai Stock Exchange and the New York Stock

Exchange, where his corresponding agent was one Francis Dupont. Finally there were profits. Xinmeng easily made over a hundred thousand a year.

It was at the SSE that Xinmeng came into closer contact with Jewish businessmen. The Elias brothers, Frank and Edmund, shared the same counter with him on the trading floor. Neither of the brothers was married. Their passion was horse racing. They were also avid bridge players.

Other Jewish businesspeople he befriended included the Kadoorie brothers, Horace and Lawrence, who were influential in real estate and utilities, both in Shanghai and Hong Kong. Benjamin Sassoon, another bachelor, with two huge German Shepherds, was a nephew of E.D. Sassoon of the Sassoon clan, which had made a fortune from the opium trade and established a real-estate empire in Shanghai. He also made friends with Myers from the U.S. News Agency and Biddy Liddell, the colourful and foul-mouthed Jewish spinster who spent more time with the horse trainers than with her friends. Among his non-Jewish friends were Watson, an American pilot, and Rosen, associated with the French consulate that ruled the French Concession.

Xinmeng became a frequent guest at the Shanghai Race Club. Apart from betting on races, he learned to play bridge and poker and regularly partnered Frank and Edmund Elias and the others.

There had been three jockey clubs in Shanghai. The earliest was the Shanghai Race Club (SRC), also known as the Recreation Club of Shanghai (上海跑馬總會). The SRC was British-controlled, and membership was exclusively for western nationals. For many years, Chinese were not even allowed to set foot in the club. The British had acquired the land sometime in 1849, and the first recorded race event took place in 1850, but it was not until about 1908 that some kind of associated membership was open to Chinese applicants.

The second jockey club was the Chinese-funded Kiangwan Race Club. The name was later changed to the International Recreation Club of Kiangwan (IRK). Planning for this club began in 1909, and the first race was conducted in 1911.

The third jockey club, located at Ying Xiang Xiang, was built in 1924. It was named the Far East Public Sports Centre and was later renamed the Chinese Jockey Club of Shanghai (CJC). The CJC was founded and controlled by the powerful gang members in Shanghai, and it was intended purely for the purpose of profiting from gambling.

By far, the SRC was the most prestigious of the three. The club was relocated twice, and each time the club's board of directors would sell the previous club site to developers for huge profits and acquire a larger acreage for a more elaborate club.

In 1861, the Shanghai Sports Industry Foundation, controlled by the British, had sent an army officer riding a warhorse to stake out an area west of the old club, forcing the local residents to give up their land. At first the foundation took only the area to be used as the racetracks for the horses. In 1863, the SRC decided to take over the enclosed area as well, approximately 466 mus (equivalent to 78 acres), consisting of several villages with about 325 families farming the land. It offered one tael (approximately one ounce) of silver for each mu of land, which is approximately one-sixth of an acre. It was an unfair deal but it was sanctioned by the Qing government.

Some 120 families refused to sell the land and did not go to receive the silver compensation. Among those rejecting the deal was one Zhao Jin-Qing whose family was said to have owned a plot of about twenty mus near Shi Pai Lou. This was the burial ground of their ancestors going back five generations.

In the Chinese tradition, ancestral burial grounds were deemed sacred. They were chosen with the meticulous calculations of geomancy, as guided by a feng-shui master. Once the deceased was buried, the remains were not to be moved or disturbed in any manner. To relocate an ancestral grave was unthinkable; it would bring ill luck to the descendants.

It was said that Zhao and the others went so far as to hire a British lawyer in 1895 and initiated a suit against the foundation. The judge's ruling, however, only directed the foundation's board of directors to up their offer by a further ten taels of silver to each owner. The owners rejected the offer again. The foundation then asked the Qing authorities to force the owners to surrender. Many of the owners resisted, but their land was expropriated nonetheless.

This area became the third location of the Shanghai Race Club. The Qing government supported entertainment for the treaty powers at the cost of local people's livelihood. It was another shameful page in the history of that period.

In the early 1920s, the SRC and the IRK amalgamated. This came about in a unconventional manner. According to the book *Jiu Shanghai de Yan Chang Du*,* one of the founders of IRK, Xu Chaohou (徐超侯), was educated in England. Because of his love for riding, he became a good friend of a schoolmate, the then-Prince of Wales, the future King Edward VIII. That year the Prince of Wales was touring the Far East, and he asked to meet with Xu, who invited his

Royal Highness to ride with him at the IRK. The invitation was accepted.

When the staff of the British consulate in Shanghai got wind of the invitation, they were alarmed. It was totally against protocol. They would not want to shoulder the responsibility if something untoward should happen to the future king. Besides, it would make the SRC lose face if the prince should ride at the Chinese club and not at the club that was frequented predominantly by His Royal Highness's subjects.

The British Consulate asked Xu to withdraw his invitation to the Prince. Xu refused. The IRK board seized the opportunity and negotiated the amalgamation of SRC and IRK to smooth over the situation. The amalgamation allowed the SRC members full membership privileges at the IRK, but the privileges were not reciprocal. The IRK members were given only limited use of the SRC facilities.

The SRC club was complete with lounge room, shower/bath facilities, restaurant, bar, tennis court, swimming pool, billiard room, poker room, tea room, and dance hall. It was a one-stop luxury recreation centre.

Xinmeng secured a membership at the SRC. He went there often to play bridge or poker, and he was always there on race days. Frank and Edmund Elias placed heavy bets, but Xinmeng was more fascinated by the horses. He also fantasized about riding one.

"Come with me to the stables, XM. I'll let you talk to Aaron the trainer," said Biddy Liddell, extending an invitation. "He's the best. He'll tell you all about the horses."

Biddy, a legendary figure in Shanghai, dressed always in riding attire – boots, gloves, whip, cap, and all. She walked like a man, gestured like a man, smoked like a man, and swore like a ruffian. She rode, she betted, she spent most of her days on horses or lingering at the stables. She knew all the trainers and everyone's horses.

As she led Xinmeng through the gate to the stables, she explained why she thought the good trainers were all Jews.

"Western-style horse racing is a new sport in this city. There are no native experts. You can train apprentices to groom the animals, but a trainer requires extensive knowledge about the horses and many years of experience dealing with them. One has to know how to talk to the horses, you know. When the SRC first started, they had to look to India and Iraq to import the Indians and Jews here to do the job. For some reasons, the Indians, over the years, all went to join the police force as security guards or took other jobs. But the Jews stayed. Some of the trainers are second generation."

"Does that mean they were born here in Shanghai?" asked Xinmeng.

"Quite so. I was born here too; so were Frank and Edmund," said Biddy. "I guess our British accents fooled you."

"I often wondered at the fluency of your Shanghai dialect," Xinmeng replied.

"Especially my swearing, huh?" Biddy burst out laughing loudly.

Aaron was in his mid-forties. Though his family had originated in Baghdad, his father, Daniel, had been a horse trainer for the Sassoon family in India. When the Sassoon clan began shipping opium from India to Shanghai, Daniel migrated with them. He was already an old man when the SRC started horse racing. But he was still good with the horses and Aaron benefited much from his knowledge and expertise.

"What can I do for you, Mr. Zhao?" asked Aaron after the introduction.

"Cut out the bloody formality, Aaron. This is my friend XM," chided Biddy.

"Yes, Aaron, everyone in the club knows me as XM. So, you too, please."

"Very well then, XM, what is your interest in horses?" Aaron asked again.

"I've become very fond of horses. Maybe you can teach me a thing or two," said Xinmeng. "I wouldn't mind buying one to ride and race."

"Ride and race! Mmm . . ." Aaron broke out into a broad smile. "You're in luck, XM. You come at an opportune time. Do you know Commissioner Jarvis, the vice-chief of police for the International Settlement?"

"I've met him at the club a couple of times, but I wouldn't say I know him," Xinmeng answered.

"Mr. Jarvis owns this horse, Little Joe," Aaron said. "Come with me. I'll show you."

Xinmeng and Biddy followed Aaron to the fourth stall down from where they were.

"Look at this beauty! Isn't he gorgeous?" Aaron patted the horse as he continued. "Little Joe here is champion stock. He is fast and alert and is especially good on muddy tracks. But for some reason he hasn't won a race yet. Mr. Jarvis had entered him five times already, and each time he failed to win, place, or show. Mr. Jarvis has had him for two years now, and he is disappointed. The other day he was saying to me that, if anyone was interested, he would sell Little Joe at a reasonable price."

"I remember him from last Saturday's race. He came fifth out of eight, didn't he?" Biddy recalled.

"Yes. And it was right after that race, Mr. Jarvis told me to look for a buyer." Aaron looked down at the ground, scratching the earth with his boot and shook his head. "I don't blame him. But I can tell you, Little Joe is a winner. I'm not trying to push a sale. I have all the confidence in the world in him. He'll come ahead and soon, I tell you."

"Would you consider Little Joe a good buy, Aaron?" Xinmeng seemed to be taken by the horse. "What's the asking price?"

"Six hundred taels of silver. I guess there is some flexibility if you negotiate with Mr. Jarvis."

"Is the horse worth it?"

"Every farthing! I can vouch for Little Joe; he's going to win. If I were to buy a horse, I'd pick Little Joe as my top choice."

Xinmeng and Biddy looked at each other and smiled.

"All right. Let me sleep on it and let you know tomorrow," said Xinmeng.

"Make him an offer of five hundred and see if he'll accept," suggested Aaron. "But if you do buy him, it doesn't mean you will race him right away. You have to learn how to ride first. Let someone else race him till you're ready. And I must warn you that there is a lot of work involved if you intend to own, ride, and race a horse. You'll have to be here before dawn almost every morning to learn and train. Will you be game for that? It requires a great deal of discipline."

"I know. I'm quite aware of the rigorous training and exercising. I think I can handle that," Xinmeng replied.

"I'm sure you're also aware this is an expensive hobby. Every horse requires two people to groom, exercise, and take care of it. Good stewards do not come cheap," advised Aaron.

"Yes. I'm aware of that," said Xinmeng.

In the 1930s, the SRC, like most of the other prestigious race clubs in the world at that time, was a high-class amateur club. Amateur jockeys raced the horses, but the owners of the horses could qualify to race as well. All the beginners were issued a "red licence." When a rider had won ten races, he was issued a "black licence." The holder of a black licence could use the whip, as well as wearing boots with spurs. The red-card holders were not permitted the use of either.

Commissioner Jarvis and Xinmeng sealed the deal at five hundred taels of silver for Little Joe. Both were happy. They became fast friends at the racetrack.

Weeks passed. Xinmeng religiously attended the pre-dawn sessions for exercising and training. He enjoyed it.

As race season drew to a close, Aaron advised XM to enter Little Joe for a race on Stable Day, it being the last race day of the season. Aaron also suggested a young rider Bo Chen to ride Little Joe.

Xinmeng was extremely excited as it would be the first race for Little Joe since he had taken over ownership.

The night before the race it poured cats and dogs. The condition of the track was so bad that some of the owners were hoping they would postpone the races to another day. Stewards, trainers, riders all frowned when they looked at the ground. It was so wet, so messy. They shook their heads and sighed.

Little Joe was slotted for the second race. The first race ended with some kind of upset. There was much arguing and bickering among the owners and riders.

When the second race started, Little Joe was lagging behind. Xinmeng's heart sank as Chen rode the horse on the outside in the second-last position. At that moment, Xinmeng fully understood why Commissioner Jarvis wanted to get rid of this horse. He said to himself that he got a rotten deal.

But although Little Joe was on the outside, Chen was riding him at a flying pace, splashing up all the mud and water, and Little Joe seemed to enjoy kicking up a storm. He never faltered. He flew down the outside until he overtook all the horses and reached the finishing line, leading by two heads.

There were thunderous cheers. The spectators were incredulous. Xinmeng was beside himself and let loose all his emotions, much to the surprise of his friends.

Little Joe became the famous "mudder." He went on to win many races, even with Xinmeng as the jockey. Xinmeng was able to receive his black licence within three years of purchasing Little Joe.

In subsequent years, Xinmeng would acquire four more thoroughbreds and five Mongolian ponies.

Later, when the Japanese military occupied the Chinese-administered section of Shanghai in 1937, one of their officials would take Little Joe by force and used him to pull carriages. Xinmeng was heartbroken. Despite all his connections with the western powers, he knew no one who could exert influence on the Japanese officers. He felt helpless. He had no chance and no power to rescue Little Joe.

Chapter 18

The World at War

Japan's intrusion into China had become more and more widespread. Japan's ambition to rule all of China was clear to all. In the 1930s, Japan controlled the Manchurian railway. On September 18, 1931, it had attacked and occupied several strategic points in China's northeast Manchuria region. By February 1932, Japan had conquered all of Manchuria and had set up a puppet state Manchukuo (Manchu Kingdom). Puyi, the Qing dynasty's last emperor, who had abdicated twice as emperor in his boyhood, was installed as the puppet head of Manchukuo. The natural resources in the area were Japan's prime target, in particular, the coal mines as well as the gold mines along the Heilongjiang River (Black Dragon River). Manchukuo became the base from which Japanese power was to extend over the entire Chinese domain.

Japan did not formally declare war on China; it simply sent more troops and more residents into the country, so sure was it that China would not be able to resist. Neither did they set up Japanese governments in the regions they occupied; there were only puppet governments with their collaborators as officials.

In 1937, Japan created an incident at Lugouqiao (Marco Polo Bridge) on the outskirts of Peking (Beijing) and used it as pretext to march into Peking and Tianjin. In the fall of the same year, the Japanese military employed similar tactics to pick fights with Chinese soldiers in and near Shanghai. They entered Shanghai and occupied the Chinese-administered area of the city. For the time being the British retained their authority in the International Settlement and the French over the French Concession. Thus began Japan's eight-year grip on Shanghai.

Nanking (Nanjing) fell after Shanghai, and the Nationalist Government under Chiang Kaishek moved to the interior city of Chungking (Chonqing) in Sichuan Province.

In the West, the Second World War began in 1939, when Hitler invaded Poland. In the Pacific region, the war between Japan and China had started much earlier, and by 1937 Japan ruled Manchuria and occupied most of the major cities along China's eastern coast.

Anti-Japanese sentiment had flared high throughout China. Time and again in large cities, thousands of students marched in the streets, calling for the Nationalists and the Communists to form a united front to fight the Japanese. But, Chiang Kaishek was preoccupied with obliterating communism from China. He compared the Japanese invasion to a treatable disease, Communists to deadly cancer cells. The latter was more of a threat to his power as the head of the Republic. Therefore he directed his resources to fighting the Communist guerrillas instead.

Chiang's strategy backfired. In December 1936, he was held against his will in Xi'an, Shaanxi Province, by General Zhang Xueliang of the Northeastern Army. Chiang was coerced into agreeing to stop the civil war and combine his forces with that of the Communist army to battle the Japanese.

Xinmeng's eldest daughter was born around the time the Japanese military invaded Shanghai. As a matter of fact, all of his five daughters were to be born during the Japanese occupation of Shanghai. Xinmeng's brokerage firm was doing well and suffered no setbacks for the time being.

On the surface, Shanghai appeared unchanged under Japanese occupation. Decadent lifestyles carried on as usual; the crime rate was unabated; gang power was on the rise. But beneath the surface of endless pleasures and vices, the anti-Japanese undercurrent gathered force. The occupier set up a puppet government in Shanghai and recruited a network of supporters who condoned and participated in many of the Japanese atrocities – primarily the secret killing and torturing of anyone who they suspected as being anti-Japanese. Wang Jinwei, a former official under Chiang, shamelessly collaborated with the enemies and was targeted as traitor number one by the whole nation.

Underground resistance grew in the city. Attempted assassinations of Japanese collaborators, countered by the execution of resistance activists, became frequent occurrences.

At the same time as the intense international espionage and spy activities seeped into every nook, the city's craze for dancing, horse racing, dog racing, gambling, and prostitution reached an unprecedented high. Nightclubs and dance halls sprang up one after another, each outdoing the previous one in grandeur and opulence.

In February 1940, Xinmeng, the Nie siblings, the Li brothers, plus Yan Tigang, with their respective spouses, had a brush with the Japanese presence. They decided to meet for a Lunar New Year celebration. Since they all lived in the vicinity of Yu Yuan Road, they decided to go to the Paramount Ballroom Hall for some fun.

During their undergraduate years, Xinmeng and his friends had frequented the Astor House or Yipingxiang for tea dances and cabarets, but in 1932 a businessman by the name of Gu Lianchenput had put down seven hundred thousand taels of silver to build the extravagant Paramount Ballroom Hall at 218 Yu Yuan Road.

The architect, Yang Xiliao, modelled his design on some of the most luxurious nightclubs in New York at the time. The structure was built with steel and reinforced concrete, with an elaborate ventilation system that completely recycled the air of the entire building every ten minutes. There were eighteen thousand light fixtures in total, programmed to change colour and intensity as desired.

The main dance floor was eight hundred metres square with a ceiling eight metres high. It was named the "thousand dancers hall," though in actuality it could accommodate only a few hundred at a time. Steel plates supported the dance floor and functioned in the same manner as the suspension in automobiles. The bouncing effect made the dancers experience a surreal floating sensation as they moved around the floor. It added to the intoxicating atmosphere.

Two smaller dance floors flanked the main one. Each could take about two hundred people. On the upper level was a colourful stained-glass floor, lit from underneath.

When guests were about to leave, they would give their car licence numbers to the service manager, who would then flash the numbers from the tower of the building and the chauffeurs of the cars, parked nearby, would drive to the entrance to pick up their masters and company. The Paramount was an amazing dance hall.

For the holiday season, dinner tickets were, as a rule, double the usual charge, at about fifteen dollars each, but the cost was not a problem for these young revellers. Upon arrival, they bumped into a group of about six Japanese military officers in uniform. Teddy and Ronnie looked annoyed and suggested that they go somewhere else. Most Chinese avoided Japanese soldiers. Tigang, however, looked at the two tables that the captain had prepared for them in a nice spot a distance away from the Japanese officers' table and said: "This will do. We are far away from the 'Lou Bu Tou' (turnip heads). Anywhere we go we may end up in a similar situation. Let's sit down and order drinks."

"What did you call them, Tigang? Lou Bu Tou? Turnip heads? Why?" asked Lisa.

"Haven't you heard? Most people call the Japanese soldiers Lou Bu Tou in private. For two reasons: their ugly caps, wider at the bottom and narrower at the top makes the soldiers heads looks like turnips, and also because of the Japanese fondness of eating turnips. Just a derogative name for these creatures."

Everyone sat down. It had been a while since the whole group had been together, and there was a lot of catching up and many reminiscences. When the band played a waltz or a slow foxtrot, they would all get up and dance. During the intervals they played musical chairs between the two tables, with each one trying to talk to everyone else.

The evening went on merrily; everyone was having fun. The seven young couples enjoyed the music, the food, and the company. It was quite like old times.

The band started to play "Orchid in the Moon" – a tango. Only a few couples stepped onto the floor to show off their skill at the fancy steps. Peiting was eager to do his bit, but his wife was shy, knowing too well that Peiting's exaggerated body movements and head jerking would look foolishly comical, and she did not want to be part of it. While he pleaded with her in an attempt to drag her away from the table, quite unexpectedly, there was a sudden scuffle on the dance floor and *bang*!

A shot was fired and a woman fell to the ground.

Everyone headed for the exit. There were screams and confusion everywhere. Xinmeng and his group quickly left the Paramount before the police arrived. They speculated that it had to be one of the Luo Bo Tous venting his anger at someone. What a disappointing way to end what had been an otherwise thoroughly delightful evening, they grumbled.

The next morning it was headlines on every newspaper:

"Paramount's Popular Top Taxi-Dancer – Chen Manli 陈曼莉 – Gunned Down by Japanese Officer for Refusing to Dance with Him . . ."

This was the official version. Rumours abounded following the incident. A more intriguing story surfaced that Chen Manli was, in fact, an undercover agent sent by the Nationalist government in Chungking to work among the Japanese officials. She was actually shot by an underling of Wang Jinwei, the Japanese collaborator, in retaliation for an earlier assassination of one of Wang's people.

Such were the goings-on in Shanghai. Whatever the lifestyle, it was always accompanied by a constant edge of fear.

Shanghai, being a treaty port that required neither visa nor passport to enter, attracted all who, by choice or by necessity, came to seek adventure – or survival. Along with the adventurers came refugees from a number of countries.

The Russian Jewish refugees had arrived first. From 1881 to 1917, during the tsarist rules of Alexander II, Alexander III, and Nicholas II, waves upon waves of anti-Jewish violence spread throughout the Russian Empire. In major cities like Kiev, Warsaw, and Odessa, as well as smaller cities and villages numbered in the hundreds, Jews suffered persecution at the hands of Christians and government officials. During these pogroms, Jewish homes were destroyed and families were reduced to destitution. Many were killed, and large numbers of men, women, and children injured.*

Purportedly, about two million Jews left Russia. A portion of them went to Manchuria, mostly to the city of Harbin, where they built a community of thirteen thousand by 1920. After the Russian Revolution of 1917, many White Russians also escaped to Harbin where they, jointly with the Japanese, carried out anti-Semitic acts. As a result, the Jews in Harbin felt compelled to leave. Most of them headed south to Shanghai. The number was estimated at about seven to eight thousand.

Then, in the 1930s, Jews from a number of countries in Europe also began to make their way to Shanghai.

While Japan spread its wings over continental Asia, Adolf Hitler, who had become Chancellor of Germany in 1933, was moving to achieve absolute Nazi German domination of continental Europe.

In 1938, Germany had ended the Sino-German Alliance with the Republic of China. Germany recalled all officers working with the Chinese army and ceased all shipment of arms to China. It then struck an alliance with Japan and recognized Japan's authority in Manchukuo.

Persecution of Jews in Germany had begun as soon as Hitler took power. The Jews were stripped of their citizenship and deprived of all privileges. Their properties and businesses were confiscated and their livelihoods taken away from them. The Jews' survival hung in the balance. They started to leave the country.

On March 12, 1938, German troops had crossed into Austria. The Viennese welcomed Hitler with an unrestrained outpouring of fanatical enthusiasm. When Hitler held an election in Austria on April 10, 1938, 99.73 per cent of Austrians voted in favour of Germany's annexation of Austria.

In May 1938, the Nuremberg laws, which forcibly segregated Jews in Germany and deprived them of all rights, privileges, and possessions, were enforced in Austria. The Nazi authorities set up a Property Transfer office with a few hundred employees to blatantly and aggressively confiscate Jewish properties, businesses, and bank accounts.

SS Lieutenant Adolf Eichmann, in charge of the new Centre for Jewish Emigration in Vienna, coerced the Jews to emigrate and to turn over their assets to the Nazis.

It was in Austria that the Nazis formulated a method, combining economic expropriation with expulsion of Jews. This became the standard practice in other Nazi-occupied territories. Those who were unable to leave were transported to concentration camps or termination camps.

The situation in Europe deteriorated rapidly.

The Jews' only chance for survival was to leave Nazi-occupied territories. Frantically, they scrambled to get out of Germany, Austria, Poland, Hungary, the Netherlands. But alas, an unkind world did not receive them well. Many countries set quotas for Jewish immigrants; others refused them outright. Shanghai was one place that offered a thin ray of hope to those who had nowhere to go.

The early refugees travelled by train to Italy and sailed on Italian ships to Shanghai. Others came by way of Siberia through Japan. As German power spread in Europe, the journey became more convoluted and more difficult. Being stateless and penniless, they were totally destitute.

While Shanghai had the best and the latest to offer to a small portion of the privileged citizens and the super-wealthy foreigners at this time, by and large, the living standard of most of the residents in the city was far below that of the major European cities such as Berlin, Vienna, and Warsaw. The newcomers were hard hit by the cultural shocks that awaited them on their arrival.

Those who had some possessions with them were able to manage a frugal life. Most were deprived of their belongings, and their hardship was beyond words. They were first placed in the *heime*,* which were barrack-like buildings that accommodated over a hundred beds in each dormitory. Later, they were moved into the Hongkew (Hongkou) area, a poverty-stricken district, where disease and overcrowding were rampant.

It was common that several families were crammed into tiny living spaces, most of which were without sanitary facilities. Language barriers and lack of opportunities forced them to scrape out a subsistence living. For the more than twenty thousand European Jewish refugees, life in Shanghai was deplorable. They suffered and they endured. At the same time, they gained courage and fortitude. And they survived.

Even managing to leave their countries was not an easy task for the persecuted Jews. They would have to show proof of their passage and a final destination visa in order to get permission to exit. In some places they had to pay a hefty sum for the exit visa. The alternative was the concentration camp.

With most countries limiting or barring Jewish immigrants, getting a destination visa became a major hurdle for those who wanted to leave. In the midst of the hostility and oppression, a number of decent human beings rose to the challenge and extended a helping hand to the helpless Jews.

Dutch Consul Jan Zwartendijk and Japanese Consul Chiune Sugihara were both stationed at Kovno, capital of Lithuania, in 1939. By then, the only exit route left for the Polish Jews was by way of Lithuania through Siberia and Japan to a country that would receive them.

Aware of the fact that the Dutch colony of Curacao required no visa, the consul stamped "no visa required" for Curacao for the refugees. The Soviet Consul allowed the refugees transit through Russia, on condition they must also obtain transit visas from Japan in order to reach their destination.

For twenty-nine days in July and August of 1940, Japanese Consul Chiune Sugihara, defying orders from his superiors forbidding him to issue transit visas, signed and stamped transit visas at the rate of three hundred a day for the Polish Jews. Even when he was ordered to leave Kovno, he continued to issue visas from the train.

It was estimated that Sugihara issued a total of about six thousand transit visas to the refugees. Out of those, twenty-five-hundred recipients eventually reached safety in East Asia. Among them, the entire Mir Yeshiva, as well as members of yeshivas from Kletsk (Byelorussia), Telsh (Lithuania), Lublin, and Lubavitz (Byelorussia) sought haven in Shanghai.

Dr. Ho Fengshan was appointed Chinese Consul General in Vienna in May 1938.

At the time there were more than 185,000 Jews living in Austria, out of which about 170,000 were residents of Vienna, which had the third-largest Jewish community in Europe. Vienna became the centre for the emigration of Austrian Jews.

Ignoring an order from the Chinese ambassador in Berlin to stop issuing visas to the Jews, Ho persisted with his liberal visa policy, stamping visas to Shanghai for all who asked.

Purportedly Ho issued about four thousand such visas. On the strength of Ho's visas, some were able to obtain release from concentration camps; others used the visa to purchase passage to leave. Yet others managed to use the Shanghai visa to obtain transit visas from other countries, such as Italy. Ho knew well that the Shanghai visa was issued in name only, because, in fact, a visa was not needed to enter Shanghai. But the visa served the purpose of expediting exit from Austria. Most of these recipients ended up in the Philippines, Palestine, or England.*

December 1941 was an ominous month. On the morning of December 7 (Hawaiian time), the Imperial Japanese navy conducted their now-notorious surprise military strike on the U.S. navy base at Pearl Harbor, Hawaii. This was Japan's pre-emptive strike to prevent the U.S. Pacific Fleet from trying to stop Japan's planned invasions of the Philippines, Malaya, Singapore, and Hong Kong.

The United States declared war on Japan, and entered the war in both the European and Pacific arenas. In Shanghai, the Japanese military now occupied, in addition to the areas under Chinese administration, the International Settlement, which was governed by the Municipal Council, with strong British influence. Murders, espionage, and gang wars became part of the daily routine. Night curfew was imposed more often than not. Ordinary people lived in fear; students – many of whom participated in anti-Japanese manoeuvres – and underground activists put their lives on the line, expecting to be shot or tortured without notice.

By then, the Jewish refugee population in Shanghai had exceeded twenty-five thousand. Together with the wealthy traders and businesspeople and the Russian Jews who came via Harbin, the Jewish count was nearing forty thousand. It was too high for Hitler's liking. Because Germany and Japan were allies, Hitler was counting on the Japanese to help him with his plans for the eliminations of Jews in Shanghai.

In the summer of 1942, Hitler sent Colonel Josef Meisinger to Shanghai with a mission – to help the Japanese solve the Jewish refugee problem there.

Josef Meisinger had been the chief of the secret police in Warsaw in 1939. Known as the "Butcher of Warsaw," he was responsible for the death of an estimated hundred thousand Jews in Poland. In the words of a fellow Nazi, Hitler's spymaster Walter Schellenberg, writing in his memoir, *The Labyrinth*, Meisinger was "one of the most evil creatures" on earth. Meisinger's atrocities in Warsaw appalled even his superior. Schellenberg had collected a huge file on Meisinger and he described the latter as being "so utterly bestial and corrupt as to be practically inhuman."*

It was Reinhard Heydrich, one of the main architects of the Holocaust, known as "Hitler's hangman," who intervened and saved Meisinger from court martial and possible execution. In 1942, Meisinger was posted to Tokyo as the chief of the Gestapo for Japan, China, and Manchukuo.

Meisinger was only too ready to repeat what he did in Warsaw and obliterate all Jews in Shanghai from the face of the earth.

The Japanese authority in Shanghai had created a Jewish Affairs Bureau for the purpose. The co-authors of *The Fugu Plan* report that, at the initial meeting, Meisinger was insistent that, for the good of the German-Japan alliance, "the entire Jewish plague must be eradicated from Shanghai."

Meisinger put forth his plan. The Japanese military was to round up all the Jewish refugees on Rosh Hashanah, the Jewish New Year holiday, which was to begin at sundown on September 1. The soldiers were to surround the synagogues, where most of the Jewish refugees were expected to gather. The captives would then be eliminated in one of three ways devised by Meisinger.

For one, the Jews, stripped of clothes and belongings, were to be loaded on dilapidated ships, towed out to sea, and left to perish. Or the Jews could be put to work at the salt mines, with minimum sustenance. From their European experience, Meisinger knew that the labourers would not last long. Alternately, a concentration camp could be built on the island of Chongming at the mouth of the Yangtzie River, and there "the Jews would be permitted to volunteer for medical experiments . . . on the human nervous system's tolerance for pain, for example."*

It was a wicked plan. Tsutomo Kubota, the director of the Bureau of Stateless Refugess in Shanghai, took time to ponder the proposition. The Japanese vice-consul, Mitsugi Shibata, was shocked by the extent of Meisinger's brutality and his determination to carry out the senseless killings. Shibata's conscience would not allow him to see such atrocities take place. At the immense risk of being charged with treason, Shibata alerted the Jewish leaders of the impending calamity that was about to descend upon them. He urged them to use whatever connections they had to lobby the Japanese higher-ups.

The Jews frantically pulled out all their connections to the influential Japanese officials. Dr. Kaufman in Harbin managed to reach the Japanese Foreign Ministry and the upper ranks of the army. Others negotiated with Tsutomu Kubota to stop Meisinger's madness.

But, in the end, it was chiefly because of the "fugu plan" mentality prevailing amongst the upper echelon of the Tokyo government that this Final Solution was thwarted.

During the Russo-Japanese War of 1904, Japan had found itself in trouble. With a much smaller army and limited resources, it soon realized that it would be defeated. In desperation, the vice-governor Takahashi of the Bank of Japan tried to secure loans from the international market in London to fund the campaign in Manchuria. Much of Takahashi's efforts were in vain until he met Jacob Schiff from the United States.

Schiff, a Jewish-American banker, held a grudge against Tsar Nicholas II for the pogrom against the Jews of the Russian town of Kishinev. He arranged loans totalling $196 million for the Japanese war chest against Russia. As a result, Japan was able to defeat the Russians and the two countries signed the *Portsmouth Treaty* in September 1905.

Schiff's ability to raise such a huge amount of money left a strong impression on the top thinkers in Japan regarding Jewish power.

In 1919, when Japanese soldiers were sent to Siberia to fight with the White Russian soldiers against the Communists, they were introduced to a book entitled *The Protocols of the Elders of Zion*. The *Protocols* was an anti-Semitic fiction that falsely described a Jewish plot to take over the entire world. Two young Japanese officers, Captain Norihiro Yasue and naval officer Koreshige Inuzuka, in particular, took the book literally and believed every word of it.

They were persuaded that the Jews were in the midst of a conspiracy to take over the world. They were led to think that the Jews were behind social instability and Communism; the Jews were cornering the wheat market and had control of world capital. They were convinced that the awesome sum of $196 million loaned to Japan by Jacob Schiff was sufficient proof that the Jews had direct connection to and power over the president of the United States. They also found other sources claiming that the Jews excelled in trade, commerce, manufacturing, and inventions. And because of their superior intelligence, the Jews were able to reach the top in just about every field and profession.

All this "information," without verification, was fed to the higher-ups in Japanese officialdom and, between 1932 and 1940, the "fugu plan" emerged.

The "fugu plan" was premised upon Japan becoming a superpower in Asia, and the Jews were to play an indispensable role in assisting them to achieve that goal. The Jewish refugees from Europe would be placed in the newly formed Manchukuo to lead in technology, skill development, management, and production of superior quality goods, and the American Jews were to provide them with the capital and a liaison to the head of the United States. It was at best a plan based on total delusion.

Although by 1942 the plan was no longer being actively pursued, it had already so affected the mindset of the Japanese authorities in Tokyo, and hence the officials in Shanghai, that they were not prepared to carry out the drastic measures against the Jews that Meisinger suggested. Jews might still play a role in Japan's broader plan of becoming a world superpower, which was far more important than Japan's alliance with Germany. The Japanese government refused to take part in exterminating the Jews in Shanghai. Meisinger's plan fizzled out.

Instead, the Japanese authority in Shanghai ordered all "stateless refugees" and those who had arrived after 1937 to be confined in a ghettoized area in Hongkew (Hongkou). By 1942, all Jews who were U.S. or British nationals were also to be held in camps.

The Hongkew ghetto was a concentration camp of sorts. Because of the overcrowding, living conditions became even worse. They lacked everything: accommodation, food, sanitation, and health care.

The Jews were not allowed to leave the ghetto without a permit issued by a Japanese officer, Ghoya, who was an assistant to Kubota, the director of the Bureau of Stateless Refugees. Ghoya was evil and belligerence personified. He was temperamental to the extreme and did his duties according to whim. He purposely made it difficult, if not impossible, for the refugees to obtain the permits.

Life for the Jewish refugees in Shanghai took a turn for the worse.

翻手為雲覆手為雨

Toronto, Canada

2012

人间烟霭浮沉

Chapter 19

Recollections

On the appointed day and hour, four of the sisters, their stepmother, Ellie, and Thomas assembled at Rhae's place.

The dining room served as a conference room for the day, with the recording machine ready to go, pens and paper neatly placed for the participants. Tea and refreshments were spread out on the kitchen table for those who wanted to partake.

Auntie Ellie had passed her nintieth birthday, but still looked youthful and energetic. She had a sharp mind and an incredible memory. Were she not a bit hard of hearing in one ear, she would have engaged a great deal more in all kinds of activities and discussions. Because of her hearing impairment, however, she had to position herself to catch all the conversation.

Rhae brought a tall glass of Auntie Ellie's favourite Bi-luo-chun* green tea and placed it in front of her on the dining table. It was Auntie Ellie's preferred drink for early afternoon. She called it her daily "fix" to boost her energy.

The others were advised to have their food and drinks in the kitchen so as not to cause interference during the taping of the proceedings.

There was an air of expectancy and excitement in the room. Everyone was eager to launch into a different period in history, and there was so much to recollect, to hear, to tell, and to discuss. Auntie Ellie took a sip from the tall glass. She was about to open her mouth when Thomas butted in.

"If you guys don't mind, I would like to be the moderator for the day." Without waiting for anyone to answer, he continued: "Auntie Ellie, can you first tell us a bit about yourself, your family, and the general background of the time when you were growing up. For recording purposes." As he said it, Thomas pushed the button to turn the machine on.

"I thought you all knew about my family. But, of course, I'm happy to tell you about my younger days and about my family.

"My maiden name was Shaw, the same as the famous Hong Kong film tycoon Run-Run Shaw, who passed away recently at age 107. No, we are not related. My father owned a gold-trading exchange called Da De Ren and he was also the Taipan, or corporate head, at Xing Ye Bank. He was well-to-do, as you probably know, and well-known in financial circles in Shanghai before the Communists came and in Hong Kong among the business people from Shanghai.

"There were five of us siblings: an older brother and an older sister before me, and a younger brother and a younger sister after me. I was the middle child. Now only my younger sister and I are still alive. She lives in New Jersey.

"Like your mother, Flora, I attended the famous McTyeire

School for Girls in Shanghai. Every girl in that school had an English name. I became Eleanor. Again, like your mother, I never graduated. When I was seventeen, my parents arranged for me to marry my first husband, Dai Mogang.

"The only reason they picked Mogang to be their son-in-law was because of the Dai family wealth. They were one of the richest, most well-established families in Shanghai.

"At seventeen, I was clueless about marriage and family. I was happy and carefree going to school . . . I started driving at fifteen . . . I had the use of a car and everything I wanted was always at my fingertips. All of a sudden I became someone's wife and boom, boom, boom . . . within six years I gave birth to five children – three boys and two girls. I was barely twenty-four.

"What did I know about bringing up children! I couldn't be bothered with them. I hired *amahs* or what they call nannies nowadays, to look after all my children. I'm sure your mother did the same with you. No fashionable woman in her right mind in the thirties and forties would personally take care of her children – that is, if they could afford the nannies. More so with those of us who had attended 'foreign' schools . . ."

"Quite true. Our mother didn't take care of us herself. We were brought up by our wet-nurses or *amahs*. Then it was Auntie Dinni who supervised us for homework or piano practice," interjected Yvette.

"I was a spoiled brat, I guess. First by my parents then by my husband."

"Tell us about your husband," Thomas directed.

"My husband was . . . I would say . . . not only was he born with a silver spoon in his mouth, he had diamonds and gold in his palms. At birth he was given a ridiculous amount of money. He knew he wouldn't need to work a single day of his life, and he didn't.

"Mogang was ahead of his time. He was a connoisseur of good wines. If he were to have chosen a profession, I'm sure he would have wanted to be a sommelier.

"He never went to school; he always had private tutors. But he spoke fluent English – speaking only, he could not read or write it. I think he picked up a lot from his English-speaking friends like the Eliases, the Kadoories, the Sassoons, and so on. Because his Chinese name sounded so close to Morgan, many chose to call him Morgan."

"The names you mentioned just now were all Jewish people. How come all Jewish friends? No Chinese friends? No English friends?" asked Thomas.

"Sure there were." Nodding to Linny and Adele across the table, Auntie Ellie continued. "Your father came by, but not frequently. He was more in touch with my father, and more regarding business than for social purposes. Mogang used to play bridge or poker regularly with the Elias brothers and some other English people. Your father would substitute once in a while when one of the regular players couldn't make it.

"There were the Parkers, English to the bone, quite haughty and very picky. The servants hated Mrs. Parker. James Parker was with Shell. Walter Whittaker was with the banking association. Another one was on the board of the Jockey Club. Can't remember his name at the moment. Among the Chinese were C.X. Chen, who owned cigarette factories; S.W. Kiung, the comprador* for Hong Kong and Shanghai Bank, and many others. Because Mogang did not go out to work, he had no colleagues or even business associates. He had drinking friends, gambling friends, racing friends . . . most of them were Jockey Club or Shanghai Club members. All nationalities. My husband truly led a life of leisure – didn't even have to look after his own finances."

"Well, the men would play cards or go to the races. What about you?" Thomas pressed.

"The wives would play Mah Jeung* if it was a Chinese group. Most of the time, the wives did not accompany their husbands. Occasionally they would arrange to go shopping or window-shopping, or go for afternoon tea or a matinee at the movies. But I was always home by dinner-time.

"The best thing about Mogang was that he never cared how much money I spent. He let me buy anything I wanted. I loved jewellery – I still do – and I bought and bought. Loads and loads of it. Some pieces were absolutely exquisite; others less so . . ."

"And what happened to them?" Thomas again.

"Lucky for me that I bought so much jewellery. Before the Communists liberated Shanghai, I took them to Hong Kong and put them in safety-deposit boxes at the Hong Kong and Shanghai Bank. Eventually I left Shanghai after the liberation. I had only twenty thousand American dollars with me when I took three of my children to Hong Kong.

"I opened a jewellery shop in Hong Kong. It was the jewellery and the twenty thousand dollars that enabled me to send my three children abroad to study. I must add that we were fortunate that Horace Kadoorie was kind enough to let my father stay in one of the Kadoorie-owned apartment units on Argyle Street, because of what my father did for them during the war. So, in the beginning, we were able to share that unit with my father before we rented our own."

"Let's leave the Kadoorie story till later. Why did you only bring three of your children? What happened to your husband? Did he not go to Hong Kong with you?" asked Thomas.

"No, my husband did not want to come to Hong Kong with us. He had all that money and he thought he could just go on like always. He didn't want any change, not realizing that all his buddies were heading south to Hong Kong. Eventually most of the money was taken away from him. For many years after that I had to provide for his living expenses from Hong Kong till he passed away. He was not very far-sighted, I hate to say.

"To answer your other question, my eldest son was already married, so there was no sense complicating his life. Besides, he was kind of nationalistic in thinking. He said Chinese should remain on Chinese soil and not go to a British colony. Very tragically, he took his own life during Mao's Cultural Revolution. Like so many others, he couldn't stand the persecution by the Red Guards, who labelled him 'a reactionary capitalist running dog.'

"My youngest son had just started secondary school; I thought it would be best for him to complete it first. A serious mistake, probably. But then hindsight is always so clear. However, I was able to sponsor him to come to Canada in the eighties when Deng Xiaoping opened up China to the outside world. By then he was married with one child.

"My eldest daughter, second son, and second daughter had all completed high school, and I wanted them to pursue higher education. After the Communists founded the People's Republic of China in 1949, children from well-to-do families had no chance of entering universities. Priority was given to members of the labouring class or peasant families. We were classified as 'reactionaries' in that society. A lot of privileges were denied us because of our 'capitalist' background. Class discrimination, wouldn't you say!

"I am extremely proud of my three children who left Shanghai with me. They all supported themselves through universities in California and Canada. They were high achievers and later pursued successful and gratifying careers. I cannot brag enough about their accomplishments . . ."

"We'll leave that to another day, Auntie Ellie. Now, let's zero in on the years during the Second World War in Shanghai," said Thomas.

"The war years were tough on everyone. The Japanese military and the puppet government officials were hated by all. I must admit, people like me did not contribute in any way to help fight the Japanese occupiers. The kind of lifestyle we had somehow kept us removed from political participation of any sort. Looking back, I now feel a bit ashamed for the lack of effort on my part. However, both my father and my husband helped the Jews during those difficult years after the Pearl Harbor incident . . ."

Rhae said excitedly: "Yes, this is what we're waiting to hear."

"My father was a good friend of the Kadoorie brothers – Horace and Lawrence – he was closer to Horace though. They were business associates as well as friends.

"My father had immense respect for Horace; he nicknamed Horace 'Mr. Charity,' because of the many charitable organizations Horace was involved with. The Shanghai Jewish Youth Association was established by Horace. He built The Kadoorie School. Helped to expand the Jewish Hospital.

Even before the mass influx of Jews from Europe arrived, he made a point of trying to improve the welfare of the Jewish community, especially the youth. A very compassionate and generous man..."

"Wait, wait. Can someone fill me in on the Kadoories. I know they were and still are big in Hong Kong. All of you lived in Hong Kong for many years and I didn't. I would like to hear a bit more about them if you don't mind." Thomas looked from one to another around the table. Linny was happy to comply.

"I happened to read up on them recently. Sir Elly Kadoorie and his brother, Elias, were Mizrahi Jews from Baghdad. They first moved to Bombay, now Mumbai, in India. In the eighteen eighties, Sir Elly migrated to Hong Kong. Lawrence was born in Hong Kong and Horace in London, England. Lawrence later became Lord Lawrence Kadoorie and Horace, Sir Horace Kadoorie. Lawrence married Muriel Gubbay, whose father was a distinguished scholar by the name of David Sassoon Gubbay. Horace never married.

"In the beginning, Elly Kadoorie worked briefly as a clerk for E.D. Sassoon and Company. Later, he joined Sassoon Benjamin and George Potts to form Benjamin, Kelly, and Potts. Kelly stood for Elly. Thus began his illustrious career.

"Elly Kadoorie's brother, Elias, died in the early 1920s, and Elias's Hong Kong Shanghai Hotel Limited was inherited by Elly and his sons. Elly's Penninsula Hotel was completed in 1929 – it became a landmark in Hong Kong and is still one of the most prestigious hotels there. The family has substantial holdings in China Light and Power, as well as many other businesses. They own a vast amount of real estate, including the entire Kadoorie Hill in Kowloon, I believe.

"Elly passed away a year before the end of the war. Lawrence died in 1993 and Horace in 1995. I would assume that it is Lawrence's son Michael, daughter Rita, or their children who are in charge of the Kadoorie empire now."

"Let me add this," said Auntie Ellie. "You cannot talk about the Kadoories in Shanghai without mentioning their residence, 'The Marble Hall,' which they built in 1924. I was invited to a couple of events there. What an incredible place!

"According to my father, Elly Kadoorie did not mean to build such a grand structure. He hired an architect who had a weakness for liquor. It must have been the influence of Bacchus that made the architect turn what was to be a graceful residence into a magnificent palace. You can imagine the surprise when Elly Kadoorie and his family returned from a trip to find that, instead of a spacious parlour as they requested, the architect gave them a ballroom* that was more than, say, twenty times what we have as a living room in a good-sized house here. I'm not exaggerating; it was huge. And a verandah that seemed to go on endlessly. It was so amazingly beautiful that it would have been a sin for Sir Elly to reject it, even though it was not what he had in mind. And I can tell you it was a wondrous experience to dance in that ballroom . . ."

"More so than the Paramount Ballroom?" Rhae asked.

"Not the same. The Marble Hall was stately, elegant, classic, with an air of European aristocratic splendour. The Paramount was mostly well-appointed, doused in luxury and opulence. It was a commercial place. Quite different.

"The Marble Hall became a landmark. Sir Elly entertained a lot there. The family left for Hong Kong in 1949, and the liberation army took over Marble Hall. It wasn't clear if the Kadoories actually donated it to the new government willingly or if it was just taken from them. It is now the Shanghai Youth Palace."

"Now, Auntie Ellie, tell us how your father helped the Kadoories?" said Thomas the moderator.

"Before I do that, let me give you some idea about the situation of the Jews in Shanghai around the mid-1930s.

"At first, there were the Russian Jews, mostly from Harbin, who began to arrive in the twenties. Most of them were not rich, but were not too badly off. Kind of middle-class. The majority of them lived in the French Concession. Many of them had businesses and opened shops in the French Concession, which, as you know, was governed by the French Consul General.

"There was, for instance, the Siberian Fur Company on Bubbling Well Road. It carried the best furs – sables, Russian broadtails, which were the craze in the thirties. Gregori Klebanov was the owner. Shanghai gets very cold in the winter and heating systems did not exist then. Sable was especially popular, because it was warm and very light. By comparison, mink was much too heavy. Broadtails were mainly for looks; they didn't provide warmth. By the way, Rhae, I saw you wearing a black broadtail full-length coat last fall. I don't recall you ever mentioned buying one. Would that be from your mother or your mother-in-law?"

"You're observant, Auntie Ellie," replied Rhae. "It was from my mother-in-law. She also gave me a short broadtail jacket. Incidentally, both were made by Siberian Furs, but probably by the Hong Kong Siberian Fur Company, which I guess must be the continuation of the store in Shanghai.

"Let me tell you about my broadtail coats. They were given

to me decades ago. I kept them in the trunk and never wore them. Then, last fall, I decided to donate them to the Salvation Army. Out of curiosity, I took them to an upscale department store just to have an opinion on their value. I couldn't believe my ears when they assessed the full-length coat at twelve thousand dollars and the jacket at eight thousand. I became selfish; I had both pieces cleaned and kept them for my own use. Stingy me!"

"Ah! I would've done exactly the same if I were you, " said Aunt Ellie. "They are beautiful. Don't feel guilty, Rhae. Now, back to the Russian Jews. They had cafés, restaurants, bakeries. They built their own synagogue. We, the natives, loved their Borscht soup, enjoyed their cabarets, and so on.

"Then, all of a sudden, there were lots more Jews, from Europe. If I remember the numbers correctly, in the ten months between the end of 1938 and September 1939, around fifteen thousand Jewish refugees arrived. Starting around the Chinese New Year in February of 1939, over a thousand Jews arrived in Shanghai every month.

"I remember my father told us that Uncle Horace was worried. As a matter of fact, it was not only Horace Kadoorie. Most of the well-to-do Sephardic Jews in Shanghai were constantly talking about the large influx of Jews and how best to help them.

"They organized committees. One of them was the Committee for the Assistance of European Jewish Refugees in Shanghai, which operated in Hong Kong. They did fundraising events and campaigned for donations. The Jewish Joint Distribution Committee, better known as JDC, which, I believe, was an American organization, opened an office in Shanghai.

It was chiefly JDC and the local wealthy Jews, the Sephardi as well as the Russian Ashkenazi Jews, that provided the majority of funds for the refugees.

"When the refugee number reached around thirty thousand, even we, the natives, began to feel the pinch of the overcrowding and the lack of infrastructure in the city. Mogang's house was in the French Concession, which was not too badly affected because it was generally a bit pricy for most of the refugees. In many pockets in the International Settlement, especially in and around HongKew, an area of low-income Chinese and a high concentration of Japanese residents, the lack of affordable accommodation, the deficiency of the sanitation system, and the poor health-care facilities reached a crisis level.

"Food shortages became acute. Especially staples like rice. Not just in the HongKew area but all over Shanghai. Every time rice was available, our cook would buy a lot and store it. Many people had to buy it on the black market, and it was usually two or three times the normal price.

"Some friends of ours owned rice fields in the suburbs of Shanghai which were leased to farmers. They stipulated that the farmers pay them in kind instead of cash. So, at harvest, our friends would personally travel to the fields and transport the rice back to Shanghai. They always hired security guards with guns to accompany them in case they got robbed on the way."

"I do remember that, during the war, quite often we did not have steamed rice for supper. The cook would make some congee with chunks of yams in it. One bowl of steamed rice can make a whole pot of congee. We were told that times were hard, and we had to eat whatever was available. Sheryl and

Adele were too young to remember, but I'm sure Rhae and Yvette do," said Linny.

"I definitely remember. I hated those yam congees, but it beat being hungry," said Rhae. "Looking back, if families like ours, comfortably well off, had to go through such a tough time, how much worse must it have been for the poor and the destitute. I've read several of the books written by the Jewish refugees describing their Shanghai experiences, and one thing that comes out loud and clear is that they were always hungry. So sad!"

"And the situation did not improve." Auntie Ellie picked up from where she left off. "Now, a few thousand of the refugees were in transit. Within months they would leave for other destinations. Still, overall, throughout the war years there were at least twenty-five-thousand European Jewish refugees in Shanghai.

"Of course, it was not the refugees that caused the food shortage. It was the war. Supplies were kept from reaching the Japanese-occupied areas. But, under the circumstances, the refugees suffered even more than they would have otherwise during ordinary times. The meagre subsidy or their little bit of hard-earned money had to stretch a long way.

"Horace and his friends were tireless in trying to solve all kinds of problems arising from the refugee situation. My father and some of his friends were called upon when Horace and his associates needed to deal with some Chinese individuals or organizations. It wasn't often, just occasionally.

"Out of the blue, Pearl Harbor happened. Sir Elly and family had gone to Hong Kong in December 1941 to escape the cold winter in Shanghai. Within hours of their attack on Pearl

Harbor on December 7, the Japanese invaded Hong Kong. The Japanese soldiers attcked from Shenzhen. After more than two weeks of fierce fighting by British, Canadian, and Indian soldiers and local volunteer militias, the governor of Hong Kong, Sir Mark Young, surrendered. A Japanese general was installed as the new governor, and the Japanese used Kadoorie's Peninsular Hotel as their command post. They remained there till February of the following year, when they moved to the Hong Kong and Shanghai Bank Building.

"The Japanese occupation of Hong Kong lasted for three years and eight months and all that time Hong Kong was under martial law. Most of the British nationals and other foreigners were sent to camps. The Kadoories were in Stanley Camp.

"Hong Kong was in total confusion. The chaos was horrendous. A lot of people from Shanghai, many of my relatives and friends, had gone there thinking they would be safe from the Japanese, and were caught between a rock and a hard place. They did not know where to turn.

"Supplies were cut off – not only food but everything. Rice, oil, sugar, flour, salt, were rationed. The Japanese began to send all the unemployed people back to mainland China.

"It was not clear whether it was due to the severity of the food shortage or for some other reason, but the Japanese authorities ordered the Kadoories to return to Shanghai. When Sir Elly and family arrived in Shanghai after eight days on a boat, crammed under the deck with two thousand others, they found that the Japanese had taken over the Marble Hall.

"Worse still, not only did they find their residence occupied, the Kadoories found their bank accounts frozen by the Japanese and some of their assets confiscated. Since they had a household staff of more than seventy, cash flow was a problem.

That was when my father stepped in to help. Being the head of Xin Ye Bank and owning a gold-exchange shop of his own, he had plenty of cash under his control. He gave a personal, unconditional guarantee on behalf of the Kadoories, enabling the bank to advance cash to tide them over. Of course, the Kadoories were well-known in financial circles; no one would ever have doubted their ability to repay. But because of the possibility of the Japanese taking over the banks, and also the fact that some of the Kadoorie assets were already in Japanese hands, the bank, even with my father's intervention, capped the amount the Kadoories could withdraw. My father then used his own funds to lend to Horace.

"It was a small gesture on my father's part, but Horace was forever grateful. In the late fifties, when my elder brother went to Hong Kong and was without a job, Horace returned the favour by providing a personal unconditional guarantee to the bank on my brother's behalf, and that made it possible for my brother to become a stockbroker.

"Of course, the Kadoories weren't the only people to have their accounts frozen. Many of the wealthy Jews were in the same predicament. It was said that the Japanese suspected them of funding anti-Japanese activities. The Japanese authorities kept detailed dossiers on all the wealthy Jews in Shanghai. Quite a number of them ran into cash problems . . ."

Rhae interrupted. "Ah! That explains why, after Pearl Harbor, the funds for the refugees seem to have dwindled. Several books mentioned that funds were not available to help the refugees. No one mentioned that those who were providing the money were actually themselves in need of help."

"Did you ever go to the Hongkew area during that time?" asked Thomas.

"My father took us there sometimes – that is, before 1943," answered Auntie Ellie. "You see, the Jews in Hongkew tried very hard to make a living. To their credit, they slowly built up businesses and opened shops. As a matter of fact, they even created a 'Little Vienna' for themselves. I think it was along Chusan Road. My father was so impressed by their determination and their resilience, he wanted us to see how people in extreme deprivation were able to remain tenacious, courageous, and creative. He wanted us, my sisters and me, to learn to endure hardship like these refugees. He felt we had too easy a life.

"There was a Café Louis on Ward Road. It was famous for whipped cream. In those days, most of the cakes and pastries in Shanghai used butter cream – a much heavier cream. We went crazy over the whipped cream – so light and so refreshing. There was also Roy's Rooftop Garden Restaurant, which was very popular and always crowded. And the Wiener schnitzel at Wiener Café Restaurant, also on Chusan Road, was out of this world. I can still see the little café on the street level, with a gigantic dentist's sign in the second-floor window. In 1943, when the Japanese made Hongkew a Jewish ghetto, we stopped going there,"

"Why?" asked Thomas.

"The Chinese did not require a pass to enter or leave the area the way the Jews did, but the Japanese soldiers were very cruel towards the Chinese. They treated Chinese like dirt, always displaying their conquerors' smugness. The Chinese had to bow to the soldiers whenever they came into contact with them. A soldier could stop a Chinese at any time, take his belongings from him, or beat him up for no reason, or even bayonet him at will. There were Japanese soldiers posted in Hongkew, plus all the Bao Jia – resident security guards. It just wasn't safe for us to take leisurely walks in Hongkew.

"There was this Captain Ghoya, who was authorized to issue passes for the Jews. He was one beastly creature, hated by all. He called himself the 'King of the Jews,' and abused his power to no end. He was temperamental and unpredictable, and acted on whim. He made a lot of people suffer, and he took pleasure in it. But, to his credit, he never sent any Jew from Hongkew to prison. The Shanghai prison was like a death cell; very few people survived in there."

"Did the Kadoories relocate to Hongkew at all?" queried Thomas.

"I don't think so. My father vaguely mentioned that they were in and out of camps, but I don't know if he was referring to their experience in Hong Kong or if they were required to be in those camps in Shanghai that were set up for foreign nationals. They were powerful people with a lot of connections. I never heard about them being ghettoized in Hongkew.

"I remember that, in the fall of 1942, diplomats and officials of the so-called 'enemy nations,' the British, Americans, Dutch, and so on, were repatriated, and then all enemy nationals who remained in Shanghai had to wear armbands to identify their country of origin – the Americans wore red with the letter 'A,' the British wore 'B,' the Dutch wore 'H,' and nationals of the colonies and protectorates of enemy nations wore 'X.'

"Throughout 1943, all enemy nationals, as well as nationals of Iran, Iraq, and other neutral countries were required to move to camps. There were at least seven or eight camps* for these people. I was told that the Columbia Country Club Camp and the Long Hua Camp were the best camps to be in. Others included Zaibei, Pudong, Yangzhou . . . Altogether about eight thousand foreigners spent a year or two in those camps. Now that I think about it, the Kadoories, being either Iraqi or British, would have definitely been ordered to one of those.

"By the way, these camps were in no way like the Nazi concentration camps in Europe. There was no deliberate starvation, no torture, no killing. It was just a method of keeping them together, most likely for security purposes. Also, these people did not require permits to leave the camps as those in Hongkew did.

"It was during this period, 1943 to early 1945, that my husband and I and our children left for Anhui Province to be a bit further away from Japanese control. We left Shanghai shortly after my husband made arrangements to hide Frank Elias and his father in our house."

"How did that come about? What about Frank's brother, Edmund?" asked Rhae.

"As soon as the proclamation was posted that all stateless Jews and those who were U.S. or British nationals were required to move to Hongkew or the camps, Frank came to my husband and said there was no way that he would subject his father, who was near eighty, to such humiliation. He begged Mogang to think of a way to help them out.

"Frank was very much a spendthrift. He wasn't one of the super-rich Sephardi; he was a money broker of sorts. But he lived high. He rented six penthouse units in Haycourt, which was a luxury apartment building, just for himself, his brother, and his father. Typical Shanghai buffoonery behaviour – pretending to be richer than he really was. The Eliases had neither the status nor the influence to get the appropriate connections to help them. Both brothers were bachelors then; Edmund married an Englishwoman when he travelled to England after the war.

"Our house was in the French Concession on Avenue Joffre in Nongtang, or Lane, #1390. We had a huge place, three-stories with fifteen bedrooms and five modern bathrooms fitted with the latest fixtures and so on. It was the equivalent of three ordinary houses. The best part was that the Japanese soldiers were not likely to come knocking on our door to search for Jews. Mogang assigned two suites on the third floor to Frank, his father, a nurse, and a houseboy. They were to stay inside at all times. Before we left for Anhui, all the servants were instructed to provide the guests with everything they needed and to look after them during their stay. Frank and his father lived quite comfortably there for close to two years, hosting drinking or poker parties and entertaining friends quite frequently.

"As for Edmund, he was unlucky. He was caught by a soldier when he went home the day after the proclamation came into effect. He ended up in Hongkew. After a good part of a year, he managed to obtain a day pass – he probably bribed someone. He left the ghetto and never returned. They all stayed at our house till the Japanese surrendered in August 1945. By then we were also back from Anhui."

"What would have been the penalty if the Japanese officials were to find out that Jews were hiding in your home?" Thomas asked.

"I have no idea. I don't think Mogang ever considered such a possibility. In hindsight, I realize it was a rather risky undertaking. We could all have ended up in jail, I suppose, or worse. But then, I don't think there were that many cases of Jews hiding in Chinese households."

"Well, we didn't hide the Jews in our house, but about half a dozen of them came regularly to our house during the last year of the war," Linny said.

"Why?" asked Thomas.

"In 1943, the Japanese proclaimed that all shortwave radios were to be handed over to them. They forbade people to listen to Western media, the BBC, or Voice of America. My father handed in his shortwave radio, but kept another very good radio in his bedroom. A friend of his knew how to install a shortwave receiver and did it for him. My father listened to the BBC or VOA most nights.

"As the war in Europe deteriorated for Hitler, father's Jewish friends were anxious to know what was happening. So, almost every two weeks or so, Horace Kadoorie, Benjamin Sassoon, Eric Myres, Freddie Goldstein, and some others would arrive at our house in the evening and stay till quite late."

"I remember that every time these people came the atmosphere was kind of tense and mysterious, and we children were sent to bed quickly. The guests were ushered right into my father's bedroom, where they sat on the lounge or the bed to listen to the radio," Rhae interjected.

"The first couple of times I had no idea what was going on," continued Linny. "Later I found out from my amah, Ming. Rhae and Yvette will remember our house in Yong Quan Fang. The gates of the complex, where our house was, faced the gates of the City West Secondary School across the street. That school was occupied by the Japanese military. Day and night, two Japanese soldiers with bayonets and a huge Alsatian dog patrolled back and forth in front of the gates . . ."

"I remember that vividly. None of the children from Yong Quan Fang would walk past the school gates. We always crossed over to our side of the street to avoid the soldiers and the dog," said Yvette, before Linny continued:

"Because the soldiers were always there, all cars and pedestrians coming into or leaving our complex were watched closely. We all felt we were under constant scrutiny. One wrong move and we could face severe consequences. There had been instances where the Japanese soldiers barged into our complex demanding information or explanation.

"Father was extremely cautious. He wouldn't want the soldiers to take note that there were foreigners coming to our house on a regular basis. He would send Niu-Niu, the chauffeur, to fetch his Jewish friends after dark, so it was not as noticeable who was in the car. Then there would be a special set-up in the living room that would help to explain why those guests were in the house, if the Japanese should pay a surprise visit."

"This is very intriguing. How come I didn't know any of this?" said Adele.

"You were too young. You wouldn't remember even if you saw everything. Besides, you were usually already in bed when the guests arrived," explained Linny. She went on.

"The maids would set up a poker table in the living room on the ground floor, and a few decks of cards with one deck spread out on the table, gambling chips, cognac snifters, cigars, and ashtrays. Even the gramophone was ready to be cranked. But the guests didn't play cards or listen to records. They had maybe one drink, and then headed straight to father's bedroom on the second floor.

"The cook, Ah Fang, would then be sent to the front gates to strike up a casual conversation with Junior San, the security guard, and chat with him for some time. He might even bring a bottle of Mao Tai to share with Junior San. The idea was to post him there to watch the soldiers across the street. Should there be any suspicious looks, movements, or actions, he would hurry back to the house and alert my father and his friends, and all of them would come down to the living room and take up their places at the poker table, smoking and drinking, pretending they were having a good time.

"Luckily, there was never any mishap. Amah Ming, Ah Fang, and the other four servants were all so loyal they would never have breathed a word of this to anyone.

"Because of the shortwave radio, Father and his friends heard about the latest happenings about twelve hours ahead of most people. Often war news was censored by the Japanese, and the general public never came to hear it. The night they heard that the Japanese had unconditionally surrendered, they were ecstatic. They went wild like little kids, laughing, cheering, shouting, hugging, and crying. It was so emotional. Then they went downstairs to the living room and started celebrating – emptied three bottles of Hennessy XO cognac and two bottles of Glenfiddich single-malt Scotch. They stayed till almost dawn, too excited to sleep."

Hearing that, Auntie Ellie said excitedly, "When news broke the next day, the entire city went crazy. Everyone was out on the street, jubilant that they were finally rid of the Japanese yoke of eight long years. We had just come back from Anhui about a week prior. We were certain that the war was going to end soon when the Americans dropped the atomic bombs in Japan, so we left Anhui. We were so happy to be home!"

Linny spoke again. "I remember father took us for a ride to the Hongkew area the next day. Eight of us squeezed into his Pontiac. Father drove, mother and I sat in the front, and the four of you and Aunt Dinni sat in the back. When we got close to the Garden Bridge, the traffic was impossible, with throngs of pedestrians and lines of cars barely moving. It was slower than a snail's pace but no one minded. Everyone was euphoric.

"On some streets, Japanese women knelt on both sides of the street with their belongings spread out in front of them on the pavement, hoping to sell them before they were returned to Japan. They were humbled and sad. It was a pitiful sight. Many wept as some Chinese spat on them or kicked them to let out the anger that had been bottled up over the eight years under Japanese oppression. That scene is burned into my memory. I felt very sorry for them.

"Father thought it was better not to leave the car, so we circled around the area and came home. It was an unforgettable afternoon.

"Later we were told that some Jews spat on Captain Ghoya and were cheered by all. One person even hit him.* Father remarked that no amount of insults or injury could ever make up for all the unfair treatment Ghoya had inflicted on the Jewish refugees."

"Did you girls go to Hongkew during the occupation?" asked Thomas.

"I don't recall visiting the area. Definitely not after it was designated a refugee ghetto when Japanese soldiers were everywhere," answered Linny. "You see, we were constantly cautioned not to be anywhere near any Japanese. It was common knowledge that the Japanese soldiers had a tendency to look for 'flower maidens.' We young girls would be prime targets.

"We did, however, go to the French Concession for Russian food. That was when we were first introduced to non-Chinese cuisine. Oh, pardon me, actually the first non-Chinese food Rhae and I tasted was Japanese food. Rhae and I were taken to a real Japanese restaurant once, could even be in Hongkew. We all sat on tatami mats with our shoes off and were served by geishas.

"But we went to the Russian restaurants more often. We called it the 'Big Feast,' or 'da cang.'* It always started with borscht, and the second course was always a fish, followed by a main course and dessert. For some reason I don't remember any of the main courses or even the desserts. Maybe we were full after the fish course."

"I don't even remember the fish. Only the soup. I loved it. So rich and tasty," said Rhae. "I vaguely recall a Fieker Café Restaurant on Avenue Joffre. The name stayed with me because it sounded like 'flying guest' in Chinese. Aunt Dinni said it was an Austrian Jewish restaurant. Very well-known. It was not just the Jews who frequented it, but all the other foreigners too. As a matter of fact, Chinese celebrities like Madam Sun Yatsen and her sister Madam Chiang Kaishek used to go there as well. Now I haven't the faintest idea what we ate there. Isn't it weird that I remember the name of the restaurant and not the food."

"Shanghai being such a cosmopolitan city in those days, you girls, including Auntie Ellie, were lucky to be exposed to many cultures early on in your lives," remarked Thomas.

"I've often thought about that," responded Yvette. "I sometimes wonder, if the Japanese had not ghettoized all the refugees in one area, would we have had more interactions with the refugee children, and they with us, and become better acquainted with each other's cultures. It would have been marvellous if the refugee children had picked up some Chinese culture or language and we some of theirs. From the books I read, almost all the children had no opportunity to learn Chinese, neither language nor culture. It was too bad. Some were in Shanghai for over ten years and remained totally segregated."

"I doubt if they would have attended the same schools as we did. For one thing, their parents would have insisted on them learning their religion and their own culture first. They would have attended the Jewish schools. For another, the schools in Shanghai were not free. Some tuition fees were quite high; not many of the refugees would have been able to afford it." Linny added, "However, there might have been more social interaction, which would have benefited both of us, I'm sure."

"From all accounts, the Jewish diaspora community in Shanghai, Russian, Austrian, or German, had an exceptionally vibrant cultural life. It was incredible that their creativity blossomed under such adverse conditions," said Rhae as she fingered through a pad of notes in front of her and pulled out a piece of paper covered with writing. "Yesterday, I jotted down some notes on their intellectual and cultural activities during the refugee years.

"There were a lot of publications – newspapers, magazines, books, even a calendar, or Almanac. *Our Life* was an influential periodical, whose founding editor was David B. Rabinovich. It was edited in English, Yiddish, and Russian. Impressive, eh! Ossie Lewin from Germany was the chair of the European Jewish Artists Society. He founded and edited the *Shanghai Jewish Chronicle*, which in November 1945 changed its name to the *Shanghai Echo*. It ran from 1939 to 1949 and was the longest-running Jewish newspaper in China. Sorry, I have to clarify. It was the longest-running refugee-founded-and-operated paper. To differentiate, there was *Israel's Messenger*, an influential publication that had a great impact on the Shanghai Jews as well as on Jews in the Far East in general. It was founded by wealthy Serphardi Jews, N.E.B. Ezra, M. Myers, and L. A. Levis, and lasted for more than three decades, from 1904 to 1936.

"Then there was the *8-Uhr Abenblatt*, or *8 O'Clock Evening News*, a German newspaper run by the Central European Jews and the semi-monthly *Gelbe Post*, or *Yellow Post*, founded and edited by Adolf Joseph Storfer. Yet another eminent Jewish scholar, Y. Tonn, founded *Asian Seminar*; he was devoted to adult education.

"As far as books go, *Selected Short Stories by Jewish Authors* was published in 1943. *Farvoglte Yidu*, meaning *Wandering Jews*, was a Yiddish title, also published during World War Two.

"These cover only part of the literary output. I was surprised to read that a certain Horst Levin actually managed to secure a spot on the local radio and hosted a regular program on XMHA.

"There were also countless outstanding performances of plays and concerts, most of which took place at the Lyceum Theatre, which was the best western-style theatre in Shanghai. The performances were for fundraising purposes. They had a Refugee Orchestra, with many string players and not enough woodwind and brass players. The violinist Alfred Wittenberg was so revered he became a professor at the Shanghai Conservatory of Music. He stayed in Shanghai till his death in 1953. The Italian Jewish violinist and conductor Arrigo Foa and the German cellist Walter Joachim were in Shanghai for a long time too. Another prominent Jewish composer Aaron Avshalomov was born in Siberia and lived in China for thirty years, mostly in Shanghai.

"And there were artists, cartoonists . . . A painter by the name of David Bloch gave himself the Chinese name of White-Green-Black (白绿黑) – based on the pronunciation of his last name in Chinese. The Austrian painter Friedrich Schiff became quite well known after the war.

"The city was brimming with talent. It was such a shame that they did not receive a wider exposure, so that a broader audience could appreciate their accomplishments.

"In particular, I want to single out Karl Steiner. Steiner was a apostle of Arnold Schoenberg, the musician and artist and the leader of the Second Vienna School, who developed the 'twelve-tone' method of music composition that influenced many twentieth-century musicologists and critics, including composers like Anton Webern, Alben Berg, and Canada's Glenn Gould. Steiner too taught at the Shanghai National Conservatory of Music."

Linny took up the topic, "It's interesting that, in the same way the Shanghai art world was and still is very connected to Paris, the Shanghai music scene definitely has strong ties to the German-Austrian school of music. I imagine that a lot has to be attributed to these refugee musicians who taught at the conservatory in Shanghai, handing down their heritage to their pupils there. Remember our piano teacher in Shanghai, Mrs. Diao? Her music teacher Mario Paci, who was the conductor of the Shanghai Municipal Symphony Orchestra, traced his music lineage all the way back to Liszt. So our training must also be quite Germanic. That may explain why Rhae is so fond of Bach's music."

"Quite so," said Rhae. "But I think the Shanghai music scene was also very much influenced by the Russian school of music. I remember our cousin Josephine and a few of my schoolmates all had Russian piano teachers."

Then picking up from what she was saying before, Rhae continued, "Anyway, after the war, Steiner came to Montreal, along with other refugee musicians from Shanghai – Julius Schloss, Franz Kraemer, the Joachim brothers, and others. Steiner taught at the McGill Conservatory of Music from 1964 to 1989. My friend Sylvia studied under him for years. Steiner died in 2001. I want to mention him because of his Canadian connection. I often wonder how many of the Shanghai Jewish refugees ended up in Canada."

"A few at least, I guess," said Adele. "Last December I was at an old synagogue on Bellevue Avenue near Dundas Street for the launch of a book entitled *Shanghai Escape*, by Canadian author Kathy Kacer, published by Second Story Press. The book is based on the true personal experience of Lily Toufar, who left Vienna with her parents on the eve of Kristallnacht, November 8, 1938, to go to Shanghai. They lived there for ten years. In 1948 they received visas to go to South America. En route to their destination, they stopped over in Toronto to visit their relatives and they never left. Lily and her family were at the launch. I felt quite emotional when I shook her hand and I couldn't find the right words to say to her."

"I'm sure there are many others," said Linny. "The only thing is that most of these survivors are all quite elderly by now. In their seventies? Eighties? Even older?"

Thomas, who had been listening intently, spoke up. "Can I backtrack a little? From what all of you were saying, I gather there were three waves of Jews that came to Shanghai: the Baghdad Sephardi – very wealthy, the Russian Ashkenazi – comfortable middle class, and the Central European Jews – the poor and deprived."

"That's correct," replied Rhae. "But if you really want to be technical, there were four waves. The refugees from Europe can be split into two groups: the Central European Jews from Germany and Austria and the Eastern European Jews from Poland and Lithuania.

"The reason I say that is because from what I gathered I understand that the ones who really suffered the most were the German and Austrian Jews. They were absolutely destitute when they arrived in Shanghai. The Polish and Lithuanian Jews were among the last group to arrive in 1941. Because there had been a Polish government in exile represented by Ambassador Tadeusz Romer for a period of time, the Polish Jews had some kind of 'backing,' so to speak. They did not want to be grouped with the 'stateless refugees,' because they claimed they were Polish nationals and should be counted as 'enemy aliens' instead.

"They were able to receive support from a number of Polish organizations, such as EastJewCom (the Committee for Assistance of Jewish Refugees from Eastern Europe), the Council of American Rabbis, the Polish Aid Society, and the Russian Jews. Other funds were funnelled by the Polish government in London via the international Red Cross. During the first two years they were in Shanghai, they did not try very hard to settle down and make a living. Instead, they were hopeful that the war would soon end and their government would help to transfer them back to Poland.

"There were about a thousand of them. The largerst portion of that group were the academics, including members of various yeshivas, such as the entire Mir Yeshiva of about 250 members and others. They were much better off than those from Germany and Austria."*

"That is very interesting, Rhae. But right now my question lies elsewhere," said Thomas as he turned to Ellie and asked, "Auntie Ellie, you mentioned that many other wealthy Jews in Shanghai went through a difficult period with cash-flow problems. Can you tell us more about these people? Who were they? Any other personal friends besides the Kadoories and the Eliases?"

Auntie Ellie pondered for a moment, and Yvette said, "Let's take five. I want fresh coffee and some snacks."

Everyone left the table to stretch their legs and headed for the kitchen.

Chapter 20

Sassoon and Hardoon

A fresh glass of Bi Luo Chun was brewed for Auntie Ellie, and she took a few leisurely sips. When everyone was back at the table, she picked up from where she left off.

"I can name a few well-known Sephardic* Jews – the Ezras, Solomons, Abrahams, Shamoons; they all used to work for the Sassoons, and later struck out on their own. But, no, I did not socialize with any of the others personally. My father might have had dealings with them, but not Mogang or me. The three names that most people in Shanghai would recognize are Sassoon, Hardoon, and Kadoorie.

"The Sassoons were huge. There were two Sassoon companies – David Sassoon and Sons, commonly known as the Old Sassoon Company, and E.D. Sassoon, known as the New Sassoon Company. It was founded by David Sassoon's grandson Sir Jacob Elias Sassoon.

"David Sassoon was born in Baghdad in the late eighteenth century. It was said that he was the son of a wealthy banker, Saleh Sassoon, who was the treasurer or a minister to the then-governor of Baghdad. When the governor was overthrown, Saleh took his family and travelled to Bombay, now Mumbai, in India. David Sassoon became a member of the East India Company, the British trading arm in India, and for a short time was granted sole monopoly rights to all manufactured cotton goods, silk, and opium.

"David Sassoon and Sons was first established in Bombay, in the early nineteenth century, and a branch was set up in Shanghai in the mid-nineteenth century. In the beginning, it mainly traded cotton goods for China's tea. China, however, did not want cotton goods or any other merchandise like Wedgwood pottery or woolen products exported by Britain. China asked for silver in return. Queen Victoria didn't want Britain's insatiable thirst for Chinese tea to deplete Britain's silver reserve. The large trade deficit* became a major concern to Queen Victoria, who decided to forcibly export opium from India to China. David Sassoon earned his huge barrel of gold from trading of a product that was banned by the Qing government."

Upon hearing the mention of opium, Adele jumped in. "There is a recent perspective on the Opium War, based more on supposition than supportable evidence. It is interesting nevertheless. Sorry, Auntie Ellie, please let me break in for a minute.

"We all know that the most ridiculous and unacceptable part about the first Opium War was that Britain refused to recognize China's anti-opium laws as legally binding. Hence the wars and all the unfair treaties China had to sign.

"In most of the historic writings, it says that the Scotsman William Jardine was the principal player, who went to London and lobbied the then-foreign secretary, Lord Palmerston, to order the British fleet to China. Jardine's company, Jardine Matheson and Company, held a quarter share of the opium imported into China. The company profited enormously from the opium trade. Incidentally, the company still exists and, with its subsidiaries, operates in Hong Kong and all over the East.

"'But since the repatriation of Hong Kong in 1997, more and more people are pointing a finger at the Sassoons as being the culprits who prompted the British throne and the British parliament to send troops to China.

"True enough, the Sassoons made tons of money from opium trades. The end of opium importing into China would have cost them dearly. Also true was the fact they had strong ties to both the British royalty and the British parliament. They were known as the 'Rothschilds of the East' and were notably powerful in England. But most official records do not name them as the instigators of the war, even though they stood to gain enormously from the outcome. I thought that was interesting."

"I question the validity of such an accusation. Last year I read a book *Flowers in the Blood* by Gay Courter. It is a historic fiction, with the main plot woven around a member of the Sassoon family in Calcutta. The book mentioned that the Sassoons did not suffer much loss when Lin Zexu, the emperor's envoy to deal with the opium problem in Canton, burned all the opium shipped by the British merchants. It says that Jardine & Matheson Co. was the big loser. So it would make more sense that Jardine would be the one who would lobby for British military intervention. But then, this book is a novel. The Sassoon family in the book was based in Calcutta, not Bombay." Rhae expressed her opinion on this issue.

"I do remember that one of father's friends was a Sassoon. Benjamin Sassoon. I think he was a nephew of Victor Sassoon, wasn't he?" asked Yvette.

"Yes, Uncle Sassy, we used to call him," answered Linny. "He was quite dark with tight curly hair. I think all of us remember his two German-shepherd dogs. They were huge. We were terrified of them.

"He left almost immediately after the war for San Francisco. When I went to Los Angeles in 1957, I stopped over in San Francisco and visited him. He received me warmly. I spent a night at his house. His assistant from Shanghai, Lillo, and her husband shared the house with him."

"So sorry to have butted in like that, Auntie Ellie. I wanted to bring up this new interpretation," apologized Adele.

"Quite all right, Adele," replied Auntie Ellie. "It was interesting to hear what you said about the new perspective on the First Opium War. Come to think of it, it does make some sense. Whether or not the Sassoons were responsible for Britain's sending the fleet, they certainly benefited from the consequences.

"The Sassoons became very big in Shanghai. Sir Jacob Sassoon built the Ohel Rachel Synagogue* in the twenties in memory of his deceased wife. I think this synagogue is still standing.

"Sir Victor Sassoon built a chain of apartment blocks and hotels, as well as his Tudor-style country house, which has the Shanghai Zoo beside it now. And, of course, there were the Sassoons' famous Peace Hotel, originally called the Cathay Hotel, and the Embankment House, an Art Deco block on Suzhou Creek.

"Apart from what Linny said about Benjamin Sassoon, I heard that Victor Sassoon, the one who was injured in the First World War, left Shanghai in 1941 and sold most of his holdings in Shanghai and India in the late forties. All proceeds were transferred to the Bahamas. I believe he lived in the Bahamas till his death in the sixties. I have no idea if his descendants still live there. He was not married when he lived in Shanghai.

"The Sassoons preferred to employ Jews to work for them. David Sassoon was the one who brought many of the other Sephardi to Shanghai. Kadoorie used to work for them. So did Hardoon, who at one stage was known as the richest Jew in the Far East."

"Any information on the Hardoons?" asked Thomas.

"Plenty!" volunteered Linny. "His life was fascinating. I read an article online, written by Katya Knyazeva: '*Silas Hardoon: Opium Dealer, Rent Collector and Once the Richest Man in Asia.*' She described Hardoon as one of the most colourful members of Shanghai's Jewish community and 'something like a precursor to Warren Buffet combined with Caligula.' Get the picture, Tom?

"Here is also a sixty-page booklet in Chinese on the life of Silas Hardoon. Have Adele translate it for you if you wish; I'll give you the gist of it now." Linny handed Thomas a little booklet with no title on its white cover and continued, "But, with no publication information or bibliography, I wonder how dependable it is. I take the content with a grain of salt.

"The author is not very kind to Hardoon. Among the Sephardi Jews, Hardoon was probably the best known to most ordinary Shanghai residents. His full name was Silas Aaron Hardoon. He was born in Baghdad in 1851 into a poor family.

His father used to work for David Sassoon in Turkey. When he was five, the family moved to Bombay, where Hardoon himself later worked briefly for David Sassoon. He came to Shanghai on his own in his early twenties and stayed in Shanghai for sixty years. He was eighty-one when he died in 1931.

"In the beginning he worked as a clerk at the Old Sassoon Company. Because he was smart and very astute in business, he soon became a senior staff member in charge of rental real estate and all lease agreements. In his thirties, he joined Victor Sassoon's New Sassoon Company at a managerial level and stayed there for more than ten years. He looked after both the real-estate sector and the opium trade of the company.

"He founded his own company at the beginning of the twentieth century, while still working for Sassoon. Every penny he saved he invested in real estate or land. To give you some idea of the kind of gains that land speculators made, Stella Dong's* book on Shanghai says that an investment of fifty British pounds in land in 1850 was the equivalent of something like twenty-thousand British pounds by 1862 – 400 per cent in twelve years.

"Hardoon's company also dealt in opium. People described him as having a sharp mind, with a good sense of what was coming in the future. They also described him as swift to take action and ruthless. Due to his business acumen, every time there was a crisis and property values plummeted, he would buy at a low price, both for himself and for his boss, Victor Sassoon, mostly in the International Settlement area. He became the 'real-estate king' of Shanghai.

"Around 1911, he left E.D. Sassoon and Company to concentrate on managing his immense real-estate empire, which consisted of enormous amount of land, residential apartment buildings, office blocks, hotels, and warehouses. His tenants loathed him, because, in the early days, he used to go personally to collect rent and would badger any tenant who was even one day late in paying. According to some, he also insisted on collecting rent based on the Chinese lunar calendar, which would give him an extra month every so many years. As you know, the Chinese lunar calendar is a lunisolar calendar which, in order to synchronize with solar calendar, has a thirteenth month every few years.

"Several things set Hardoon apart from the rest of the Sephardi. He married a Eurasian prostitute, Liza Luo Jialing. Some claimed that Liza Luo's French father, Issac Roos, a sailor, was in fact Jewish, but that was never verified. Purportedly, Liza's father left and her mother died when she was very young. She had to struggle for survival. She lived in a poor lane house, supposedly owned by Hardoon, who met her while collecting rent. They were married within weeks of their first meeting. From then on Liza influenced Hardoon in everything he did.

Liza Luo considered herself totally Chinese. She was heart and soul into Buddhism and she was a very manipulative person. She managed to steer Hardoon towards Buddhism. So devout were they that every winter they would join all the monks and nuns, who lived on the compound of their residence 'Hardoon Gardens,' also known as 'Aili Garden,' for a month-long abstinence from eating meat. Liza Luo would spend the whole month in prayer.

"Liza also influenced Hardoon to embrace a Chinese lifestyle. He was more integrated into the Chinese culture and society than any of his fellow Sephardi. However, it was not integration into the the world of ordinary people, but that of the privileged class.

"Hardoon's marriage turned out to be vastly beneficial to him. His wife led him to important connections. It is hard to believe, but a well-known prostitute of that period, especially an Eurasian woman, would very likely be well-connected to the rich and the powerful. With Liza as his cultural coach, Hardoon was able to access connections, first to the Qing court and later to the presidents of the Republic government, harnessing important liaisons with many prominent personages. He befriended powerful gang leaders as well.

"Hardoon always valued connections. As soon as he arrived in Shanghai, he went to register with the British Consulate, seeking protection. Later, he did the same with the French Consulate. Through his wife's grasp of the nuances of Chinese culture and protocol, Hardoon was able to reach the highest echelon in the Chinese government. So much so that, during the last years of the Qing rule, the palace actually sent him gifts of eunuchs to be his servants. Liza and Hardoon spared nothing in maintaining their connections – lavish entertaining, expensive gifts, or generous philanthropic donations to certain Chinese-Buddhist causes. They were never miserly.

"But that was only towards those with whom they cared to associate. Towards their subordinates and servants, they were cruel and unforgiving. Liza, in particular, behaved as if she were the Empress Dowager Cixi – totally without compassion, and at times almost inhuman in her punishment of the servants. Hearsay has it that Liza actually whipped two bondmaids to death for displeasing her or disobeying her orders.

"The Hardoon Garden, their residence, was legendary. It sat on about twenty-eight acres of land that had some eighty scenic points of interest. There were pagodas, pavilions, a Buddhist shrine, and rooms for sutra-reading, plus ponds, bridges, and more than eight thousand trees, maintained by more than two hundred workers. About ten Buddhist monks and ten Buddhist nuns were housed permanently on the compound. They spent their days chanting prayers for the master and the mistress.

"In the lunar seventh month of 1917, when Hardoon was 66 and Liza 54, they decided to celebrate their joint age of 120. For twenty days they entertained their friends and associates. Food was catered by three restaurants, plus their own kitchen. It was estimated that over a hundred thousand meals were served. Guests were invited to watch magic shows, opera performances, storytelling sessions, acrobatic performances . . . The scale of the celebration was unprecedented.

"When Hardoon died in June 1931, overnight all of Hardoon Garden was painted white for mourning.* From the entrance to the main house, seven different orchestras or bands played for the visitors. Apart from rabbis, monks from several famous temples brought dozens of their disciples with them to pray for Hardoon's soul. So did the Muslim Qur'an scholars from the Yong He Palace of Beijing.

"It was estimated that Hardoon's estate was worth something to the tune of one hundred fifty million U.S. dollars in 1931. Mind-boggling in those days. This booklet says that his coffin cost forty thousand dollars and the marble headstone installed in Hardoon Garden cost well over five thousand. Hardoon's burial on his own property scandalized the Jewish community. Not too long after Hardoon's death, Hardoon Garden was burned down. Liza died in 1941, and her funeral expenses were just as extravagant as her husband's.

"Interestingly enough, Hardoon was not as generous with the Jewish community as he was with the Chinese. He did, however, build the Beth Aharon Synagogue in 1927. By the time the synagogue was put to special use, from 1941 onward, both Hardoon and Liza were dead. The vaults of Beth Aharon housed hundreds of Jewish refugees, while the large sanctuary accommodated the three-hundred-odd rabbinical students from Belaurus and Mir Yeshiva, so that they could continue their studies. The synagogue was torn down in 1985. It was a real shame!

"Liza and Hardoon had no natural children of their own. Liza adopted a number of Chinese children, and Hardoon adopted ten or eleven non-Chinese children, mostly of Russian origin. On Liza's death, the British authorities took many chests of valuables and possessions from the Hardoon residence. The Japanese authorities cleaned up the rest.

"Their adopted son George Hardoon inherited most of the properties and assets. In 1948, when he tried to raise the rents tenfold, it caused such an uproar among his tenants that they refused to comply. Shortly afterwards George Hardoon moved to Hong Kong, before the Communists took over Shanghai in 1949.

"In the 1950s the PRC government built the Sino-Soviet Friendship Hall on the former Hardoon Garden site. Now it is the Shanghai Exhibition Centre.

"One of Hardoon's adopted sons now lives in Toronto. He is in his eighties. Don't know his name."

"You're a good storyteller, Linny," commented Thomas when Linny concluded her narrative on Silas Hardoon. "This has been a productive afternoon. Another chapter of history opened up for me. I certainly enjoyed listening to Auntie Ellie's take on the Japanese occupation of Shanghai. Personal anecdotes are always fascinating. And all of yours too. I didn't realize that you all went through quite a bit during your early years. One more question . . ."

"What about?" asked Adele.

"Auntie Ellie, you talked about the Russian Jews arriving in Shanghai. But you didn't mention why they left Harbin. From what I understand the Russian Jews had settled comfortably there in the early 1900s. Why did they leave?" said Thomas.

Rhae put up her hand.

"I can give you a bit of information there. I just finished reading *The Jews in Harbin*, loaned to me by my friend Harriet Morton. You're right. The Harbin Jewish community from around 1910 to 1920 was the largest Jewish community in the Far East. At that time Russia leased a concession of Manchuria to build the Chinese Eastern Railway, which was an extension of the Trans-Siberian Railway. The tzar, wanting economic growth along the railway line, had allowed Jews to migrate to Manchuria without restrictions. In 1879, the first Jew arrived in Harbin and within five years there was a total of about eight thousand. For a while, the Jews enjoyed a peaceful life in Harbin and suffered no discrimination. They built schools, a cemetery, a library, a hospital, and two synagogues. So rich was their cultural life, Harbin became known as the 'City of Music.'

"Then, with the Bolshevik Revolution and the civil war that followed, many anti-Semitic White Russians also arrived in Harbin, and trouble began between them and the Jews. In 1928, there was an economic crisis, because of the transfer of the railway rights to the Chinese government, and this drove some of the Jews out of Harbin, but not in large numbers. It was after the Japanese occupation of Manchuria in 1931 and the founding of Manchukuo in 1932 that the fascist White

Russians and the Japanese jointly targeted the Jewish community once again. The Jews suffered expropriation of property, kidnapping, extortion, torture, and even murder at their hands. The persecution was so bad that the Jews began to leave en masse . By 1937, of the up to twenty thousand Jews that had been in Harbin, only about five thousand remained. Some went to Tianjing and the rest headed for Shanghai."

"Ah! that explains it. It was just a little bit of a missing piece in my mind," said Thomas. "Thanks for the clarification, Rhae."

"It was fun reading up on it," replied Rhae. She looked at her watch. "We did accomplish a lot in one afternoon. I think we deserve a good meal. What say you?"

"If we don't have anything more to add, I'm all ready for a scrumptious meal," said Adele. "Where?"

"Let me book a table at the Mandarin Golf and Country Club. It's less crowded and less noisy there. And the food is reasonably good," Rhae replied.

"Excellent choice!" said Yvette. "Let me call Sheryl to see if she can join us. I'm sure she's finished with whatever she was doing. She'll be sorry that she missed this afternoon's session."

Yvette took out her cell phone to make the call.

Sheryl arrived at the golf club before the rest of the group. She sat at the table and waited.

Compared to most private golf clubs, the Mandarin Dining Room was modest in size, with simple, elegant décor. There were about seventy seats. The windows offered a vista of the golf course, and the room was bright and airy. This was the only golf and country club in Ontario that was owned by mostly Hong Kong immigrants.

Sheryl was filled in on the proceedings of the afternoon. She genuinely felt sorry that she had not been there to participate. During the course of the dinner, they rehashed some of the points and argued over some other issues until Linny's cell phone rang.

The call was from her son Wes in New York. Wes was a sculptor, a web designer who held a professorship at one of the universities. The second generation had been kept abreast of what their parents had been doing and researching. Among them, Wes and Rhae's son, Neal, also living in New York, were the two most interested in the family's possible lineage from the Kaifeng Jews.

Wes's call was to inform everyone that he had just sent in his DNA for analysis; the result would be back in a few weeks. He was curious to find out his ancestral makeup.

"That reminds me," said Adele upon hearing the news. "Auntie Muriel called from San Francisco the other day. She was offered a discount deal for three DNA analyses. Her daughters are not keen on doing theirs; only her granddaughter Denise and she are game for it. She asked if I wanted to be the third person. I'll be sending mine in once I receive the package from her."

"That'll be super!" Sheryl said enthusiastically. "We'll have analyses from three generations. We can compare them. If need be, I wouldn't mind having mine done."

"Sounds like fun." said Yvette.

"The more I think about it – that is, our possible Jewish ancestry – the more I feel like taking a trip to Kaifeng to see how things are with the remaining Jewish descendants there. My good friend Grant Guo, the news anchor at Rogers OMNI

Television, is from Kaifeng. When he heard about my interests in the Kaifeng Jews, he put me in touch with his sister, Guo Changying, who is a professor at Henan University. Grant thinks his sister can arrange for me to meet one or more of the contemporary researchers on the history of the Kaifeng Jews. That's pretty exciting. I wouldn't want to miss this opportunity.

"I may then go to Shanghai to revisit some of the Jewish sites as well as dropping in on our Uncle Charles. He's ninety-eight now, isn't he? I wouldn't mind chatting a bit with him about the war, if not particularly about the Jewish issue. Last year when I had lunch with him, he told me a lot about our maternal grandfather, Yan Shulong. It was fascinating! Uncle Charles still takes walks every day and reads a lot of history books. I'm amazed that his eyesight and his hearing are still as sharp as can be at his age."

"Let me know if you need me to collect your mail when you're away," offered Sheryl.

"Thanks, Sheryl. I'll let everyone know once I have an itinerary," replied Rhae.

Kaifeng, Shanghai, and New York City

———•———

2013

心在清涼中

Chapter 21

Kaifeng

Rhae stopped over in Beijing to spend a few days with her colleagues in the film industry. Wang Damin, her co-producer of a television drama series a few years before, had planned her Kaifeng itinerary and arranged for a reliable chauffeur, Jian, to pick her up at the Zhengzhou Airport, the closest one to Kaifeng.

It was Rhae's first trip to Henan Province. There was a lot to learn.

Henan covers a large portion of the fertile North China Plain. It was the cradle of Chinese civilization and its history goes back five thousand years. The Xia Dynasty (2100 BCE to 1600 BCE approximately), China's first and largely legendary dynasty, was established within the boundaries of present-day Henan Province. Many of the capitals of the subsequent Shang Dynasty (1600 BCE to 1100 BCE approximately) were in this province. Shang was the first literate dynasty of China. Its last and most important capital, Yin – modern-day Anyang – was where Chinese writing first came into being.

From the Shang Dynasty onward, Henan remained China's cultural, economic, and political centre until the eleventh century. Four of China's eight great ancient capitals – Luoyang, Anyang, Kaifeng, and Zhengzhou – were all located within Henan. The other four were Xi'An in Shaanxi Province, Beijing in Hebei Province, Nanjing in Jiangsu Province, and Hangzhou in Zejiang Province.

Zhengzhou, about a one-hour drive from Kaifeng, had become the capital of Henan Province in 1954, replacing Kaifeng. The airport was relatively new and therefore well-equipped with the latest technology. Impressive, Rhae murmured to herself as her eyes scanned the architecture. Service was fast and friendly.

Amidst a sea of placards with personal or corporate names on them, Rhae spotted the chauffeur, Jian, holding one with her Chinese name on it. Rhae was used to meeting her drivers this way, both in China and in Europe.

The highway from Zhengzhou to Kaifeng was also newly constructed and looked like a North American superhighway. The signage was bilingual, but here it was in Chinese and English. Impressive! Rhae muttered a second time. There was hardly any traffic. She lay back and enjoyed the leisurely ride, chatting occasionally with Jian about what was going on in Kaifeng.

There had been no lack of tourists who were interested in the early Jewish settlement in this city. In the last decade or so, a few universities in China had begun to offer Jewish Studies in their curriculum. Consequently, there had been a resurgence of interest in the Kaifeng Jewish community of the past. Organized groups, mostly from North America, came to visit Kaifeng, purely for the purpose of learning about this piece of history. Jian knew exactly what Rhae was interested in. He promised to make the necessary arrangements for Rhae to meet some of the remaining families of Jewish descent.

As soon as she checked in at the hotel, Rhae called Professor Guo Changying at Henan University. Professor Guo came to the hotel almost immediately, accompanied by her colleague Professor Liu Bailu.

Rhae was delighted to meet Professor Liu in person. Professor Liu had done a great deal of research on the ancient Kaifeng Chinese Jews. His specialty was the study of the four Kaifeng Jewish steles, on which he did his Master's thesis. Rhae was looking forward to hearing more about the steles from him. Professor Liu was also one of the four editor-compilers of the book *Gudai Kaifeng Youtairen, or The Ancient Kaifeng Jews*, which had been published in November 2011 by the People's Publisher and Distributor of Beijing. Professor Guo had sent Rhae a copy of the book as soon as it was published. It was from this book that Rhae had learned about the latest research on many of the issues and points of interest regarding the Kaifeng Jewish community. Rhae found it invaluable in providing an interesting contemporary approach to this ancient community.

The three spent the whole afternoon discussing and exchanging views on the Kaifeng Jews. To add to what Rhae already knew, Professor Liu pointed out that, from 1643 onward, there were large movements of Kaifeng Jews, as entire clans moved to Jiangsu and Zejiang provinces. Did the aftermath of the 1642 flood cause depletion of the community? Professor Liu thought that it was likely, but he and his co-researchers felt the change from the Ming Dynasty to the Qing around 1644 was more of a factor in the Jews' migration out of Kaifeng. The new conquerors, the Manchus, rode in from the northeastern edge of China's border. Sweeping as they did, from north to south and from east to west, they sent droves of people running as they approached a city or a town; the Jews in Kaifeng were no exception. Large numbers went south and southeast to Jiangsu or Zejiang provinces.

They talked about Zhao Yingcheng's unprecedented success at the imperial examinations in 1650 and his subsequent appointment to Xingbu Langzhong, making him the pride and joy of all Kaifeng residents – the Israelites in particular. Professor Liu did not agree with Rhae that the incident was a turning point that marked the acceleration of the Jews' assimilation into Chinese culture. However, he believed that the incident did play one part in the assimilation process, among so many other factors.

Rhae made a mental note that she must discuss these points in more depth with her sisters and brother-in-law.

The discussion moved from the assimilation of the Jews to the influence of Confucianism on Judaism. It was intensive. Rhae felt that her brain was brimming over with ideas. She would need some quiet time later to ruminate on what they had talked about and to sort out her own thoughts.

It had been a busy, non-stop day. Despite the flight, the long ride, and an instant meeting with the professors, Rhae felt invigorated. It was inspiring to be in the place where the people who were possibly her ancestors had settled, lived, and worked for so many centuries.

Early the next morning, Jian came to fetch Rhae from the hotel and they headed to the site of the former synagogue.

The synagogue itself had virtually disappeared around 1864. On the site was a hospital. However, one small corner of one side of the former temple was still in existence, and it was the residence of the Zhao descendants, who kept a sort of Jewish memorial centre.

At the corner of the street was a sign in Hebrew and Chinese pointing to the former location of the synagogue. Passing through a narrow lane, Rhae and Jian arrived at a stone entrance marked "Teach the Torah Lane s. # 21." It led to another lane that took them to the small rooms that had been part of the former Qing Zhen Si.

Ester Guo Yan, a young girl in her twenties, tall and slim, with a fair complexion, came out to greet them. She was a granddaughter of the Zhao clan, her mother being one of five Zhao daughters. Her grandmother – Chi Shuping, widow of Zhao Pingyu – her mother, and she were now occupying the site. The three or four tiny rooms were divided into their living quarters and the *Kaifeng Jewish History Memorial Centre*, of which Ester was the proprietor.

The walls of the centre were covered with Star of David memorabilia, available for various amounts. There were stacks of little leaflets about the history of the Kaifeng Jews, selling for RMB 50.00 each, or approximately $7.00 US (2013). Interpretation of the booklets cost the same amount, as did any discussion with Ester about the Kaifeng Jews. There was a hand-drawn rendition of the layout of the former synagogue and a model that was probably intended to be the Holy of Holies.

Rhae spent some time with Ester's mother and her grandmother, who were delighted that Rhae had the same last name, Zhao.

"And your great-grandfather was from Kaifeng? We must be related!" they insisted excitedly. It was a distinct possibility, Rhae thought. If they were, then this had to be the place where her great-grandfather had lived and grown up. She tried to feel something that spoke to her from the surroundings, but could not. It was interesting that this family also had five daughters, just like her family. As a matter of fact, she noticed the small Shirley Temple dimples in Ester's mother's cheeks, quite similar to her own. It could not be mere coincidence, she speculated. However, even if she tried, she could not come to any definitive conclusion about the possible relationship between this family and hers.

Two of Ester Guo's cousins had studied the Hebrew language and religion and had emigrated to Israel about a year before. Rhae figured that policies in Israel must have changed since the 1980s. Back then, a joint delegation from the United States and Israel had come to Kaifeng to assess if there was a genuine Hebrew community in this city. The conclusion was negative, based on some crucial observations. In China the Jewish lineage was determined according to the father's bloodline, whereas everywhere else the Jewish bloodline goes by matriarchal descent. Then there was the lack of knowledge of the Hebrew religious rites and the absence of observance. The joint delegation could not confirm that the Kaifeng Jewry was a community of genuine Hebrew faith.

Since then, there had been volunteers who came to Kaifeng from the United States and Israel to give instruction on the Hebrew language and religion. It was not clear to Rhae whether those who emigrated from China to Israel were considered as "converts" to Judaism, and were therefore qualified for Israeli immigration, or whether they were treated as descendants of

Israelites of bygone years, and were accepted by Israel for that reason.

Ester also hoped to emigrate at some time in the future. However, she could not quite explain why she wanted to go to Israel. She did not display any discernible interest in the country, nor did she show any enthusiasm about the Hebrew religion. Apart from the content of the leaflets she sold to tourists, mostly about the Kaifeng Jewry, her knowledge about Israel, Jewish history, or Jewish customs was extremely limited. Did she just want to leave China, as so many others do? Or was she genuinely driven by her ancestry to want to seek her roots, Rhae wondered to herself. But for the time being, Ester was happy and enthusiastic about running the centre. It was a good business. Very entrepreneurial, Rhae nodded in silence.

Ester mentioned a fundraising project to build a synagogue, but did not say anything about a concrete plan, details, strategies, or who was involved.

Upon leaving, Rhae picked up a few leaflets and paid accordingly.

Outside, on the main street, Jian pointed out a stone plaque that commemorated the site of the former synagogue, Qing Zhen Si, with a bit of the history of the Kaifeng Jews carved on the reverse side.

Standing there, viewing the plaque, Rhae realized that she was the first of her family to return to this ancient city from which her great-grandparents had embarked on a long journey into an unknown future in the mid-nineteenth century. So much had happened; so much had changed.

Rhae looked around. With its modern cityscape, Kaifeng was no different from most of the twenty-first-century cities in

China. It was difficult for Rhae to envisage an ancient temple standing at the spot. The synagogue had been built in 1163, and had undergone at least a dozen major reconstructions. By the same token, the city itself had undergone many reconstructions as well.

When the Jews first arrived in Kaifeng – the capital at the time – its population was around six hundred thousand, and it was said to be one of the largest cities in the world. During the Ming Dynasty, Kaifeng's population was close to a million. After the horrendous flood of 1642, the city was almost deserted. Now the population of the metropolis of Kaifeng is around five million, some eight times the number of people walking the streets when the Jews first built their synagogue. Kaifeng was the hub of China then, very much in the limelight. Now Kaifeng is one of the mid-sized cities in the country. It had lost much of its former glamour and prominence.

Jian drove Rhae to another family of Jewish descent. The Li Clan was headed by a woman in her fifties, who claimed that her family descended from the Levi clan. They occupied a fair-sized house with a spacious courtyard. The residence was also presented as a "Jewish Household," with a plaque to that effect at the front entrance. In the parlour, a Menorah set and a Passover Plate stood on display, and a Star of David was painted on the wall, indicating the family's Hebrew faith.

Li's husband was not of Jewish origins, but said he followed his wife's tradition of abstaining from eating pork or shellfish. His last name was You 游. In the past, when meat was rationed, the family had to obtain the same kind of ration coupons as the Muslims – that is, coupons for lamb and mutton only – to avoid eating pork.

Li estimated there were approximately a hundred people of Jewish descent remaining in Kaifeng, though some of Rhae's sources placed that number at a few hundred. They all knew one another and associated in some way. Through conversation, Rhae detected a certain resentment towards Ester and her family on the part of this small community. The idea of using one's ancestry to earn money did not sit well with most of them.

Were they envious of the fact that Ester and her family inherited the little corner of the synagogue and managed to capitalize on it? Did they think it was wrong to profit from history? Was it because it was their collective history, and now only one family benefited from it? Or did they genuinely feel their history was sacred and should not be mixed up with mundane commerce?

Rhae came away with more questions than answers. She would have had to stay in Kaifeng a lot longer before she would be able to approach the different clans with questions on such sensitive issues. On this first visit, no one would open up to her about the conflicts or disagreements among the different clans.

However, one thing was clear to Rhae. As she had learned from the professors the day before, the Kaifeng Jews, as keepers of a tradition, were extremely protective of their religion, their religious artifacts, and their holy scrolls.

The Jesuits in the seventeenth and eighteenth centuries had observed that the Kaifeng Jews believed that to sell their holy scriptures was to sell their god. In 1721, a French Jesuit, Father Domenge, stayed in Kaifeng for seven months, hoping to obtain a set of the Jews' holy books. He even bribed a certain Ai Wen, who promised to sell Domenge four scrolls that belonged to him but were kept in the temple. When Ai tried to take the scrolls from the temple, he was stopped and literally chased out of the synagogue as a traitor.

Another Jesuit, Father Gaubil, tried without success to borrow the holy books for just one day. Regardless of what terms he offered to the Jews, they would not consider it. James Finn, in his book *The Jews in China: Their Synagogue, Their Scriptures, Their History, etc.** records the claim of a Portuguese Jesuit, Giampolo Gozani, that the Kaifeng Jews took care of their Holy Scriptures better than they did their gold or silver. In view of this, it is not difficult to understand the community's displeasure with Ester and her family.

According to Li, because the Hebrew religion is not one of the five religions – namely, Catholicism and Protestantism, considered as two religions, Islam, Buddhism, and Taoism – officially recognized by the Chinese government, they cannot perform their Hebrew ceremonies in a religious institution. The lessons taught by volunteer teachers have been sporadic. They now hold a gathering every Friday evening in a school, with around forty people attending. Regrettably, only a small portion of the time is devoted to the Hebrew religion during this gathering. It is mostly singing, dancing, and food.

Rhae was annoyed with herself for not having found out about this weekly activity before she left Toronto. If she had known, she would have arranged her itinerary to include a Friday, so she could have met more members of this surviving group. What an opportunity wasted! Her schedule was booked solid for the next two weeks; there was no way she could juggle it to delay her flight to Shanghai, and the chance of coming back for it was slim. She felt like kicking herself.

Rhae managed to have only a brief telephone conversation with one of the members of the Shi 石 clan. They were unable to meet in person. She thought that, if she were to stay for the Friday meeting, she might have a chance to meet members of all five remaining clans, and she was very tempted to change her itinerary. In the end she decided against it; it required too much maneouvring, and somewhere along the line some other things would have to give.

That afternoon, Rhae visited the state-run Kaifeng Museum and saw three of the carved steles, or stone tablets, in the upstairs section devoted to Jewish history. No photos were allowed. Disappointing. Nonetheless, just looking at these steles prompted Rhae to think back to the conversation with Prof. Liu the previous day.

These steles were priceless, Prof. Liu had said. The Jews had them inscribed to record their origins, their history, their culture, and their philosophy, all of which was wrapped up in their religion. And for posterity, the steles told even more about the Kaifeng Jews.

Contemporary Chinese scholars Chen Changqi and Wei Qianzhi had more or less established the Jews' arrival in Kaifeng in the year 998 CE. One hundred and sixty-five years later, in 1163, their synagogue was completed. It remained their pride and joy. To the Jews, their religion was all-important. It set them apart from all other religions, including the Muslims. They made every effort to keep their practices and holy objects intact and the synagogue in good condition. They succeeded for close to eight hundred years.

The many repairs on and reconstructions of the synagogue were evidence of the Kaifeng Jews' devotion. From 1163 to 1688 there were at least twelve repairs and reconstructions; from 1653 to 1688 alone there were four repairs. It was only after 1850, when the last rabbi died and the synagogue was beyond repair, that the community scattered.

For her last day in Kaifeng, Rhae had to decide between a visit to either the Shaolin Temple or the city of Luoyang. They were both about the same distance – approximately a hundred kilometres – from Kaifeng, but in two different directions.

Luoyang had been another ancient capital during the Han and Tang dynasties. It is famous for the nearby White Horse Temple, the earliest Buddhist Temple in China, established in 68 CE during the East Han Dynasty. Luoyang's other attraction is the peony festival in late April. As it was early March, peony blossoms were not yet in season.

Rhae asked Jian to drive her to the Shaolin Temple at the Song Mountain 嵩山, one of the five ancient sacred mountains* in China.

According to ancient Chinese belief, mountains housed spirits. Some considered mountains to be "pillars" that held up the sky. Others saw them as links connecting earth to heaven. Mountain gods were venerated throughout the ages.

The Shaolin Temple was founded towards the end of the fifth century CE by Buddhabhadra, a Buddhist monk from India. It was also allegedly the birthplace of Zen Buddhism, which was started by another monk from India.

Many of the Wu Shu (martial-arts or kung-fu) techniques are said to have originated from here. As the car drove past the huge square of the Wu Shu Academy below the temple, Rhae was involuntarily hypnotized by the sight of thousands of students in uniform repeating one or another body movement in unison. This kind of practice should be introduced in all schools, she thought – not so much for the sake of acquiring martial-arts techniques but for physical fitness, discipline, and mental alertness.

Rhae recalled that, during her early years in Shanghai, both in primary school and later at McTyeire Girls School, the entire school – teachers, staff, and students – was required to do twenty minutes of physical exercise each morning before class. But this will never happen in North America, she told herself. Any regimented training in schools is likely to be strongly opposed by some groups for sure. Such is the system of western democracy.

The Shaolin Temple was destroyed and rebuilt many times. Now it was very much a tourist spot. Halls rose to seven different levels, all exquisitely maintained with income from tourism.

As Rhae climbed the stone steps to each of the seven levels, her mind wandered from one religion to another, and how each played out in her family.

Her likely ancestors travelled thousands of miles to Kaifeng, bringing with them their Hebrew faith. They were respected and admired for the observance of their religious practices. After her great-grandparents migrated to Nanchang, her grandfather Gande had become a member of the Methodist Church, bringing all his children into the Christian fold. Some of Rhae's aunts remained devout churchgoers all their lives, but her father, Xinmeng, quickly shed his Christian observances once he settled in Shanghai.

Rhae and her siblings grew up in a non-religious environment, although the servants would venerate some Chinese gods or goddesses, and their mother, Flora, occasionally burned some incense in memory of her father. Once a year, Flora did a ceremonial offering to the Earth God, during which all the children were required to kneel and do three kowtows.

One year, when Rhae was about seven or eight, Aunt Sara, a devout Christian living in Nanjing at the time, came to visit. She tried to instill some Christian beliefs into her nieces and discouraged them from idol worship. That year both Rhae and Linny decided to forego the ceremony of kneeling to the Earth God. Their mother became so enraged that she threatened physical punishment. Rhae, admitting her gutlessness, caved in. She quickly did her three kowtows and ran off. Linny, stubborn and wanting to stand her ground, refused to do the same. She got a severe beating from their mother. Physical punishment was a way of life in those days. Rhae still didn't know whether their mother was incensed because they refused to venerate the Earth God or because she was upset that Aunt Sara's influence encouraged her nieces to disobey their mother – an in-law power struggle of a kind.

Rhae and her siblings did not attend church, nor were they affiliated with any religion. After the Communists took over Shanghai in 1949, Rhae's family fled to Hong Kong, where it was extremely difficult to gain admission to good schools. Mother Conleth, the headmistress of St. Rosa of Lima School, run by the Franciscan order, took a leap of faith and admitted all five sisters. At the time, none of them could communicate in English or in Cantonese, the dialect used in Hong Kong. Within a year, all five were baptized at St. Teresa's Church in Kowloon. For about ten years, they attended daily Mass and were known for their devotion and diligence in many of the church's activities.

Now, forty years later, only one of the five remained a

devout practising Catholic. The other four had not only become lax, but two of them totally abandoned Catholic teachings and turned to Buddhism and Daoism, not as religions, but as philosophies.

Rhae meditated on what the Dalai Lama once said: that all major religious traditions teach people to add value to humanity; it is the different cultures and histories that provide people with different approaches. Something like that. She could not remember the exact words. She tried to find a link between the Dalai Lama's theory and her family's change of religious direction from one generation to another.

China has never had a national religion. Daoism began in China but only a small percentage of the population practised it in the past or practises it at present. In their grandfather's case, as in their own, choice of religion was made as much because of timing and circumstances as through any deep thought.

Both her grandfather's move to Methodism and the sisters' conversions to Catholicism were, subconsciously perhaps, somewhat out of convenience and a bit of necessity. At the time of their baptism, all five of them genuinely believed in all the Catholic teachings and eagerly bowed to all the Church's demands – blindly almost. She and her sisters, as well as their grandfather, were in their early teens when they were baptized – an impressionable age when minds can easily be led and swayed. They were influenced and impressed by the dedication and selflessness of the Franciscan nuns, as their grandfather had been by the Methodist missionaries. It was "the singer" more than "the song." And, as the Dalai Lama had said, all religions emphasize the bettering of oneself; in their teachings basically all religions sing the same song, but with different wording, different tunes, or different accompaniments. When asked by the Brazilian theologian, Leonardo Boff, which was the best religion, the Dalai Lama's answer was "the one that gets you closest to God. It is the one that makes you a better person." The Dalai Lama went on to explain that the religion that makes a person more compassionate, more sensible, more detached, more loving, more humanitarian, more responsible, more ethical, is the best religion for that person. Rhae supected that neither her grandfather nor she and her sisters really thought about self-improvement through religion. Their embracing of Catholicism, or Methodist Christianity in the case of her grandfather, was more about outward behaviour, about ceremonies and rituals. Rhae also wondered which major religion she or each of her siblings would have chosen if they had been exposed equally to others. As different as they were, she would not have been surprised if she and her four sisters had ended up following five different religions. She chuckled at the thought. There would have been endless fierce arguments, that was for sure.

As she descended from the seven levels of temple halls and made her way to the Pagoda Forest, which was the burial ground for the eminent monks throughout the ages, Rhae's mind continued to dwell on religion, philosophy, and spirituality.

China is not, and has never been, a religiously-oriented nation. Several schools of philosophy, however, have flourished since the early days. Each had gone through many years of thinking resulting in several bodies of thought. Of note are the two best-known philosophies – Daoism and Confucianism. Both began in the sixth century BCE.

It is generally believed that Laozi, the founder of Daoism,

was a senior contemporary of Confucius, who consulted him and showed great respect for him. Laozi is credited as the author of DaoDeJing – 道德经, the *Book of the Way and Virtue*.

Dao means "The Way," a metaphysical term that refers to an indescribable force or energy that cannot be felt. Yet it encompasses the entire universe. Dao promotes the strength of a soft approach over violence, spontaneity over deliberation. Dao often advocates non-action. Many of its thinking on ying and yang, the elements of water, vegetation, fire, earth, and metal, point to a "Way of Nature" and were later absorbed into the principles of Chinese traditional medicine. Rhae always perceived Dao as being metaphysical, abstract, and mystical. Of late, Rhae, Adele, and Thomas had all been attracted to Daoism.

To Confucius, born in 551 BCE, The Way means the "Way of Man" – the way of ancient sages and kings, the way of virtue, the way of how to live this life. Confucianism deals more with man's moral, social, political, and spiritual behaviour. It lays out detailed protocols to be observed between ruler and subjects, parents and children, husband and wife, brother and brother. It stresses ceremonial requirements and rites for important events, such as funerals, periods of mourning, and such. Confucianism became the most influential philosophy, and it has permeated the Chinese mindset from ancient times to the present.

Regardless of whether China has a national religion or not, however, spirituality has existed in all of the philosophies that have flourished in China. There have always been definite concepts about "man" and "heaven," whether "heaven" represents a supreme being, a force in nature, or some kind of leader or overlord. From the ancient belief that virtue determined whether a person was rewarded or punished, to continuing supplications to nature or to ancestors, to a ready resignation to destiny or fate – spirituality has undeniably always been a part of the lives of the people.

But, does it exist in present-day China? Rhae wondered. Since the dawn of the twentieth century, westernization has led to major changes in traditional values and beliefs. Marxism and Leninism surged forward. Materialism surpassed idealism. Currently, China's own brand of social-market economy seems to encourage nothing but consumerism and the gaining of wealth. Rhae sighed at the fact that the whole country now seemed bent on making money, money, money . . . China's soul seemed to her to have been snatched away and discarded somewhere.

As they approached Kaifeng on their return from the Shaolin Temple, it was still light. Rhae asked Jian if he could take her to the bank of the Yellow River, which, more than once, had brought disaster on the inhabitants of Kaifeng.

The Yellow River begins in China's western province of Qinghai. It is the second-longest river in Asia after the Yangtze River – approximately 5,464 kilometres. Up to 1946, there had been 1,593 floods in the river's 2,540 years of history, and it had shifted course about twenty-six times. The floods and course changes were caused primarily by the fine-grained loess the river carries from the loess plateau. By the mid-twentieth century, flood management improved, and the river itself lost much of its power.

In the twenty-first century, the mighty Yellow River no longer poses a threat to the city. In Kaifeng, the river has receded some distance from its former banks, and the water level is substantially lower. Jian's car drove onto the sand of the exposed former riverbed. Rhae walked along it, trying to visualize the body of water that had gushed down to destroy the synagogue and washed away the holy scrolls along with everything else in sight. It must have been terrifying.

In the plane en route to Shanghai, Rhae lay back in her seat with her eyes closed. All the thoughts that had surfaced in the previous three days ran through her mind, crisscrossing, bumping into one another: religion ... philosophy ... spirituality ... Confucius ... Confucianism and Judaism ...

Prof. Liu had reminded her that, all factors notwithstanding, the most notable thing that had spearheaded the Kaifeng Jews' assimilation into Han society was none other than Ru Xue 儒学,* which represents a traditional Chinese philosophy that is primarily based on Confucianism, with elements of Daoism and feudalism. In Ru Xue, the Confucian philosophy is applied to how to properly live this life on earth. Rhae dwelt on this for a moment.

Twentieth-century Chinese scholars agree that the serious assimilation of the Kaifeng Jews began in the fifteenth century at the beginning of the Ming Dynasty, and the process from partial acculturation to a near-total merging with Confucianism took hundreds of years, encompassing language, culture, social structure, marital-practices, ideology, identity ...

It became clear to Rhae that it was precisely because Judaism, as some suggest, is all-inclusive, involving theology, history, culture, philosophy, language, art, science, architecture, social structure, familial concepts, proper behaviour, as laid out in the Encyclopedia Judaica,* that Chinese Ru Xue would logically appeal to the Jews. The educated Israelites embraced Confucianism with little reserve, as an inscription on the

1677 stele acknowledges: "Chinese Judaism was based on Dao of the Heaven-Human relationship and was incorporated with the principles advocated by Confucius and Mencius." As author Wang Zhigao rightfully claims in his article, "The Assimilation of the Kaifeng Jews," in the book *The East Gate of Kaifeng: A Jewish World Inside China,** "Confucianism had gone [deep] into the minds of Kaifeng Jews."

Wang also pointed out that the later steles referred to their God as *Tian*, ("heaven"), not *Jahweh* ("Jehovah"), marking "the infiltration of traditional Chinese customs and ideas such as ancestor veneration, [and] seasonal festivities." The steles actually use Confucian ideology to explain the Hebrew religion. Historian Donald Leslie, co-author of the book *Juifs de Chine,* commented on the tone of the inscription of the last two steles as being "Judaism clothed in Confucianism," and pointed out in addition certain Daoist elements.

As well, the "Confucianization" is reflected in the last reconstruction of the temple. Jesuit priest Gosani's letter to Joseph Suarez in 1704, as found in Bishop White's book *Chinese Jews*, mentioned that the synagogue bore some resemblance to the churches of Europe. The synagogue built in 1163 must have been very different from these later versions. Rhae imagined that it would probably have incorporated features that expressed the Israelites' Persian origin or even a touch of Indian artistry.

By the beginning of the eighteenth century, the synagogue might have had some features of European churches, but was more Chinese in structure and decor. The reconstructed version, which is known from the 1722 sketches of the interior and exterior of the temple by French Jesuit Domenge, clearly shows the incorporation of typical features of a Chinese temple

– courtyards, pavilions, halls, and doorsills, and other details. Inside the temple were displayed numerous plaques awarded by the emperors or distinguished officials, as well as poetic couplets expressing religious sentiments. An Anglican visitor to Kaifeng in the nineteenth century described the interior to Bishop William White, who, in his book *The Chinese Jews*, described: "A large carved and gaily painted table upon which was erected a small pavilion lacquered and gilded, and in this pavilion was the Emperor's tablet carved with dragons and containing the characters Dang Jin Huang Di Wan Sui Wan Sui Wan Wan Sui (may the present emperor live forever)." This was unmistakably Chinese.

Name change was another major step in the process of assimilation. It occurred widely from the early Ming Dynasty onward. Single-syllable Han names replaced much longer Hebrew names. This was not deliberate, but came about because Hebrew was no longer their first language. As early as the sixteenth century, Ai Tian from Kaifeng told Jesuit priest Matteo Ricci that, because they had to study Chinese classics, they had no time for Hebrew.*

Along with name changes, mixed marriages became more frequent. These marriages began with those scholars who participated in the Imperial examinations: it was generally acknowledged that, very likely because of postings in areas where there were no Israelites, the officials of Jewish background did not have much choice. Then there was also the Confucian doctrine of matching families of similar social status. This influenced the marriages of these officials and their offspring. The first officially recorded case of a mixed marriage between a Jew and a Han was that of a daughter of Zuo Tang

左唐 to a Chinese official, Wang Zhilang 王侍郎, whose post was equivalent to a present-day vice-president of a board. Since Zuo Tang, born in Yangzhou, was the first Jew to pass the Second Level of Civil Exams, as Rhae and her sisters had discovered in Dr. Liu's book, his subsequent posting would have raised his social status. His daughter was expected to marry someone with a posting of similar ranking.

Professor Liu had reminded Rhae that polygamy, too, probably began with the scholars who received postings. In his book he mentioned a known case in the late Ming Dynasty, when one Zhang Mei 张美, a Jew, had six wives, four of whom were not of Jewish descent. Professor Liu had also confirmed what Wang Zhigao wrote in his article "The Assimilation of the Chinese Jews": the Jews followed the Chinese rites in marriage, death, and burial.

Sitting on the plane, with her eyes still closed, Rhae slowly sorted out the various points of interest about the Kaifeng Jews that Professor Liu had discussed with her days before. Rhae said to herself that she must tell Adele and the others about this one very significant issue that she and her siblings had entirely overlooked. Had the professors not been so emphatic about it, Rhae would still be in the dark and not have thought about it.

"Why did the Muslim community survive and propagate, whereas the Jewish community did not?" Professor Liu had posed the question to her at the very end of their meeting. Yes, indeed, why? Rhae's mind was a blank for a moment.

The Jews never had planned to propagate their religion, but the Muslims took a different approach, Professor Liu had hinted. He then went on to explain how these two different mindsets affected the communities.

During the late Ming Dynasty, the emperor imposed restrictions on trade and interchange of any kind with foreign countries. When fewer and fewer Muslim scholars arrived in China, the Muslim community started a movement that would ensure the survival and continuation of their existence in China. Strengthening their religious traditions, they used this as the springboard to set out to establish their religious education system in their temple. They groomed and nurtured the promising youth; they combined a medieval Islamic teaching system with a Chinese private-tutoring system, which led to a Muslim religious system with a Chinese slant. They encouraged translations of Islamic writings into Chinese, merging Chinese philosophy with Islam and claiming that the two shared their origins.

Ah! It finally dawned on Rhae that, while the Jews became increasingly more submerged in Confucianism – or more specifically the Ru Xue – giving up their own teachings, the Muslims strengthened Islam and amalgamated Islam with Confucianism. The end result: the number of Jews dwindled, while the number of Muslims grew exponentially.

满怀忧爱国忧民
悲愤情情怀

Chapter 22

Uncle Charles

From 1991 onward, each time Rhae had visited Shanghai, the city looked different. There were more high-rises, more developments, more people. By 2011, the population of Shanghai had reached twenty-three million, more than half of Canada's total population at the time. With each visit, Rhae also noticed that the people in general had turned more fashion-conscious. Over the two decades from 1991 to 2012, European designers had assembled a chain of boutiques along Huaihai Road. Shanghai is once again at the forefront of fashion, as it was between the wars, when it was known as "the Paris of the Orient."

For forty years after the Communists took over Shanghai in 1949, the central government in Beijing had done nothing to revitalize the city or upgrade its infrastructure. Back in 1991, when Rhae had come to Shanghai for the first time after forty years of absence, the city was just beginning to come out of its shabbiness. She distinctly remembered a little girl pointing at her and calling her "Foreigner!" There had been discernible differences in clothing, carriage, behaviour, and demeanour between the locals and people from the West.

Now, in 2012, that gap had narrowed. She no longer stood out as an outsider.

Whenever Rhae was in Shanghai, she would take her Uncle Charles to the Four Seasons Hotel for a buffet lunch. Uncle Charles, in turn, would reciprocate with coffee at a nearby Taiwanese café.

Uncle Charles was Rhae's maternal uncle, the brother of her mother, Flora, very much a product of the Shanghai of the early twentieth century. He grew up a carefree young man with no worries, no cares, and no responsibilities, frequenting nightclubs, watching Hollywood movies, eating western processed meat, sipping coffee, and enjoying European pastries. All of these, status symbols at the time, came to a stop when the Communists took over Shanghai. His "decadent" lifestyle was turned on its head. He and his wife were forced from their well-appointed luxury apartment in the French Concession and assigned a two-room portion of a flat shared with two other families in a concrete building with concrete walls, concrete floors, concrete stairs, and no elevator. In one of the rooms was a television set and a table for eating. In their bedroom was a bed, one night table, and a chair for reading – the bare necessities in modern life. It was a far cry from the opulence they had enjoyed before the liberation.

For close to fifty years, Charles had lived a frugal life. He had survived all of Chairman Mao's anti-whatever movements; he had survived the Cultural Revolution; he had survived his wife's death. The highlights of his days now consisted of a daily two-hour walk in the neighbourhood and reading. At ninety-eight, he remained a healthy, lean old man, who still enjoyed his walks and read books on history.

They were sipping coffee after lunch when Rhae mentioned her book. Uncle Charles nodded in approval.

"What a meaningful task! Both the Kaifeng Chinese Jews and what happened during the Second World War are not widely known, even here in China. Those of us who lived through that war mostly remember only the Japanese occupation, and are not too aware of what actually happened in Europe at that time. The younger generation of today knows much too little about world history. Unfortunately, nowadays, they are obsessed with money only. It's such a shame!"

"Give me your take on the Second World War, Uncle Charles. Anything you remember or that you experienced," asked Rhae. Uncle Charles stirred some more sugar into his cup. His face took on a pensive look.

"I was twenty-four when the war started – a thoughtless young man with no sense of patriotism or world politics. Looking back, I was pretty much an idiot, who knew nothing about anything. I was just coasting along aimlessly in life. You probably know that I didn't finish high school. When I was sixteen, my father forced me to marry the daughter of one of his business associates in an attempt to save his three money houses from possible bankruptcy. I never did a day's work in my life. Somehow I just muddled through. I was not a productive member of society, you would say. The Communists were not completely wrong when they labelled me a "parasite."

"We lived in the French Concession, and therefore we were not that affected by the Japanese occupation till maybe 1943. Anyway, at the time, I didn't pay attention to what was going on, but my neighbour, James Fan next door, was a senior government official in charge of some kind of liaison with those who oversaw the Hongkou, or Hongkew, area. He used to tell me about the Jewish refugees there and how they struggled. We used to dine at the Peace Hotel once a week, and he always told me some news about the refugees. All the numbers and statistics he pulled out did not make any impression on me then. It was forty years later when I read up on what happened during that period and everything became clear.

"Hongkew used to be an industrial area. When the Japanese invaded Shanghai in 1937, the battles left a good part of the Hongkew industrial buildings in ruins. The replacements were poorly constructed, but they were eventually turned into housing units for the residents there. The area was terribly polluted. Because of poor sanitation, due to lack of facilities, plus the heat and high humidity in summer, the whole area was rife with disease: typhoid, cholera, dysentery, and typhus, which was spread by ticks and fleas carried by rodents that ran rampant in Hongkew. But the rent was cheap. About a hundred thousand of the poorest Chinese and some seventy thousand Japanese lived there.

"When the European Jews arrived, fleeing Hitler, those who could afford it rented in other neighbourhoods in either the International Settlement or the French Concession. The destitute ended up in Hongkew, either renting dilapidated quarters with small rooms or living in the five or six Heime set up there. "Heime," as you probably know, are what the refugees called their settlement houses. I believe it is a German word. At the Heime, they accommodated as many as 150 beds in a room and many of the rooms had little sunlight or fresh air.

"The U.S. organization, Joint Distribution Centre, commonly known as the JDC, was the main body to help out, with steady funding of about thirty thousand American dollars each month for these refugees. They provided three meals a day and a subsidy of ten Chinese Yuan each month. The exchange rate was approximately twenty-four Chinese yuan to each American dollar. The meals would consist of coffee, bread, and margarine for breakfast; soup, meat, bread, and sweets for lunch; soup, bread, and fruits for dinner. In 1939, more than two thousand refugees were totally dependent on the JDC and other organizations.

"After Pearl Harbor, in 1941, funding became scarce, as communication with the west became difficult. Meals were reduced from three to two a day and then to only one meal a day. By April of the following year, meals were limited to the elderly, the sick, and the children only. After that there was no communication from the JDC.

"I was very touched when I read about the refugees putting out a plea to their fellow Jews in Shanghai in a 'self-help' program. They asked each family that cooked their own meals to offer one meal to the needy. Those who did not cook at home were asked to contribute thirty Chinese yuans, or about a dollar and a quarter in U.S. funds each month for those in need. Bars, restaurants, cafés, as well as suppliers of goods and merchandise were to add a ten-percent surcharge to donate to the poor. The response was good. They also set up some kind of 'kitchen fund.' I read somewhere that, in November 1942, they were able to provide some five thousand hot meals every day. Quite remarkable.

"In February, 1943, around Chinese New Year, came the proclamation that all stateless refugees were to move to the Hongkew ghetto. The deadline was May 18. Many of those who lived outside Hongkew exchanged spaces with the Chinese who had been living inside.

"That year was probably the worst year for the refugees. By winter, most of the aid organizations were on the verge of bankruptcy. The International Red Cross wrote to Washington and stressed that Shanghai was in a desperate situation. The worst hit were the German Jews, with more than five thousand on the brink of starvation and even more living in privation. By the beginning of 1944, most of these people were living on one meal a day.

"The JDC did not resume funding till early 1944. It probably took that long for all parties involved to plan and then negotiate a way for U.S. funds to reach Shanghai. By then, the equivalent of US$25,000 in Swiss francs was wired over from Switzerland every month. It was good that they used Swiss francs as currency, because inflation was hitting the roof, and the Chinese yuan was worthless."

"It is amazing you remember all the numbers, Uncle Charles," exclaimed Rhae.

"Most of the details I mentioned I found in *Juifs de Chine* by Dr. Donald Daniel Leslie and Joseph Dehergne. I read the translated version by Geng Sheng.* I made a point of remembering the dates and the numbers just because, at the time when all this happened, I was so clueless about the sufferings of those who actually lived so close by me. I feel ashamed to this day that I was so oblivious to the desperation of people around me. I became more aware in my old age.

"I also want to tell you about one incident from that period that stuck in my mind. I didn't see it first-hand. My housekeeper, Ah Lang, whose family lived in Hongkew, told me about it.

"As you know, in June 1944, the Allies landed at Normandy, and it was the beginning of the end for the Germans. On

May 8, 1945, Germany surrendered. But the Japanese did not follow suit. So the Americans increased their bombing of the Japanese-occupied areas. One day in mid-July, a bomb hit the refugee area in Hongkew. Thirty-odd refugees, along with a few hundred Japanese and four thousand Chinese residents, were killed. It was devastating to everyone. But what was amazing was that all the survivors in the area, be they Jews or Chinese, helped and supported one another. Ah Lang said she was incredulous when all the Jews came to help them and treated them on equal terms.

"We all know that at that time Chinese, most of the time, had to bow to foreigners. All foreigners displayed an air of unmistakable superiority towards the Chinese, treating them like dirt. And there they were, these westerners, treating the Chinese as if they were family members – helping with medical care, sorting out debris, sharing whatever they had with those who lost everything. Ah Lang was so touched by the Jewish refugees, she sobbed as she told me the story, saying repeatedly 'They treated us like their own.' Ah Lang's mother-in-law was injured by a piece of debris, and two Jewish men carried her to the shelter. They lost some belongings, but everyone survived."

"What a touching story!" agreed Rhae.

"A couple of years ago, I made a point to read about the Jews who remained in Shanghai after the war. By 1945, about three thousand returned to Europe, and more than ten thousand were still in Shanghai. By October 1949, when the Communists took over Shanghai, there were still a couple of thousand Jews waiting to leave China. In the early fifties, a few hundred moved to Israel and about a thousand to other destinations. Some five hundred or so Jews had no family or relatives to go to, and the JDC continued their support for them. Max Leibovich was the last of the refugees who stayed, and he died in Shanghai in early 1982; he was in his seventies. Some of my numbers may be fuzzy, but you can verify them in *Juifs de Chine*."

"I certainly will, Uncle Charles. Thanks so much for all this."

"Not at all, Rhae. I'm delighted to have an opportunity to talk to someone interested in history. It gives my old brain a bit of a spark.

"By the way, would you also be interested in knowing some of the details of the Japanese occupation of Hong Kong? Very recently, I watched a short photo-documentary video presented by a Mr. H. Lau. It portrayed Hong Kong during the three years and eight months of Japanese occupation of the island. A lot of the information I did not know before."

"Please do, Uncle Charles. I know very little about the Hong Kong situation during that period," Rhae said.

"In 1936, the total population in Hong Kong was about one million. After Japan's invasion of Beijing and Shanghai in 1937, masses of mainland Chinese flooded Hong Kong. In 1941, Hong Kong's population swelled to one million six hundred thousand.

"On December 8, 1941, the day after Pearl Harbor, Japanese bombers flew from Canton airport and bombed Hong Kong. Hong Kong was defended by British, Canadian, and Indian soldiers and Hong Kong volunteer militia.

"On February 20, 1942, the Japanese proclaimed Hong Kong a Japanese-occupied area. They moved their command post from the Peninsula Hotel to the Hong Kong and Shanghai Bank building, and the Japanese flag was hoisted. They arrested about seven thousand foreigners and soldiers and placed them at the Shum Shui Po Camp in Kowloon or the Stanley Camp on the Island.

"The Hong Kong and Shanghai Bank, the Charter Bank ... all major foreign banks ... were closed, and two Japanese banks were opened. Hong Kong dollars were considered illegal. Everyone had to change their money to Japanese currency. In January 1942, the exchange rate was two Hong Kong dollars to one Japanese yuan; by July of the same year, the exchange rate became four to one. By 1943, only Japanese currency was allowed.

"The Japanese took control of all the big hospitals, public transit. Because of the shortage of food and other necessary items, the Japanese began to deport people from Hong Kong. Within one year, they managed to send some five hundred thousand people out of Hong Kong and Kowloon. Everything was rationed.

"Japanese became the official language in Hong Kong. They started to change the street names to Japanese names. All students from kindergarten up had to learn Japanese.

"The Japanese authority was free to confiscate people's assets at will. The soldiers could arrest any able-bodied male on the street and force him to do labour. They could enter people's residences and rape women. On Locke Road they had several 'Comfort Centres,' which offered forced sex services to the Japanese soldiers.

"In 1944, due to the severe shortage of everything, rationing stopped. It became a free market; people had to pay exorbitant amounts on the black market for their daily needs.

"By the time Japan surrendered in 1945, the population in Hong Kong was down to six hundred thousand. When the British resumed control of Hong Kong, there were many billions of Hong Kong dollars' worth of Japanese currency that became totally worthless."

Uncle Charles kept shaking his head long after he finished his recounting of the Hong Kong episode.

"At least in Shanghai they did not use Japanese as the official language. We didn't have to study Japanese in school either. And we didn't experience a massacre and other atrocities that took place in Nanking," sighed Rhae. "Those were the dark years for all Chinese."

"Indeed!" echoed Uncle Charles, who continued to shake his head.

"You may be interested to know, Uncle Charles, that in Toronto there is now an organization called Toronto Alpha, formed specifically to propagate, among other world issues, the truth of what the Japanese did in China during the Second World War. The Nanking massacre, the bio-experimentation in Manchuria, and so on."

"That is commendable," said Uncle Charles." Maybe one day the whole world will get to know the truth of what the Japanese did in China. Up to now the Japanese government has kept denying any wrongdoing by creating a false history. The ordinary Japanese people have no idea of the atrocities their soldiers carried out in China. It is shamefully unfair."

The next day, Rhae took Uncle Charles for an outing. They walked through the former "Little Vienna" area on Chuson Road, which was now a neat residential district with no hint of the historic events that had taken place here in the nineteen thirties and forties.

The two of them tried to enter the former Kadoorie residence, the Marble Hall, now the Shanghai Youth Palace. However, due to extensive renovations, the entire building was covered with bamboo scaffolding and shrouded in a green net. A tour inside was not possible. Rhae was disappointed not to be able to see the grand ballroom that Auntie Ellie had described with such fondness. However, Uncle Charles suggested it was probably no longer a ballroom, but was sectioned off into bits and pieces to serve many functions. She and Uncle Charles ended the day at the Jewish Museum, viewing exhibits and reading up on the details of the Jewish history in Shanghai.

It was a fitting way to round out their discussions of the previous day.

人生何處不相逢

Chapter 23

Interlude

Before heading home to Toronto, Rhae took a detour to New York City. She had contacted Rabbi Marvin Tokayer and Mary Swartz by phone while in Shanghai and had arranged to meet them on her way back to Canada.

Rabbi Tokayer and Mary Swartz had co-authored the book *The Fugu Plan*, which provided a lot of material previously unknown to Rhae. It was in its pages that she had learned about Colonel Josef Meisinger, the Gestapo's liaison in Tokyo, and his efforts to convince the Japanese to exterminate all Jewish refugees in Shanghai. The book also discussed why the Japanese government resisted this proposed "final solution."

It was a warm afternoon in Manhattan, and the traffic, as always, was horrendous. The three sat in the Tick Tock Café, sipping tea or coffee and chatting in the casual, relaxed atmosphere. This was the first time Rhae had met the two in person, and she found them just as she had pictured them – warm individuals, happy to share their wealth of knowledge. She felt very much at ease in their company.

Rabbi Tokayer and Mary Swartz are both noted scholars who spent many years in the Far East. Mary, a member of the Tokyo Jewish community, had been a professional writer since the seventies. Rabbi Tokayer, a historian, had for more than thirty years been a worldwide lecturer on "the unknown Jewish experience in the Far East." In addition, he was now leading "tours through Jewish eyes" to the Far East on a regular basis. His latest publication was a book entitled *Pepper, Silk and Ivory: Amazing Stories About Jews and the Far East.*

Rhae intended to discuss the use of content from *The Fugu Plan* in her book, but she was quickly diverted into a discussion of the Kaifeng Chinese Jews. The focus was on the Kaifeng holy scriptures.

Rabbi Tokayer explained the three different kinds of scriptures that existed in Kaifeng, in the form of books as well as scrolls. The Square Scripture, or Fang Jing, were mainly written using Hebrew and the Hebrew alphabet on thick Chinese rice paper. Many of these did not survive the floods, as they disintegrated easily when mould set in. The Miscellaneous Scripture – or the Shan Jing – and the Torah – or the Zheng Jing – were in the form of books as well as scrolls. The books were in loose leaves with a silk surface, and there were indications that they originated in Persia. The parchment scrolls were of a more lasting quality and were wound around sticks on each side with handles at the top and bottom.

The Torah contained the five book of Moses – Genesis, Exodus, Leviticus, Numbers, and Deuteronomy – setting out early Hebrew history. The Torah in Kaifeng indicated Persian origin because the scripture was divided into fifty-three chapters only, whereas the European version is divided into fifty-four chapters. The Miscellaneous Scripture and the Square

Scripture (Fang Jing) explained the weekly observances: the religious laws, rites, prayers, calendars, ceremonies for holy days, and even genealogy. These were not exactly scriptures in the true sense of the word. The writings again indicated Persian origin.

He pointed out that the 1663 stele had stated that, in 1653, thirteen Torah scrolls were installed in the ark of the newly rebuilt synagogue of the Kaifeng Jews after the 1642 flood. As the synagogue disintegrated in the late nineteenth century, these scrolls scattered all over the world. Seven of the thirteen are known. They are in the possession of The British Library London (#2 bet); Cambridge University Library in Cambridge (#4 dalet); the Bodleian Library in Oxford (#5 he); the Osterreichische Nationalbibliothek in Vienna (#6 vov); the Library of the Jewish Theological Seminary of America in New York (#7 zayyin); the Bridwell Library in the Perkins School of Theology at the Southern Methodist University in Dallas (#12 yod-bet); and the Library of the American Bible Society in New York, (one unnumbered Scroll) respectively. A catalogue of the Sassoon Collection shows a total of seventeen Torah scrolls in its possession, two of which are associated with the Kaifeng Jewish congregation. Rabbi Tokayer then recommended a book, *The Torah Scrolls of the Chinese Jews* by Michael Pollak, as an excellent source of information about the history and the whereabouts of all the Scrolls. Rhae made a note to order the book.

Rabbi Tokayer posed a question. Why were the Jesuit priests from the sixteenth century onward so interested in getting possession of these holy scrolls? Rhae realized that she and the professors in Kaifeng had not touched on this issue during their discussion. She recalled reading somewhere about some missionaries who had wanted to reach the Jews to convert them to Christianity, but the rabbi pointed out that this was only much later, possibly in the nineteenth century.

Rabbi Tokayer explained that for many, many years, the Catholic Church had suspected that the Hebrew scriptures had been tampered with after the birth of Christ. The Church harboured a notion that Jesus was actually definitively mentioned in the Old Testament but, because the Jews did not accept him as their Messiah, they had deleted the relevant sections, to deny his authenticity as the Messiah. When Matteo Ricci, an Italian Jesuit who was one of the first missionaries to China, discovered the existence of Kaifeng Jews in the sixteenth century, it was believed that these Jews had left Persia before the birth of Christ. Therefore, the Catholic Church thought the Torah brought over from ancient Persia by the Kaifeng Jews had to be the original Old Testament and would, therefore, prove their supposition. Consequently, they were persistent in trying to get these scrolls in order to discover the truth.

However, the Jesuits were not able to obtain any clue from the Kaifeng Jews regarding the Messiah promised in the scripture. The Kaifeng Jews were greatly surprised when told that Jesus the Messiah had already come. The chief of the synagogue declared that they did not expect the Messiah for another ten thousand years. They were not aware of a Jesus as Messiah in their scriptures; they said that there could have been a mention of a holy man named Jesus, son of Sirach, but did not know this Jesus in any other context.

In the memoir of Gabriel Brotier,* an eighteenth century Frenchman who published a book on the Jewish settlements in China in 1771, in Latin, it was stated that the Kaifeng Jews had the profoundest reverence for all their books. But there was one Pentateuch that they venerated more than all the others. Purportedly it was three thousand years old and was the only ancient relic left in the possession of the Kaifeng Jews. The Jesuits sent one priest after another trying to purchase or borrow this scroll, but without success.

However, Père Gosani,* in a letter to Joseph Suarez, dated November 5, 1704, described an occasion on which he showed his European Bible to the Kaifeng Jews. They compared the descendants from Adam down to Noah and the respective age of each, and found a perfect conformity between the two. Names and chronologies were the same in both copies.

It was not until the mid-nineteenth century that Reverend George Smith, Anglican Bishop of Victoria, Hong Kong, asked the Anglican missionary in Shanghai to send two Chinese converts to Kaifeng to acquire the Torah Scrolls and other writings. It was found the scripture was the same as those used in Europe. There had not been any deletions or alterations. So much for the unfounded theory.

"I believe there is an ancient scroll in the Jewish Museum in Toronto," Rabbi Tokayer said. "It is known as the Chinese scroll. You should check it out. I'm not sure if it came from Kaifeng. Toronto holds a good collection of relics from Kaifeng, both at the Royal Ontario Museum and the Jewish Museum. It's worth a visit to both – if not for your book, then to add some depth to your understanding of the Kaifeng Jewish community."

Shortly after arriving back in Toronto, Rhae contacted the Royal Ontario Museum and inquired about their collection of Kaifeng relics. Unfortunately, these were all in storage and not on display. However, she was able to secure images of a number of the pieces in their possession, including a rubbing of two of the steles.

The Jewish Museum to which Rabbi Tokayer had referred was the Reuben and Helene Dennis Museum, housed inside the Beth Tzedec Synagogue on Bathurst Street in Toronto. Rhae had had a conversation with the curator some months earlier. She felt it was time to pay them a visit.

The museum opened in 1965 with the acquisition of the renowned Judaica collection of Dr. Cecil Roth, a Jewish historian and editor-in-chief of the *Encyclopedia Judaica*. Dorion Leibgott was the curator. But it was a gentleman named Ralph Berrin who showed Rhae many of the exquisite items on display and explained the meaning and significance of each.

The museum consisted of one large room. Glass display cases were mounted on the walls surrounding the room. In the middle there were several display tables and columns, all encased in glass. There was a collection of ketubah (Jewish marriage contracts), each of which was a unique historical document. There were silver Torah ornaments, rare Esther Scrolls, Chanukkah lamps, a circumcision chair, items for various holy days ... over sixteen hundred artifacts altogether, Rhae was told.

"Come this way, Rhae." Ralph walked towards a glass display table and searched for the right key to open the case. "This is our Chinese Esther scroll. As far as I know, this is probably the only one of its kind in existence today."

He carefully removed the scroll from the case and spread it out on top of the glass. Rhae saw a long stretch of parchment with Hebrew writing going from right to left. In between sections of writing, as well as at the top and the bottom where there was no writing, figurines, motifs, and designs decorated the scroll, and all of them, without a doubt, were Chinese. She could not help marvelling at this.

"Definitely Chinese," Ralph continued. "But because there is no signature and no date, both of which usually accompany the scroll, we do not know where it originated. Neither can we tell how old it is. It is estimated to be from the late eighteenth or early nineteenth century. The scroll is made up of parts of two scrolls with Sephardic script. The illustrations were most likely painted by a Chinese artist later on in China. I believe Dr. Roth acquired it in London, England. Someone offered to sell it to him there. No details of its origin. But we don't think it has any connection with the Kaifeng Jewish community."

"May I take some photos?" Rhae asked.

"Yes, but no flash, please."

萬物苦旱待甘霖

Toronto, Canada

2013

身外何足言　人間本無事

Chapter 24

Welcome-Home Noodles

The "welcome home" noodle dinner for Rhae took place at Adele and Thomas's home in the east end of downtown Toronto. A neighbourhood of racial and ethnic diversity, with people of all colours speaking many languages, it was a true reflection of the rich social fabric of the Greater Toronto Area (GTA). Canada's pride lies in its diverse ethnic, racial, and cultural citizenship, and the GTA is very much a showcase of this.

As more newcomers had arrived in the city over the late 1990s and early 2000s, pockets of one group or another staked out their preferred areas. Those from Hong Kong, Taiwan, and Mainland China reached from Scarborough, in the east end of the city, north to Markham and northwest to Richmond Hill, creating five or six Chinatowns in the metropolis. Those of Greek descent spread along Danforth Avenue, the eastern extension of Bloor Street, a major mid-town thoroughfare, giving the area a distinct Greek flavour. Immigrants from Korea favoured properties along Yonge Street and Bloor Street West. Little Italy stretched west of the Annex in central

Toronto, and for many years those of Italian origin monopolized Woodbridge, an enclave north of Highway 7 around Islington Avenue. South Asians concentrated to the west of the city in Mississauga and Brampton. Wealthy Russians liked expansive spreads of land on the outskirts of the GTA, as well as the posh neighbourhoods in the area of Bayview Avenue and York Mills Road. Since the turn of the twenty-first century, Iranians and other Muslim groups had increased by thirty percent in York Region to the north of the city. As waves of immigrants poured in, the original Jewish market, which had occupied the southwest quadrant of College Street and Spadina Road, changed from Jewish to Chinese to Vietnamese to Latin and South American, as well as Caribbean and African Canadian. The last forty years of the twentieth century saw the makeup of Toronto morph from an Anglo-Saxon majority to a vibrant and colourful combination of all backgrounds and all heritages.

Since the dawn of the new century, trends had moved towards fusion, be it in food, culture, relationships, or business. Mixed marriages had increased, global intercultural interactions flourished, and the newly developed or redeveloped neighbourhoods tended to be home to all races and ethnicities. Adele and Thomas had searched for such a community. They enjoyed associating with their neighbours from all corners of the earth. It was one of the reasons they picked this particular location when they left Seattle to settle in Toronto.

Their house backed onto a pond frequented by Canada geese almost all year round. The brood had multiplied from a pair to a few dozen in a matter of about five years. Reeds and various water plants covered the banks. It was picturesque. Sitting in the kitchen or on the porch or relaxing in the garden at the lower level, the scenery was one of tranquility and of peace. At sunset, it was extraordinarily beautiful, with silhouettes of tall grasses gently swaying in the breeze against a flaming orange-red sun disappearing over the horizon.

Adele tended an extensive vegetable garden. In summer and fall there was no shortage of home-grown fruits and vegetables.

Inside the house, the décor was Oriental, accented by Chinese curios, calligraphy, and Chinese paintings, some of which were Adele's own works. On the side table was a framed wedding photo of Xinmeng and Flora, the sisters' parents. Xinmeng was in tails, and Flora was in a white full-length gown with a semi-Chinese top, the fashion of the day then. It was the era of the most famous Chinese-American Hollywood movie star of the 1920s and 1930s, Anna May Wong, who was the rage in Berlin and London and was hailed as the most beautiful Chinese woman in the world. Many of her wardrobe designs combined western fashion with a Chinese motif and they were widely copied in Shanghai. The bridal bouquet trailed down to the floor.

The best man and two groomsmen flanked Xinmeng on one side; the maid of honour and two bridesmaids flanked Flora on the other. Two flower girls and a ring bearer stood in the front.

Flora wore a long necklace of imperial jade, a gift from her father, Yan Shulong. Because it was a black-and-white photo, the brilliant translucent green of the stones did not show. Pity!

In 1967, during Chairman Mao's Cultural Revolution, the Red Guards confiscated this necklace, along with all of Flora's diamonds, rubies, sapphires, and other jewels. When the Cultural Revolution was finally over some ten years later, the government gave back a pittance in RMB, or Chinese yuan, as compensation for the items taken from the owners. It amounted to something like fifty yuan, equivalent to about seven U.S. dollars for one carat of diamond. It was almost incredible that, in the frenzy of the Red Guards' raids on families during the height of the Cultural Revolution, they had actually taken detailed and accurate records of the valuables removed from each family. Looking back, such actions, sanctioned by the head of state, amounted to no less than open robbery, as most items were later sold and the proceeds were kept by the state.

In the nineties, the sisters were told that people had spotted their mother's necklace for sale on the Hong Kong market. It was worth millions of Hong Kong dollars then. No one knew who had possession of it now.

Adele had made copies of this wedding photo for all the sisters, but she was the only one who had it framed and displayed in the living room. Each time Rhae visited her sister, she never failed to look at it with intense interest. On this day, she once again scrutinized every person in the photo and was struck by how very modern her mother looked for her time. Her eyes lingered on the photo as she took her seat at the dining table.

For this occasion, Adele and her daughter Elaine had prepared three different kinds of noodles: Henan broad noodles in an extra hot and spicy soup; cold Shanghai thick noodles with plenty of sesame oil; and Cantonese chow mien, topped with an assortment of ingredients. As was typical of Chinese meals, there were many dishes of meats, vegetables, and seafood. Quite a feast!

As always, everyone was keen to listen and to offer responses as Rhea gave a very detailed account of her journey and her encounters. Of special interest to all was her update on the contemporary Kaifeng Jews.

"When I met Ester's mother, who is the second of five sisters like us, I actually saw a resemblance between the two of us. She has the same dimples as I do and the shape of our faces is quite similar too. And she is the second daughter, as I am. I was intrigued, but I didn't say anything to them."

"Why not?" asked Sheryl.

"Well, people wouldn't want strangers barging in to claim relationship, would they?" answered Rhae. "Besides, I didn't want to complicate things, because there's no way to determine whether we're related or not. My objective of the trip to Kaifeng was to find out more about the community rather than to prove that we are of Jewish descent. I guess we'll talk about the DNA analysis later this evening?"

"Yes. Let's do that after dinner. It's interesting," said Linny excitedly.

"They actually keep very good records of births and deaths in China. If you had visited the Kaifeng municipal office, maybe you would have found something," said Adele, who was hoping to obtain more information about their great-grandfather Zhao Yidong.

"That was possible, I suppose. There were two reasons I didn't. First, information on our great-grandfather was so scanty, the only thing we know is that his name was Zhao Yidong. I'm not even sure if the name we know was the same as that registered. You know how the Chinese have several different names. I don't know his parents' names. I don't know his exact birthday, only that he was born in the year of the dog. With the Chinese calendar being different to the western calendar, if his birthday was at the very beginning or the very end of the Lunar year, it could mean a different year in the western calendar. Which means the search would have been horrendous, because I'd have had to go over a range of up to three years to find his registration.

"The second reason was that Kaifeng has gone through so many floods that washed away or destroyed tons of documents. I thought that a search would probably not turn up anything. I only had three days there, and didn't feel like spending time in a futile pursuit. Also, I was afraid of having to deal with the bureaucracy in order to access records. Since I was a "foreigner" to the local officials, there would have been endless red tape. I couldn't handle that. It would have been worse than trying to find a needle in a haystack; it would be like trying to scoop up the moon from the bottom of the sea."

"You're quite right!" concurred Thomas. "You probably would have come up with nothing."

Uncle Charles's factual details on Hongkew and Hong Kong during the war years provided some depth to the more superficial memories the sisters and Auntie Ellie had of that period. The sisters had been too young to understand the social disparity between their circle of relatives and friends and the downtrodden in the poor areas. Auntie Ellie had been too protected from the reality of the goings-on in Hongkew. The information on Hong Kong during the war years was an eye-opener for everyone.

"My in-laws did escape to Hong Kong in 1940," said Rhae. "My husband, Dean, was about two years old, and his sister barely one. Because they were not bona fide residents of Hong

Kong, and food and all supplies were terribly scarce, they were ordered deported from the colony. They decided to return to Shanghai, so my father-in-law registered with the ship company to purchase their fares. Every day the company posted a list of names of those who were to get the tickets.

"My mother-in-law used to tell me about the horrible experience they had coming back to Shanghai on a ship. They were not given much food. Each family huddled together at the bottom of the ship and slept on the floor. It was as dirty as anything. So many people got sick. She said it was a miracle they survived the journey. Looking back, she felt lucky that they were able to leave Hong Kong. The subsequent shortage of food led to many deaths from starvation. If they had stayed, they might have been among the statistics."

Yvette joined in. "Yes, Shanghai was in bad shape, but compared to other cities it was nothing. We were spared the horrors of the Nanking massacre and the biochemical experimentation on people in Manchuria. As well, we escaped the desperation of those in Hong Kong. I don't think too many starved to death in Shanghai. And we were not forced to learn Japanese at the cost of abandoning our own language."

"I can't imagine that at the end of the war there were only six hundred thousand people left in Hong Kong. The streets must have seen almost deserted then. And look at it now. Officially, the population is said to be more than seven million, not counting the illegal migrants," Linny remarked.

"Hong Kong has gone through many ups and downs. It would be fascinating if someone wrote about the past seventy or eighty years in Hong Kong from a personal perspective," said Rhae.

"Another project on the horizon?" queried Sheryl.

"Definitely not! But I wish someone would do that," answered Rhae.

When tea was served after dinner, the conversation turned to the issue of ancestry. It was on everyone's mind.

"I'm anxious to hear about the results of the DNA analysis. How did yours go, Adele?" asked Rhae.

"Unfortunately, mine is not completed yet. Because Auntie Muriel lives in the United States and I'm in Canada, there are some glitches regarding this special package deal of three for the price of one. The company is sending me a different package, and so far I haven't received it. Somehow I have a feeling this particular company is a bit fishy. They only do the analysis back about five hundred years. When a company offers three analyses for the price of one, it makes you wonder about their professionalism and their accuracy. So, mine is still an unknown. Sorry to disappoint you," replied Adele.

"What about Auntie Muriel and Wes?" asked Rhae.

"Auntie Muriel's says hers is mostly East Asian," said Yvette. "As Adele mentioned, this company only goes back five hundred years. I don't think we need anyone to tell us our family was mostly East Asian for the past five hundred years."

"Now, my turn to tell you about Wes's genetic makeup," Linny was eager to speak. "It's rather intriguing!"

"How so?" asked Thomas.

"You wouldn't believe this." Linny shook her head. "The analysis says that, on his father's side, it is Han Chinese. But on his mother's side, which means us, it is . . . listen to this . . . sixty-seven percent Chinese and the rest is Middle Eastern, plus First Nations from twelve thousand years ago. Can you imagine! What a mixed pot we are!"

"Are you unhappy with that?" asked Sheryl.

"No, I'm not unhappy. I'm just bewildered. We are still in the dark. Does Middle Eastern mean Jewish or Arab or what. And how on earth did we get the First Nations blood. As far as we know, there is no known connection to any American aboriginals in our ancestry," stated Linny.

"They can trace that far back? To twelve thousand years ago?" asked Rhae.

"It looks that way," said Sheryl. "If you follow the theory of evolution, don't they say that homo sapiens started from Africa in the very beginning, and it was later on that branches travelled to Europe or Asia."

"As I recall, in Asia one branch went eastward through India and southern China and moved along the coast northward towards Russia. About twelve thousand years ago, humans first crossed the land bridge from Asia to Alaska and migrated south along the coast to reach South America." Thomas charted the migration pattern of early humans.

"We must have shared some of the genes from way back when with the Native Americans. But since the migration route from Africa reached Asia first, before it arrived at the Americas, it is technically more accurate to say that the American Aboriginals share some of the Chinese Han genes, wouldn't you agree?" asked Adele.

"You do have a point there," said Rhae. "I'm happy that we have such a good mixture of genes from different regions. I think it has been good for us."

"Undeniably!" said Thomas. "In future, there will be even more mixes in our descendants. The combinations and permutations of all the different gene pools will produce fascinating outcomes, no doubt. This probably is happening more and more by the minute."

Auntie Ellie, who had been quiet all evening, spoke up. "This has been quite an education for me. The beginning of human beings had never entered my mind. It is really interesting. I guess I'm of a typical traditional Chinese mentality that asks not where we came from or where we go after life, but are concerned chiefly with how we fare in this life. Here and now. Practical, I guess."

"Now that the DNA analysis has not given you a conclusive answer as to whether you are of Jewish descent, are you going to do something more to try to find out?"

"I suppose we can go for even more extensive DNA analysis if we wish. But for me, it doesn't matter whether we are of Jewish descent or not. I'm happy to have found out so much about the different pieces of history and that our forefathers might or might not be part of them," answered Rhae. "When Professor Li first pointed out the possibility of our being the descendants of Kaifeng Chinese Jews, I thought it was so cool being a Chinese Jew, because that would be a 'rare breed,' but now I am more inclined to think there are countless so-called rare breeds, and some are even more interesting than ours."

"Same here," echoed Adele. "I'm satisfied that I am me. Han Chinese or Jewish or Native American or whatever."

"I wouldn't mind finding out more," declared Linny, who never gave up easily on anything. "I may go for some more tests. Just out of curiosity."

"I'm with Rhae. It has been fun and exciting to dig up historic material. Quite a collaborative exercise for all of us. I really enjoyed it. As to ancestry, I'm not too concerned," Yvette said.

"Well, I'll just take for granted that we are of Jewish descent, as well as having Native American genes somewhere along the line," Sheryl chimed in. "I bet most of the people here in Toronto are just as mixed as we are. I doubt if anyone is really and truly pure in his or her racial makeup. Appearances can be deceptive. Who would have thought that we were anything but pure Han Chinese. And Han is not pure either for that matter."

"True!" exclaimed Adele. "Look at Thomas. His skin is so fair, you could easily say he has Caucasian genes. Yet, as far as he knows, for the past five generations his forebears were all Chinese from Taishan. But who knows, maybe many centuries ago there was a mixture of some other race."

"When you are my age," said Auntie Ellie, "a lot of things don't matter anymore. To me, a person is a person. I don't care if he or she is of one particular race or another. I value the quality of the person more than anything else. Colour, creed, race, gender, age, sexual preference . . . they don't concern me."

"You are thoroughly modern, Auntie Ellie. You can be our role model. We should all be so broad-minded and inclusive," Yvette said, and everyone nodded and smiled.

"Since we did so well in finding information and sharing it, I think we should continue to do the same on another topic. It makes our retirement years a lot more meaningful than, say, going on cruises or playing mah-jeung. What think you?" asked Sheryl.

Thomas stood up and pointed a finger in the air and said in a cheerful tone: "Aha! Another project? Let me see. I would suggest that we go from Chinese Jews to Aboriginal Americans. I for one do not know enough about them, and I think it will be a fascinating subject to study. And this time I'll do my bit in getting the information."

"I second that," said Rhae.

"I'll go for it too," Yvette agreed. "I don't know how my friends can go on cruises several times a year. I think I'll limit my wanderlust to one or two at the most in any given year. This searching for knowledge and information sounds great. It'll keep my brain working."

"We can be a bit more organized this time," suggested Adele. "We should first confine the area to North America and assign different regions to each of us . . ."

Inadvertently, the five sisters, together with Thomas and Auntie Ellie, had formed a "Group of Seven" of sorts. Quite to their surprise, they actually worked well together in their search and research for material. They did not argue or bicker over details as they usually did during most of their family dinners. Maybe this was one of the reasons it was stimulating and enjoyable for them and that they wanted to tackle another topic.

A NEW ENDEAVOUR BEGINS.

Chronology of Chinese History

1. **Primitive Society – approximately 1.7 million year ago to 2100 BCE** 原始社会
   Approximately 1.7 million years ago – Yuan Mou Ren in Yunnan Province area 元谋人
   Approximately 700,000 – 200,000 years ago – Beijing Apeman near Zhoukoudian 北京猿人
   Approximately 18,000 years ago – Shan Ding Dong Ren began communal society 山顶洞人
   Approximately 4,000 years ago – legendary period of Huang Di, Yao, Sheng, Yu 皇帝 尧 舜 禹

2. **Slavery Society – approximately 2100 BCE to 476 BCE** 奴隶社会
   Xia – approximately 2100 BCE to 1600 BCE 夏朝
   Shang – approximately 1600 BCE to 1100 BCE 商朝
   Zhou – approximately 1100 BCE to 771 BCE 周朝
   Spring and Autumn Period – 770 BCE to 476 BCE 春秋

3. **Feudal Society – 475 BCE to 1840 CE** 封建社会
   Warring States – 475 BCE to 221 BCE 战国
   Qin – 221 BCE to 206 BCE 秦朝
   West Han – 206 BCE to 25 CE 西汉
   East Han – 25 CE to 220 CE 东汉
   Three Kingdoms / Two Jin / Northern and Southern Dynasties – 220 CE to 589 CE 三国 两晋 南北朝
   Sui – 581 CE to 618 CE 隋朝
   Tang – 618 CE to 907 CE 唐朝

Five Dynasties – 907 CE to 960 CE 五代
Northern Song Dynasty – 960 CE to 1127 CE 北宋
Southern Song Dynasty – 1127 CE to 1276 CE 南宋
Yuan Dynasty – 1271 CE to 1368 CE 元朝
Ming Dynasty – 1368 CE to 1644 CE 明朝
Qing Dynasty – 1644 CE to 1912 CE 清朝

4. **Republic of China – 1912 to 1949** 中华民国

5. **People's Republic of China – 1949 to present** 中华人民共和国

Chronology of Events Relevant to This Book

Year	Month	Event
998		A large contingent of Jews arrives to settle in Kaifeng, Capital of Northern Song Dynasty.
1168		Completion of the Kaifeng synagogue, the Qing Zhen Si (Clear and True Temple)
1839	March	Qing Emperor Daoguang sends Lin Zexu to Canton to deal with opium importing.
	June	Lin Zexu burns opium imported by British and American traders at Hukou.
1840	June	British invade China. First Opium War begins.
1842	August	Treaty of Nanking (Nanjing). First Opium War ends. Opening of five treaty ports: Shanghai, Ningbo, Xiamen, Fuzhou, and Canton (Guangzhou).
		Ceding of Hong Kong Island to Queen Victoria and her successors in perpetuity.
		Payment by the Qing government to Great Britain of a total of $21 million, to be made by the end of 1845.
1844	July	Treaty signed between the United States and China, giving Americans same right as the British to trade in Treaty Ports, plus a number of important additions. Article 21 states that

(continued)

Year	Month	Event
		Americans committing crimes in China can only be tried and punished by duly empowered American officials and according to the laws of the United States (extraterritoriality).
1844	October	France signs treaty with China, acquiring same rights to trade as the British and the Americans. It re-emphasizes the principle of extraterritoriality with even greater force than for the Americans.
1848		American Bishop William Boone establishes headquarters in Hongkew, an area in Shanghai, the beginning of American settlement.
1849	April	Shanghai French Concession boundaries defined; initial area of 164 acres would be expanded several times in later years.
1850s		The first Sephardi Jews arrive in Shanghai from India. Elias Sassoon opens the first Jewish Office in Shanghai.
1851–1864		Taiping Rebellion in China. Leader Hong Xiuquan claims to be a younger brother of Jesus Christ and declares himself the Heavenly King of Taiping Tianguo (Heavenly Kingdom of Great Peace).
1856–1859		Second Opium War.
1858	June	Treaty of Tianjin, with extraordinarily strict terms on China.
		A supplementary clause explicitly imposes a system of importing and selling of opium in China, despite the fact that the Chinese penal code prohibits the sale and consumption of opium.
		Part of the mainland Kowloon peninsula is ceded to Hong Kong.

Year	Month	Event
1859	October	British chief negotiator, Lord Elgin, orders his troops to burn down Yuan Ming Yuan Summer Palace in Beijing, allowing looting by the troops.
1860		Convention of Peking (Beijing) rectified.
1863		Amalgamation of British and American settlements in Shanghai.
1880		Elly Kadoorie arrives in Shanghai to work for the Sassoon Company.
1880–1917		Exodus of Russian Jews from Russia, mostly to Britain and the United States. Jewish settlement in Harbin begins in 1897. By 1920, the Harbin Jewish population reaches fifteen thousand.
1883–1885		Franco-China war.
1894–1895		Sino-Japanese War. Treaty of Shimonoseki signed in 1896.
1900		Outbreak of Boxer Uprising in China. Eight foreign nations jointly invade China.
1904–1905		Russo-Japanese War
1907		The first Russian Ashkenazi congregation is founded in Shanghai.
1908		Emperor Xuantong accedes to the throne at age six.
1910		The Sephardi community of Shanghai numbers over seven hundred under the leadership of D.E.J. Abraham
1911		Outbreak of the Republican Revolution, led by Dr. Sun Yatsen.
1912	January	Establishment of Republic of China. Qing Dynasty ends.

Year	Month	Event
1917	August	China declares war on Germany and Austria-Hungary.
1917		Tsar of Russia is deposed. The Soviet Union is established. Migration of White Russians begins. Many settle in Harbin.
1924		The Russian-Jewish population in Shanghai reaches one thousand.
1931	Sept.	Japan launches military operation in Manchuria. Anti-Japanese movement begins in the northeast provinces and spreads throughout China.
1931	onward	Migration of Russian Jews from Harbin to Tianjin and Shanghai. Approximately eight thousand settle in Shanghai.
1933		Japan establishes Manchukuo in Manchuria and places the last Qing emperor, Puyi, as puppet head.
		Hitler becomes Chancellor of Germany. Persecution of Jews begins. German Jews begin arriving in Shanghai.
1936		The Rome-Berlin Axis is announced after Nazi Germany and Fascist Italy sign a treaty of cooperation.
1937		Japan invades China, occupying Beijing, Shanghai, Nanking, and other coastal cities, initiating war in the Pacific. Beginning December 13, the "Rape of Nanking" continues for seven weeks. It is carried out by Japanese soldiers who unleashed an unparalleled storm of violence and cruelty on the civilians. An estimated 300,000 civilians, many of them children, are massacred.

Year	Month	Event
1938		Germany annexes Austria. Jews seek refuge outside German-occupied areas.
		Germany terminates the Sino-German Alliance with the Republic of China. Germany recognizes Japanese authority in Manchuria.
1939	March	France and Great Britain guarantee the integrity of the borders of the Polish state.
	August	Nazi Germany and the Soviet Union sign a non-aggression agreement with a secret codicil, dividing eastern Europe into spheres of influence.
	Sept. 1	Germany invades Poland from the west, initiating World War II in Europe.
	Sept. 3	France and Great Britain honour their guarantee of Polish borders and declare war on Germany.
	Sept. 17	The U.S.S.R. invades Poland from the east. Warsaw surrenders. The Polish government flees into exile. Colonel Joseph Meisinger begins extermination of Polish-Jews; he is nicknamed "The Butcher of Warsaw."
		By the end of 1939, seventeen thousand German and Austrian Jews find refuge in Shanghai.
1940		Germany invades Norway and Denmark, attacks Western Europe – France, the neutral Low Countries, Luxembourg – establishing the Vichy government in France.
	June	Italy enters the war and invades southern France.
	July/Aug.	The Soviet Union occupies the Baltic States, annexing them as Soviet Republics.

Year	Month	Event
	Sept.	Germany, Italy, and Japan sign the Tripartite Pact.
1941		The last of the 1,000 Polish Jews arrive in Shanghai.
	June–Nov.	Nazi Germany and its partners invade the Soviet Union.
	Dec.	Soviet counteroffensive drives the Germans from Moscow.
		Japanese navy attacks Pearl Harbor. U.S.A. enters World War II.
		Japanese troops invade Hong Kong, land in the Philippines, Vietnam, Laos, Cambodia, and Singapore.
		Hong Kong comes under Japanese rule for three years and eight months.
		European Jewish refugee population in Shanghai nears 25,000.
1942		Colonel Joseph Meisinger arrives in Shanghai with his plans to exterminate the Jewish refugees in Shanghai.
1943	February	Japanese authority proclaims all stateless refugees to be confined in a ghetto in the Hongkew (Hongkou) area.
		Japanese authority sets up eight or more camps to accommodate Foreign Nationals in Shanghai.
1944	June	British and U.S. troops land in Normandy, France. Soviet Union launches offensive on the eastern front.
1945	January	Germans are in retreat.
	April	April 30, Hitler commits suicide.
	May	Germany surrenders to western Allies and the Soviets.

Year	Month	Event
	August 6	U.S. drops atomic bomb on Hiroshima.
	August 8	Soviet Union declares war on Japan and invades Manchuria.
	August 9	U.S. drops atomic bomb on Nagasaki.
	August 14	Japan surrenders unconditionally. World War II ends.
1948		The State of Israel is founded on May 14.
1949		The Chinese Communist Liberation Army enters Shanghai at the end of May. The People's Republic of China is founded on October 1.

Notes

Text
CE (common era) is used in place of AD for years or centuries after birth of Christ and BCE (before common era) in place of BC (before Christ).

The notes below are indicated by an asterisk (*) in the text.

Preface
p. xi: The comment on the unreliability of memory is from David McRaney, *You Are Not So Smart: Why Your Memory is Mostly Fiction, Why You Have Too Many Friends on Facebook and 46 Other Ways You're Deluding Yourself*, New York: Gotham, 2012.

PART ONE:

Introduction
p. 3: **Oriental Jews** – There are a number of subgroups of Jews who all share the same basic beliefs of Judaism, but have variations in their cultural and traditional practices. Oriental Jews are descendants of Jews of East Asia, mainly of Japan and China. Other subgroups include Sephardic, Ashkenazi, Mizrahi, Yemenite, and Ethiopian.

Chapter 1: Blue-Cap Hui Hui

p. 7: **kang** 炕 – Heated brick beds that in the past were commonly used along the Yellow River in Northern China.

p. 8: **Blue-Cap Hui Hui** 蓝帽回回 – The name local Chinese used to refer to the Israelites. Hui Hui was a general term for people from the Middle East. The Jews were called Blue-Cap Hui Hui, because they wore blue during their religious ceremonies, whereas Muslims were called White-Cap Hui Hui, because they wore white during their religious ceremonies.

p. 12: **Ba Zi** 八字 – Each of the four components in a person's birth date – the year, month, day, and hour – is represented by two characters. The resulting eight characters form a person's ba zi.

In the Chinese calendar, each year is named after an animal. The first two characters, therefore, also indicate the animal symbol under which the person was born.

In China, the ba zi is important to a person's life journey. Purportedly, the eight characters map out the significant happenings in the person's life and seal his or her fate. When a person consults a feng shui master about his house, the master would base his geomantic calculations on the person's ba zi and correlate them to the house. Likewise, a fortune-teller, when consulted, will read the same ba zi before telling the client anything about his future, his past, or his present. But at no time have the eight characters been more important than at the birth of a person and at the time when a marriage is being arranged, although this is rarely the case today.

If a newborn's ba zi indicated that he or she was likely to bring conflict to the family, then measures would have been taken to remedy the situation. In an extreme case, the infant may have been given away to another family as a precautionary move to fend off the likelihood of possible calamities or catastrophe.

In the arrangement of a marriage, usually the boy's family would ask for the girl's ba zi. The girl's family could accept or deny the request. But once a girl's ba zi had been given out to one family, it could not be given to another family until it was returned from the first family. When the ba zis of prospective partners were in place, the family would call on a fortune-teller to spell out the pros and cons of the intended union. The reading was to calculate the bride's compatibility not only to her future husband but also to her future parents-in-law and future descendants. This custom had gone on for thousands of years, and people genuinely believed that their fate was intrinsically connected to and governed by their set of "Eight Characters."

p. 18: **Bao Gong** 包公 – A legendary folk hero who was famed for his righteousness and fairness. His prefecture was in Kaifeng during the Song Dynasty.

p. 21: **Mao hour** 卯时 – Between 5 a.m. and 7 a.m. The Chinese traditional way of marking time was to divide the day and night into twelve sections. Each section represents a period of about two hours. It begins with the Zi-hour 子时, from 11:00 p.m. to 1:00 a.m.

Chapter 2: Road to Shanghai

p. 28: **Grand Canal System** – The entire Grand Canal System was completed during the reign of the second Sui emperor (604–609 CE), and it connected the Yellow River, the Yangtze River, the Qiantang River, and the Huai, Wei, and Wai rivers. It linked northern China from cities like Luoyang and Kaifeng all the way to Yangzhou in Jiangsu Province. It made transportation much easier, especially for shipping the grain collected as taxes from the fertile Yangtze plain to the northern provinces, where troops were stationed.

Alongside the canal was an imperial roadway, with intermittent posts through which the emperor and his ministers in the different provinces and cities couriered their documents back and forth. It was a primitive postal service. When there was an emergency, the emperor would dispatch a fast horse to carry messages to his ministers. It was faster than travelling by water.

p. 31: **Taiping Rebellion** – This peasant movement was led by Hong Xiuquan, born in 1814 in an ethnic Hakka family in Guangdong. In despondency after repeated failure at the imperial examinations, Hong was introduced to a book on Christianity. He was impressed by the Christian doctrine of teaching people to live peacefully together. In 1843, he founded "worship God religion" and began to teach people to worship God and live a just life, that all men were equal before God. He and his close friends baptized their followers, telling them Hong was Jesus' brother and was authorized by God to rid the world of evil. Their organization expanded quickly and began to revolt against the government. In 1851, Hong established "Taiping (peaceful) Heavenly Kingdom" and began a full-scale revolution. By 1856 the Taiping army controlled most of Jiangxi, Anhui, Hubei Jiangsu – more than ten provinces. Their success went to their heads and the leadership group began to have internal conflict and dissention as to who was the ultimate leader. The Taiping movement began to disintegrate, and in the end it was defeated by the joint armies of Generals Zeng Guofan, Zuo Zongtang, and Li Hongzhang, along with western foreign troops. The Taiping Heavenly Kingdom was crushed in 1864.

p. 31: **Boxer Uprising** 义和团 – Material on the Boxer Rebellion can be found in Jonathan Spence, *The Search for Modern China, 3rd ed.*, New York: Norton, 2012, p. 235.

p. 35: **mong han yao**, "sleeping fumes" – It was a practice by thieves and robbers to put people to sleep by spraying a kind of anaesthetic smoke before they carried out their crimes. As late as the twentieth century, criminals were known to use this method in their break-and-enter activities.

p. 40: **yin piao** 银票 – A certificate issued by money house for a certain amount, cashable at other money houses.

p. 40: **money house or money farm** 钱庄 – This refers to the early form of banks in China during the nineteenth century.

p. 40: **mother's savings, or siji** 私己 – In the old days, the women of most households would try to put aside a small amount from their housekeeping money as their savings for old age.

p. 43: **Double Month party, or Shuang Man Yue** 双满月 – The Chinese customarily celebrate the birth of a newborn when the baby is one month old. Some people opt to celebrate when the baby is two months old, and this is called a "Double Month" celebration.

p. 44: **Jingdezheng porcelain** – Jingdezhen is situated in the northeast part of Poyang Plain in Jiangxi Province. For over two thousand years, it was known as the porcelain capital of the world.

Jingdezhen began producing porcelain as far back as the Han Dynasty (220–206 BCE). At the time the area was called Xin Pin. During the Northern Song Dynasty, in the eleventh century, the name was changed to Changnan. By then the porcelain from Changnan was already well known beyond the boundaries of China. It was from this name, Changnan, associated with the exquisite quality of the porcelain from the area, that the English word "china" came to represent both the finest porcelain as well as the name for the country where the porcelain was produced.

A later Song Emperor Jingde (1004–1007) decreed that all the pieces made for the imperial court be marked "made in the Jingde period." As time went on, Changnan became known as Jingde-zhen, "the Town of Jingde."

Some of the most famous types of porcelain from Jingdezhen include the almost-translucent "rice pattern" that was introduced during the Song Dynasty and the "blue and white" porcelain that began during the subsequent Yuan Dynasty.

Because of the Kaolin earth in the Poyang basin, the exquisite porcelain pieces have been described as being: "as white as jade, as bright as a mirror, as thin as paper, with a sound as clear as a bell."

Today, Jingdezhen remains a national centre for porcelain production. There is a ceramic research institute and a ceramic museum, along with five kaolin quarries, fifteen factories, and two porcelain machinery plants.

p. 44: **Poyang Hu** 鄱阳湖 – Located in the northern part of China's southeastern province of Jiangxi, it is the largest freshwater lake in China. The lake system stretches 170 km from north to south and the widest part is about 74 km. It supplies water to both Jiangsu and Shandong provinces. In the past century, the lake has been silting up badly. Nanchang, the capital of Jiangxi, used to be right at the lakeshore, but is now about 24 km (15 miles) from it.

At Poyang Hu is one of the largest migratory bird protection areas in the world, encompassing a total of 224 sq. km (86 sq. miles). Due to the mild climate, abundant aquatic plants, and unpolluted fish, the sanctuary is the winter home to the world's largest population of migratory birds. It is called Migratory Birds Paradise. Birds from Siberia, Mongolia, Japan, and North Korea, as well as the northeastern and northwestern regions of China come to stay here during the cold months. It is also home to 95 per cent of the world's endangered White Crane species, known as the Black Sleeve Cranes, or the Immortal Cranes in China.

p. 48: **mellow fruitfulness** – Taken from John Keats's poem "Ode to Autumn," which begins with the line "Season of mists and mellow fruitfulness . . ."

Chapter 3: Revelation

p. 52: **cheong-sam** – Chinese traditional attire for a female. It hugs the body and features a high collar and two slits at the sides of the lower portion of the dress. It began in the early twentieth century and is still in fashion in the twenty-first century. Many different variations of the cheong-sam have developed, some of which incorporate western influences.

p. 55: **xian nv** 仙女 – Fairy or nymph or ethereal maiden.

p. 56: **Zhu's Didactics** 朱子家训 – A classical piece of Confucian teaching, setting out the duties and obligations of each member in the family.

p. 56: **dishu** 棣书 – One of the older formal styles of Chinese calligraphy. The expression "dishu" literally means square calligraphy. It is commonly used on tombstones nowadays. Beginning in the 1990s, dishu has become popular throughout China.

p. 58: **Zhao Kuangyin** 赵匡胤 – The first emperor of the Song Dynasty (960–1127 CE).

p. 62: **Year of the Horse** – The Chinese calendar is based on a twelve-year cycle. Each year is represented by an animal, hence each person has an animal symbol 生肖 or birth-image 属相 (the likeness a person belongs to), depending on the year the person is born. The twelve animals rank as follows: Rat, Ox, Tiger, Rabbit, Dragon, Snake (Earth Dragon), Horse, Sheep, Monkey, Rooster (Phoenix), Dog, Pig.

Chapter 4: Searching for the Past

p. 66: **Sinia** – The passage from Isaiah 49: 12 mentioning "those from the land of Sinim" is now accepted as not referring to China. There is probably no Jewish reference to China before the ninth century.

(Donald Daniel Leslie, *The Survival of the Chinese Jews: The Jewish Community of Kaifeng*, Leiden: Brill Acdemic, 1973, p. 3).

p. 70: **Chong Yang Festival** 重阳节 – A traditional Chinese festival that falls on the ninth day of the ninth lunar month, hence also known as the Double Nine Festival. It began as early as the Warring State period (475–221 BCE). On this day, people customarily visit the graves of their ancestors, go hiking, appreciate chrysanthemum blossoms, and drink chrysanthemum wine. Often, families organize an outing together.

p. 73: **occupational rankings** – Social status according to one's occupation, 士, 农, 工, 商, 兵. Scholars are at the top, eligible to become government officials, followed by peasants, labourers, merchants, and soldiers. Merchants and soldiers were not held in high esteem. It behooved the Kaifeng Jews to want to upgrade themselves to the top scholarly rank.

p. 84: **assimilation** – A 1991 discussion of the Kaifeng Jews and assimilation can be found in *Gudai Kaifeng Youtairen* (開封猶太人的同化問題 '當代宗教研究' 1991年第一期), edited by Yang Meiyan, p. 227. The material on the emperor's affair with the prostitute who might have been an Israelite (page 90 here) is on pages 256–8.

p. 86: **The imperial examination system** – See Sidney Shapiro (translator, compiler, and editor), *Jews in Old China: Studies by Chinese Scholars*. Expanded edition. New York: Hippocrene Books, 2000.

Chapter 5: Life in Nanchang

p. 94: **si-he-yuan** 四合院 – In northern China most of the houses were built in the si-he-yuan configuration, that is, rooms on four sides surrounding an open courtyard in the centre.

p. 94: **aiya** 啊呀 – A common exclamation used by Chinese to show surprise, joy, regret, etc.

p. 94: **foot binding** – For more information see Rita Aero, *Things Chinese*, New York: Doubleday, 1980; John King Fairbank, *The Great Chinese Revolution: 1800–1985*, New York: Harper & Row, 1986;

Dorothy Ko, *Every Step a Lotus: Shoes for Bound Feet*, Oakland: University of California Press, 2001.

p. 100: **extraterritoriality** – An explanation of extrateritorriality can be found in Henry J. Lethbridge, *All About Shanghai: A Standard Guidebook*, Oxford in Asia Paperbacks, Oxford University Press, 1986. (First published in 1934.)

The principal of extraterritoriality was to allow foreign residents in China to be exempt from Chinese law and jurisdiction when they committed a crime in China. They were to be judged and sentenced according to the laws of their respective native countries.

The practice began with the British consular officials being authorized to arbitrate and settle the differences of their nationals with Chinese. In 1844 the United States negotiated a treaty with China. In it there was a much clearer and more concise definition of the principles of extraterritoriality.

Fourteen foreign nations, signatories to "favoured nations" treaties with China, exercised extraterritoriality privileges and rights in Shanghai: the United States, Belgium, Brazil, Great Britain, Denmark, France, Italy, Japan, The Netherlands, Norway, Portugal, Spain, Sweden, and Switzerland. Austria, Germany, Hungary, and Russia did not have such privileges.

Those with these privileges had either their own national courts or consular courts. The British had H.R.M. Supreme Court. The U.S. had the United States Court of China. All other foreign tribunals were consular courts, presided over by their respective consul generals – with the exception of France, Italy, and Japan, who had special judges appointed for the purpose.

p. 101: **Methodist missionaries** – Information is based on: William Townsend, *Robert Morrison: The Pioneer of Chinese Missions*, London: S.W. Partridge, 1890. (http://www.globalportal.umich.edu/2011/01/07/the-new-women-of-china).

In 1847, almost single-handedly, Rev. Judson Dwight Collins initiated the American Methodist Episcopal Mission in China. His passion and hard work paid off. Within years, the Methodist mission extended from Fuzhou in Fujian Province, covering six large districts with sixty stations that included Beijing, Tianjin in the north, three hundred miles along the banks of Yangtze River, westward to Chongqing. They built schools and hospitals and were among the most successful missionary groups in China.

Jiujiang in Jinagxi Province was one of the early stations. In 1892, two young female natives of Jiujiang, Ida Kahn (original name Kang Cheng aka Kang Aide) and Mary Stone (original name Shi Meiyu), were groomed by a missionary-teacher Gertrude Howe, who sponsored them to study medicine at the University of Michigan, Ann Arbor. They graduated in 1896. Not only were they the first Asians to earn degrees at the University of Michigan, but were also among the very first Chinese women ever to become Western-trained physicians.

The two women doctors returned to Jiujiang and, as representatives of the Women's Foreign Missionary Society of the Methodist Church, they opened a small hospital for women and children in Jiujiang. Ida Kahn later founded and led a new hospital in Nanchang, Jiangxi. The Nanchang Hospital became Jiangxi Provincial People's Hospital. It is now one of the top hospitals in China.

p. 104: *I-Ching* 易经 – *The Book of Changes,* one of the Ancient Chinese classics.

Chapter 8: Gande in Ascendancy

p. 127: **child bride** 童养媳 – Records show that the child-bride practice in China began as early as the Three Kingdom Period (220–265 CE). It arose from gender discrimination that led to some poor families opting to sell their daughters at an early age to be raised by a richer family as a future daughter-in-law. Polygamy also played a role in this practice. In Imperial China it was not an uncommon practice among the poor. Child brides were often treated like slaves and had to do all the menial household chores.

p. 127: **bondmaid** 丫头 – In feudal society, young girls from poor families were traded as commodities. They were bought or sold or given as gifts. Usually they worked as scullery maids. Some were promoted to become personal maids. Many were sexually abused by their masters and suffered dire consequences. It was not uncommon for bondmaids to be chosen as concubines.

Chapter 9: SOCNY

p. 131: **mus** 亩 – Plural for "mu," a measurement of a piece of land. One mu of land is approximately equivalent to one-sixth of an English acre.

p. 133: **Yuan Shikai** 袁世凯 – He was one of the most despised characters in recent Chinese history. He betrayed Emperor Guangxu 光绪, who entrusted him with the mission to suppress the power of the Empress Dowager Cixi. The Emperor had welcomed new ideas and was ready to embrace progress and advancement for the country, but his power was curtailed because the Empress Dowager was still very much in command. Emperor Guangxu had to establish his authority before he could go full speed ahead with his renewal plan for the country. The first thing to do was to strip the Empress Dowager of her supreme command. Yuan pretended to be supportive of the emperor's efforts but secretly reported the emperor's plan to his superior, General Ronglu 荣禄, who was a personal guard of Cixi. Cixi acted swiftly. The emperor was put under house arrest, and his favourite consort, Zhen-fei 珍妃, considered to be an undesirable influence on the emperor, was thrown into a well to die

p. 135: **"in search of change, of hope and of salvation for their country and the people"** – The state of affairs in China in the early twentieth century led to the birth of the Chinese Communist Party. Relevant material can be found in Jonathan D. Spence, *The Search for Modern China*, Chapters 10 to 12.

Chapter 11: A Salt Licence

p. 144: **saddle ring** 马鞍戒 – A decorative jade band to wear on the finger. The top rectangular portion resembles a saddle, and the entire ring is carved out of a whole piece of jade.

p. 144: **Qi Baishi** 齐白石 – One of the best-known Chinese brush artists of the early twentieth century.

p. 145: **Indian opium** – The best quality opium was grown in India and in Yunnan Province in China. Other opiums produced in China were of lesser quality and not as desirable. Indian opium was more costly. Users accustomed to Indian opium would not want to smoke Chinese-grown opium.

p. 150: **broomstick curse** 扫帚星 – A term used for someone considered as bad luck. A broom is considered the lowliest item in the household; it doesn't bring any joy, happiness, or wealth to people. It is used to discard rubbish, and hence is not a welcome item that people would treasure.

Chapter 12: A Knock on the Door

p. 159: **silver standards** – Silver standards indicate the standard of fineness or purity for the silver alloy used in the manufacture or crafting of silver objects or bullion.

Fine silver has a millesimal fineness of 999. It is called pure silver or three nine fine. It contains 99.9 per cent silver with 0.1 per cent of impurities. Fine silver is used to make bullion bars for international commodity trading and investment in silver.

Mexican silver has a millesimal fineness of 950. It contains 95 per cent pure silver and 5 per cent copper or other metals. From 1930 to 1945, Mexican silver had a millesimal fineness of 980.

p. 161: **Chiang Kaishek's campaigns** – Accounts can be found in Jonathan Spence, *In Search of Modern China*, Chapter 14, "The Clash."

PART 2

Introduction

p. 174: **Hong** 行 – A specialized company that dealt exclusively with foreign traders who brought merchandise to China. Most of the Hongs were stationed in Canton, the major port in south China. Because of the distance from Canton to the central government in Beijing, it was difficult for the Qing rulers to exert effective control over the Hong's activities in their dealings with the foreign traders.

p. 175: **Lin Zexu** 林则徐 – A minister sent by Emperor Dao Guang to Canton in 1839 to deal with the opium problem. His burning of the opium brought in by British traders, in June 1839, provided the British government with an excuse to dispatch a fleet of sixteen warships carrying 540 guns, four armed steamers, 28 transports and 4,000 troops that started the First Opium War in 1840.

p. 175: **BBC History** – The program aired in Britain on December 3, 2012.

p. 177: **No visa required to enter Shanghai** – The officials of the Nationalist government used to handle the passport control at the port of entry, but this had ceased to function. None of the foreign powers wanted to assume the authority for fear that the Japanese would want to participate. Consequently, there was no control at the entry point, making Shanghai a "free port." Details can be found in Irene Eber (trans.), *Voices from Shanghai: Jewish Exiles in Wartime China*, Chicago: University of Chicago Press, 2008, p. 9.

Chapter 14: Carefree Days

p. 184: **Zeng Guofan** 曾国藩 – A powerful minister and general during the late Qing Dynasty. Zeng was a native of Hunan Province and he led the Hunan army famed for their valour. General Zeng was credited with crushing the Taiping movement in 1864.

p. 190: **taipan** 大班 – A term used to refer to the head of a large corporation.

Chapter 15: Destiny Dictates

p. 195: **The Communists' "Long March"** – An account can be found in Jonathan Spence, *In Search of Modern China*, Chapter 16, "The Drift to War."

p. 196: **Fox spirit** 狐狸精 – A ghost-character, from an early Chinese novel *Liao Zhai* 聊斋, who appears at night in the form of an attractive woman, usually to entice innocent men.

p. 198: **Youtairen** 犹太人 – Jews were referred to by many different names in Chinese history. It was not until the Qing Dynasty that the term You Tai was used to denote people of the Hebrew faith. Ren means person in Chinese.

Chapter 17: Striking Out on His Own

p. 230: **Jiu Shanghai de Yan Chang Du**, "旧上海的烟娼赌" (*Opium, Prostitution, and Gambling in Old Shanghai*), compiled by the Shanghai Culture and History Research Centre, Hong Kong: Zhong Yuan Publishing Co., 1990 (ISBN 962-8277-21-9), pp. 138–39, tells of the incident that led to the amalgamation of SRC and IRK.

Chapter 18: The World at War

p. 243: **Russian Jewish refugees** – From 1821 to 1917, during the Tsarist rules of Alexander II, Alexander III, and Nicholas II, especially the latter two, wave upon wave of repeated large-scale anti-Jewish violence spread throughout the Russian Empire. In major cities like Kiev, Warsaw, Odessa (in Ukraine), as well as in countless smaller cities and villages, Jews suffered persecution at the hands of Christians and government officials. During these pogroms, Jewish homes were destroyed and families reduced to destitution. Many were killed and large numbers of men, women, and children injured.

p. 245: *heim* (plural: *heime*) – A German word that the refugees used for the barrack-like dormitories where European Jews were housed upon arrival in Shanghai.

p. 247: **The European Jewish Refugees**: – Remarks made by Michael Blumenthal, the U.S. secretary of the treasury under President Jimmy Carter at the Rickshaw Reunion, Foster City, California, April 20, 2002, p. 14. It can be found online at The Shanghai Experience and History, https://archive.org/details/20151019115312. He was a former Jewish refugee in Shanghai:

"We were in Shanghai – against our will – because the rest of the world stood by and did nothing until it was too late and tens of millions, Jews and non-Jews, lost their lives. I do not refer only to the fatal efforts to appease a criminal government whose leaders had made no secret of their evil intentions against us, their neighbors and the world. I have in mind also that virtually all countries of the world, even those who condemned anti-Jewish atrocities in words, did much too little to open their doors to shelter us."

p. 248-9: **Schellenberg's memoir** – Walter Schellenberg, *The Labyrinth: Memoirs of Walter Schellenberg*. Boston: Da Capo Press, 2000.

p. 249-50: **Meisinger Plan** – Colonel Joseph Meisinger devised three options for total extermination of Jewish refugees in Shanghai. The details are given in Rabbi Marvin Tokayer and Mary Swartz, *The Fugu Plan: The Untold Story of the Japanese and the Jews During World War II*, Gefen Publishing House Ltd. 2012, pp. 223-4 (ISBN 965-229-329-6). This book also outlines the Fugu Plan.

Chapter 19: Recollections

p. 257: **Bi-luo-chun** 碧螺春 – Literally means "Green Snail Spring." It is a fancy name for a green tea that is often rated as the best among green teas because of its tender and delicate appearance and its refreshing aroma. It originated in the Taihu area in China's Jiangsu Province. It is also produced in Zejiang and Fujian provinces. According to folklore, the tea was so named by Qing Emperor Kangxi 康熙皇帝 during one of his tours of southern China, when he became enamored with the tea's taste and fragrance. Because it is unfermented, Bi-luo-chun retains its natural colour and the leaves display beautifully when brewed in a glass. To maximize its aroma and its delicate taste, Bi-luo-chun is best brewed with water that is hot but not boiling.

p. 260: **comprador** – A native agent for a foreign business in China. The comprador oversaw the native workers, etc.

p. 261: **Mah Jeung** 麻将 – A popular Chinese board game played with tiles, purportedly invented during the Ming Dynasty by seamen.

p. 265: **Marble Hall Ballroom** – Measured 65 feet high, 80 feet long, and 50 feet wide. The verandah was 225 feet long. Evelyn Huang and Lawrence Jeffery, *Hong Kong: Portraits of Power*, Little Brown & Company Limited, 1995 (ISBN 0-316-22052-3), p. 58.

p. 273: **Camps for foreign nationals** – 1. Abandoned building of the Great China University; 2. Pudong camp for single U.S. nationals housed in the British American Tobacco Company warehouse; 3. Zhapei camp; 4. Three camps in Yangzhou, which is two hundred miles from Shanghai; 5. Longhua camp; 6. Columbia Club camp, which housed British families and U.S. missionaries; 7. A camp using a boys' school on Yu Yuan Road housed the Shanghai Municipal Council and police staff; 8. Ash Camp on Great Western Road; 9. A camp on Lincoln Avenue housed mainly the elderly.

p. 279: **Ghoya** – Purportedly he was beaten up by Max Scheldlinger after the Japanese surrender in 1945.

p. 280: **The "Big Feast," or "da cang"** 大餐 – In the Shanghai dialect, this means western cuisine.

p. 286: **Polish Jewish refugees** – Material on this group can be found in the research paper "Polish Jews in Shanghai: Politics and Community Among Survivors" by Andrew Jakubowicz in Australia.

Chapter 20: Sassoons and Hardoon

p. 287: **Sephardic Jews** – There are several subgroups of Jews with different culture and traditions. They all share the same basic beliefs but have variations in culture and practice. Sephardic Jews are descendants of Jews from Spain, Portugal, North Africa, and the Middle East. Ashkenazi Jews are descendants of Jews from France, Germany, and Eastern Europe. Mizrahi Jews are descendants of Jews from North Africa and the Middle East. Other subgroups are Yemenite, Ethiopian and Oriental. (http://www.jewfaq.org/ashkseph.htm)

p. 288: **trade deficit** – Prior to the Opium War, the British trade deficit with China was to the tune of nine million British pounds export to twenty-seven million British pounds import over a period of a few years.

p. 290: **Ohel Rachel Synagogue** – Built in 1920 and dedicated in 1921, it sits on the former Seymour Road, which has been renamed North

Shaanxi Road. It is the largest synagogue in the Far East and is now a protected architectural landmark in Shanghai.

p. 292: **Stella Dong's book** – *Shanghai: The Rise and Fall of a Decadent City*, New York: Harper Collins, 2000.

p. 295: **white for mourning** – It has been a Chinese tradition to wear white for mourning. When a death occurs in a family, the household will be draped in white silk. Mourners will wear white linen shrouds at the funeral. For a close relative, such as parents or a spouse, female members will wear a white floret made of knitting wool in their hair for as long as a year.

p. 298: ***Mandarin Golf & Country Club*** Purchased by a group of mostly Hong Kong immigrants in 1989, it was redesigned and operated as a private club.

Chapter 21: Kaifeng

p. 312: **James Finn**, *The Jews in China: Their Synagogue, Their Scriptures, Their History, etc.* London, 1843, p. 320.

p. 314: **Five sacred mountains** – In China, there are three groups of sacred mountains. This particular group of five mountains has been venerated since the Warring States Period (475–221 BCE) that predated the beginning of the Daoist (Taoist) religious organization or the introduction of Buddhism in China. The five mountains mark the five Cardinal Directions in Chinese Geomancy – East, South, West, North, and Centre, which is considered a direction.

> Tai Shan 泰山 in Shandong Province marks the Eastern Direction. Being in the East, where the sun rises, it is the most sacred of all mountains. Tai Shan itself is a deity to many people, and ancient emperors would go there to make offerings. It is the Mountain of Tranquility.
>
> Heng Shan 衡山 in Hunan Province has over seventy peaks. It marks the Southern Direction and is the Mountain of Balance.

Hua Shan 华山 the tallest of the five, spreads out over 120 kilometres near the ancient capital of Xi'An in Shaanxi Province. It has five peaks and marks the Western Direction. It is the Mountain of Splendour.

Heng Shan 恒山 in Shanxi Province is famed for its hanging temples. It marks the Northern Direction and is the Mountain of Permanence.

Song Shan 嵩山 stretches between Luoyang and Zhengzhou in Henan Province. It has thirty-six peaks and marks the Central Direction. It is the Mountain of Loftiness.

All five mountains are highly venerated by both the Daoists and the Buddhists.

p. 321: **Ru Xue** 儒学 – A Chinese philosophy combining mainly Confucianism infused with feudal practices and Daoist thoughts was the main controlling philosophical outlook of the Chinese people for thousands of year till the founding of the People's Republic of China.

p. 321: **Encyclopedia Judaica** (not to be confused with the *Jewish Encyclopedia*) – First published in 1971, it is an encyclopedia on the Jewish people, the Jewish faith, and the State of Israel, with extensive coverage of Jewish life, culture, history, and religion.

p. 322: ***The East Gate of Kaifeng*** – An article by Wang Zhigao, "The Assimilation of the Kaifeng Jews," appears in *The East Gate of Kaifeng: A Jewish World Inside China*, edited by Patricia Needle. China Center, University of Minnesota, 1992.

p. 323: **Chinese Jews** – In William Charles White, *The Chinese Jews: A Compilation of Matters Relating to the Jews of K'ai-feng Fu*. Toronto, 1942 (reprinted New York, 1966).

p. 324: ***Zuo Tang and Wang Zhilang*** – material can be found in *Gudai Kaifeng Youtairen*, edited by Yang Meiyan. Beijing, 2011, p. 36.

Chapter 22: Uncle Charles

p. 332: ***Juifs de Chine*** – Dr. Donald Daniel Leslie and Joseph Dehergne. *Juifs de Chine,* 中国的犹太人 translated by Geng Sheng (耿昇). Zhengzhou, Henan: Da Xiang Publishing (大象出版社), 2005. ISBN 7-5347-3434-7

Chapter 23: Interlude

p. 342: ***Gabriel Brotier*** – French missionary, a Jesuit priest (1723–1789). He was never in China, but he published a book with the Chinese title "认定居在中国的犹太人" (English translation would be something like "Confirmation of the Jews Living in China"). It was based on all the correspondence of the different Jesuit priests about their experiences with the Kaifeng Jews. It was first published in Latin in 1771 and was published in French in 1774. (Page 25, *Juifs de Chine* by Donald Daniel Leslie, Chinese translation 中国的犹太人, see Chapter 22 note.)

p. 343: ***Giampaolo Gosani*** – Italian missionary, a Jesuit priest who made several attempts to obtain a Torah scroll from the Kaifeng Jews without success.

Chinese Usage and Glossary

Pinyin is used for all Chinese characters except a few of the proper nouns that have been accepted in their historic spellings: for example, Peking for Beijing, Nanking for Nanjing, Hongkew for Hongkou, and some people's names, such as Chiang Kaishek for Jiang Jieshi or Sun Yatsen for Sun Yixian.

All Chinese names are presented in the Chinese way, that is, surname first, followed by given name(s). If the given name consists of two or more characters, they are spelled out as one word or hyphenated.

The surname Zhao was historically spelled "Chao," as it is in most of the earlier writings by Bishop William White and others. It is also spelled in many other ways, depending on the geographic regional pronunciations, such as: Chiu in Hong Kong, Djao in Shanghai, Chao in Taiwan, Jew or Jiu for overseas Taishan people, and so on. In this book, "Zhao" is used throughout.

Terms used to address people:

爸 ba – father
伯 bo – to address senior males of parents' generation; suffix.
弟 di – younger brother; between brothers or friends; suffix.
儿 er – denotes son or daughter, literally means "little" or "junior"; suffix.
哥 ge – older brother; used by wife to husband or between brothers or friends; suffix.
姐 jie – older sister; between sisters or friends; suffix.
老 lao – denotes seniority, often used among friends; prefix.

妹	mei – younger sister; used by husband towards wife or between friends; suffix.
娘	niang – mother.
朮	shu – father's younger brother; also to address friends of parents; suffix.
小	xiao – little or junior; between friends; prefix.
爷	ye – master

Chinese Glossary

ba	father	爸
ba zi	eight characters comprising a person's year, month, day, and hour of birth	八字
bai tian di	salute to heaven and earth ceremony in marriage	拜天地
Bao Gong	Magistrate Bao, a Song Dynasty legendary minister	包公
Dishu	a formal style of Chinese calligraphy	棣书
Han	the largest ethnic group in China (currently 93 per cent)	汉
Hangzhou	a major city in southeast China	杭州
Hui Hui	beginning in Tang Dynasty, people from the Middle East were referred to as Hui Hui	回回
hutongs	lanes that connect houses in northern China	胡同
Jin Yuchen	the main character in the first part of the book	金玉琛
Kaifeng	the city where a Jewish community existed for about 900 years. It is in the province of Henan, China	开封

Kublai Khan	the Mongol leader who conquered China to establish the Yuan Dynasty in 1271 CE	忽必烈
Lao Jin	Jin the elder, father of Jin Yuchen	老金
Lao Zhao	Zhao the elder, father of Zhao Yidong	老赵
Mao Shi	5:00 a.m. to 7:00 a.m. in Chinese time	卯时
niang	birth mother	娘
Ningpo	one of the five treaty ports along the Chinese coast	宁波
nongtang	a complex of houses in Shanghai	弄堂
Pan Ying	a rascal who tried to kidnap Jin Yuchen	潘瀛
Qing Dynasty	the Manchu dynasty from 1644 to 1912 CE	清朝
Qing Zhen Si	Clear and True Temple, name of the synagogue in Kaifeng	清真寺
Shanghai	the major port at the mouth of the Yangtze River	上海
Shaolin	a temple complex in Henan province famed for martial-arts techniques	少林
nvqiangren	superwoman	女强人
Taiping Rebellion	an uprising against the Qing government 1851–1864	太平天国
Tiao Jin Jiao	pluck-the-sinew sect – name for the Hebrew religion	挑筋教
xian nv	ethereal maiden, fairy	仙女
Xiao Gao	Gao junior, the guide to Shanghai	小高

Xiong	last name for the Xiong family; literally means "bear"	熊
Youtai	current Chinese name for Jewish people	犹太
Yuan Dynasty	the Mongol dynasty lasting from 1271 to 1368	元朝
Yuxi	Jin Yuchen's brother	玉玺
Zhao	one of the last seven Jewish names in China	赵
Zhao Gande	major character in the book, son of Jin Yuchen	赵乾德
Zhao Kuangyin	the first emperor of the Song Dynasty (960–1276)	赵匡胤
Zhao Wengui	one of the two ambassadors sent by Kaifeng Jews to Shanghai to study the Hebrew language and religion	赵文贵
Zhao Xinmeng	major character in the book, son of Zhao Gande	赵信萌
Zhao Yidong	major character in the book, husband of Jin Yuchen	赵义栋
Zhao Yingcheng	historic Kaifeng Jewish character who attained high political position in 1650 CE during the Qing Dynasty	赵映乘
Zhu zi jia xun	a classical piece of Confucian teaching, written by Master Zhu, setting out the duties and obligations expected of each member in the family.	朱子家训

Bibliography

An Xiaofeng, ed. *Zhong Guo Shang Xia Wu Qian Nian* 中国上下五千年, Yan Bian Education Publisher, 2000. (ISBN 7-5437-3914-3)

Applebaum, Isaac, and Dorion Liebgott, *Art and Tradition: Treasures of Jewish Life*. Toronto: Beth Tzedec Congregation, 2000. (ISBN 978-0968748305)

Chan, Anthony B. *Perpetually Cool: The Many Lives of Anna May Wong (1905–1961)*. Maryland: Scarecrow Press, Inc., 2003. (ISBN 0-8108-4789-2)

Curry, Andrew. "Roman Frontiers," *National Geographic*, September 2012, pp. 106–27.

Dehergne, Joseph, and Donald Daniel Leslie. *Juifs de Chine* 中国的犹太人 (Chinese translation). Translated by Geng Sheng. Zhengzhou, Henan, China: Daxiang Publishing Company, 2005. (ISBN 7-5347-3434-7)

Dong, Stella. *Shanghai, 1842–1949: The Rise and Fall of a Decadent City*. New York: HarperCollins, 2000. (ISBN 978-0688157982)

Ershiwu Shi Xinbian 二十五史新编 Hong Kong: Chunghwa Book (Hong Kong) Ltd. Co., 1998, 2011. (ISBN 978-962-231-924-0)

Falbaum, Berl, comp. and ed. *Shanghai Remembered: Stories of Jews Who Escaped to Shanghai from Nazi Europe*, Momentum Books, 2005. (ISBN 978-1-879094-73-8)

Heppner, Ernest G. *Shanghai Refuge: A Memoir of the World War II Jewish Ghetto.* Lincoln: University of Nebraska Press, 1993, 1995. (ISBN 978-0803223684)

Holocaust Oral History Project. "The Remarkable Story of Chiune and Yukiko Sugihara and the Rescue of Thousands of Jews," from a photo exhibit of the *"Visas for Life" Project*, 1995. (ISBN 0-964-8999-0-6)

Huang, Evelyn, and Jeffery, Lawrence. *Hong Kong: Portraits of Power.* New York: Little, Brown & Company, 1995. (ISBN 978-0316220521)

Israel Ministry of Foreign Affairs. *"Visa for Life: Diplomats Who Rescued Jews."* Courtesy of Yad Vashem, The Holocaust Martyrs' and Heroes' Remembrance Authority.

"Jews in Shanghai." Exhibit coordinated by Stephen Siu, The Chinese Cultural Centre of Greater Toronto, 2001.

Kacer, Kathy. *Shanghai Escape.* Toronto: Second Story Press, 2013. (ISBN 978-1-927583-10-4)

Kraus, Gerda Gottfried. "The Story of the Gottfried Family," as told by Gerda Gottried Kraus . Vancouver, B.C.: Vancouver Holocaust Education Centre.

Kremer, Roberta. *Diplomat Rescuers and the Story of Feng Shan Ho.* Vancouver, B.C.: Vancouver Holocaust Education Centre, 1999.

Lethbridge, H.J. *All About Shanghai: A Standard Guidebook.* Oxford in Asia Paperbacks. Hong Kong: Oxford University Press, 1986. (First published in 1934.) (ISBN 978-0195815948)

Li, Jingwen, Zhang Likang, Liu Bailu, and Zhao Guanggui. *Gudai Kaifeng Youtairen* 古代开封犹太人 Beijing, China: People's Publishing Company, 2011. (ISBN 978-7-01-010368-6)

Middagh, Stephanie, and Cara Zurzolo. *Shanghai Connection: "Creating a Refuge During the Holocaust"* (Project) Jewish Heritage Centre of Western Canada. Winnipeg, Manitoba, Canada, 2001.

Miller, Freida. *Shanghai: A Refuge During the Holocaust.* Teacher's Guide to the exhibit by the same name at the Vancouver Holocaust Education Centre. Vancouver. Canada, 1999. (ISBN 1-895754-37-2)

Needle, Patricia, ed. *East Gate of Kaifeng: A Jewish World inside China* 汴梁祖风. Minneapolis: University of Minnesota China Center, 1992. (ISBN 978-0963108708)

Pan Guang, comp. and ed. *The Jews in Shanghai* 犹太人在上海. Shanghai Pictorial Publishing House, 2005. (ISBN 7-80685-502-5)

Pan Guang, ed. *The Jews in Shanghai* 犹太人在上海. Shanghai Pictorial Publishing House, 1995. (ISBN 7-80530-177-8)

Pan Guangdan 潘光旦教授. *Zhongguo Jinnei Youtairen De Rugan Wenti: The Chinese Jews of Kaifeng* 中国境内犹太人的若干问题：开封的中国犹太人, 1953.

Qu Wei 曲伟 and Li Shuxiao 李述笑. *The Jews in Harbin* 犹太人在哈尔滨. Heilongjiang Social Science Research Centre. Translated by Xu Chenghan and Zhao Weiqing. English editor: Dan Ben-Canaan (Israel). Beijing Social Science Documentation Publishing House, 2003. (ISBN 7-80190-078-2)

Ristaino, Marcia Reynders. *Port of Last Resort: The Diaspora Communities of Shanghai.* Palo Alto, Ca.: Stanford University Press, 2001. (ISBN 978-0804738408)

Shanghai Cultural History Research Centre 上海文史研究馆, *Old Shanghai: Opium, Gambling, Prostitution* 旧上海的烟赌娼 Hong Kong: Zhongyuan Publishing Co., 1990.

Shanghai Zhanggu Cidian 上海掌故词典 Shanghai Cishu Publishing Co., 1999. (ISBN 7-5326-0513-2)

Shapiro, Sidney, trans., comp., ed. *Jews in Old China: Studies by Chinese Scholars.* New York: Hippocrene Books, 1984, expanded edition 2001. (ISBN 978-0781808330)

Spence, Jonathan D. *The Search for Modern China*. New York: W.W. Norton & Company, 1991. (ISBN 978-0393307801)

Spence, Jonathan. *Chinese Roundabout: Essays in History and Culture*. New York: W.W. Norton & Company, Inc., 1993. (ISBN 978-0393309942)

Sun Qinan 孙琴安. *Shanghai Bailemen Chuanqi* 上海百乐门传奇. Shanghai Sociology College Press, 2010. (ISBN 978-7807456568)

Tokayer, Marvin, and Mary Swartz. *The Fugu Plan: The Untold Story of the Japanese and the Jews Suring World War II*. Jerusalem/New York: Gefen Publishing house Ltd., 2012. (ISBN 978-9652293299)

Wald, Shalom Salomon. "China and the Jewish People: Old Civilizations in New Era." Strategy Paper. Israel: The Jewish People Policy Planning Institute, 2004. "中国和犹太民族：新时代中的古文明" (ISBN 965-229-347-4)

Walfish, Barry. *As It Is Written: Judaic Treasures from the Thomas Fisher Rare Book Library* Exhibition Catalogue. University of Toronto: Thomas Fisher Rare Book Library, 2015. (ISBN 978-7727-6114-9)

Wang, Jian. *Shanghai Jewish Cultural Map* 上海的犹太文化地图. Shanghai Jingxiu Wenzhang Pubisher, 2010. (ISBN 978-7-5452-0496-4)

White, William Charles. *Chinese Jews*. Toronto: University of Toronto Press, 1942, 1966.

Xu Hongxin 许洪新. *Shanghai Lao Nongtong* 上海老弄堂 Shanghai Science Technology Studies Publisher, 2004. (ISBN 7-5439-2303-3)

Xu Xin. *The Jews of Kaifeng, China: History, Culture and Religion*. Jersey City, N.J.: KTAV Publishing House, 2003. (ISBN 0-88125-791-5)

Xu Xin, with Beverly Friend. *"Legends of the Chinese Jews of Kaifeng"* New Jersey: KTAV Publishing House, 1995. (ISBN 978-0881255287)

Xue Liyong 薛里勇, *Old Photos of Shanghai: Old Schools* 上海旧影 – 老学校 Shanghai People's Art Publishing Co., 1999. (ISBN 7-5322-2053-2)

Yang Hao and Ye Lan, eds. *Jiu Shanghai Feng Yun Ren Wu* 旧上海风云人物. Shanghai People's Publishing Company, 1992. (ISBN 7-208-01242-3)

Ye, Shuping, and Zheng Zuan. *Old Fashions of Shanghai* 上海旧影. People's Arts Publisher, 1998. (ISBN 7-102-01958-0)

Ye Xiaoshen. *Photos of Old Shanghai: Immigrants World* 上海旧影 移民世界 Shanghai People's Arts Publisher, 1999. (ISBN 7-5322-2117-2)

Zhang Wei'e / Wu Li, comp. *A Guide to Shanghai.* Translated by Cheng Runming / Zhan Yunzhao. Hong Kong: Joint Publishing Co. (HK) & Shanghai Scientific and Technical Publishers. Joint Publishing Co. (HK), 1984. (ISBN 962-04-0226-X)

Zhang Wenjing and Zhang Shiling. *"Forever Nostalgia: The Jews in Shanghai."* China, 1998 (pamphlet).

Zhao Xiangbiao, Liu Songlin, and Zhang Mangong, comp. and ed. *Tuwen Zhongguo Tongshi* 图文中国通史 Urumji Xinjiang Youth Publishing House, 1999. (ISBN 7-5371-3592-4)

Film

"Shanghai Ghetto." Dana Janklowicz-Mann and Amir Mann. Docudrama. Presented by Rebel Child Productions, Documentary NVG-9695.

Online

Asianartmall.com
Canadian Encyclopedia
Encyclopedia Britannica
PBS.org
Picturechina.com.cn
The Rickshaw Express – "Visas for Life" project, 2001
Salars.cn/BBS
Ushmm.org
Visas for Life project. *The Remarkable Story of Chiune and Yukiko Sugihara and the Rescue of Thousands of Jews.* motlc.wiesenthal.com/site/pp.asp?c=hkLTJ8MUKvH&b=475921

Wedding photo of author's parents, Djao Singming and Florence Rita Yen. The characters Xinmeng and Flora are based on this couple.

(Left) Remaining corner of the burnt down Western Mansion in Nanchang. (Right) Paramount Ballroom Hall on Yu Yuan Road, Shanghai.

The official front door of #15 Yong Quan Fang.

Entrance to Yong Quan Fang complex in Shanghai.

(Left) Silas Aron Hardoon (1851–1931) real-estate tycoon in Shanghai. (Right) Sir Elly Kadoorie (1867–1944) influential leader of Sephardic Jews in Shanghai (courtesy of Goldstaub family).

Marble Hall, Kadoorie's residence in Shanghai, now Shanghai Youth Palace (courtesy of Goldstaub family).

Sleeping quarter in a Heim *for European refugees during WWII in Shanghai (courtesy of Goldstaub family).*

(Left) Eric Goldstaub in Shanghai, 1940.
(Right) Eric's mother (courtesy of Goldstaub family).

Zhao descendants in Kaifeng: (left to right) mother, author, grandmother, Ester Guo.

Entrance to Zhao residence, the only remaining corner of the former synagogue – the True and Clear Temple.

Plaque over the doorway of the Li residence, indicating a Jewish household.

Li family: (left to right) daughter, Li, her husband, You, and son-in-law.

Author standing on former river bed of the Yellow River near Kaifeng.

Side panel at the Shanghai Jewish Museum.

The Oriental Scroll. Courtesy of Reuben & Helene Dennis Museum, Beth Tzedec Synagogue, Toronto.

Rabbi Marvin Tokayer, the author, Mary Swartz, 2015.